MW01007561

The Quality of Government

The Quality of Government

Corruption, Social Trust, and Inequality in International Perspective

BO ROTHSTEIN

THE UNIVERSITY OF CHICAGO PRESS   CHICAGO AND LONDON

BO ROTHSTEIN is the August Röhss Chair in Political Science at the University of Gothenburg in Sweden. He is the author of several books, including, most recently, *Social Traps and the Problem of Trust.*

The University of Chicago Press, Chicago 60637
The University of Chicago Press, Ltd., London
© 2011 by The University of Chicago
All rights reserved. Published 2011.
Printed in the United States of America
20 19 18 17 16 15 14 13 12 11   1 2 3 4 5

ISBN-13: 978-0-226-72956-5 (cloth)
ISBN-13: 978-0-226-72957-2 (paper)
ISBN-10: 0-226-72956-7 (cloth)
ISBN-10: 0-226-72957-5 (paper)

Library of Congress Cataloging-in-Publication Data

Rothstein, Bo, 1954–
    The quality of government : corruption, social trust, and inequality in international perspective / Bo Rothstein.
        p.   cm.
    Includes bibliographical references and index.
    ISBN-13: 978-0-226-72956-5 (cloth : alk. paper)
    ISBN-10: 0-226-72956-7 (cloth : alk. paper)
    ISBN-13: 978-0-226-72957-2 (pbk. : alk. paper)
    ISBN-10: 0-226-72957-5 (pbk. : alk. paper)   1. Political corruption.   2. Quality of life—
Political aspects.   I. Title.
    JF1081.R684 2011
    364.1'323—dc22

                                                                    2010052566

♾ This paper meets the requirements of ANSI/NISO z39.48-1992 (Permanence of Paper).

TO JONATHAN AND ISABELLE

Contents

Preface and Acknowledgments

It has been a long downward spiral. I used to study pleasant things like social policy, the welfare state, comprehensive education reforms, active labor market policy, and the general prerequisites for social solidarity and political equality. By a series of unexpected events, I stumbled into research on social capital and trust. From there it became important for me to understand why distrust (in government as well as in "other people in general") is so widespread around the world. The part of the world where I've grown up, lived, and worked—the Nordic countries— is exceptional in having comparatively high levels of social capital and social trust. My intellectual journey resulted in this book and took me to the land of dysfunctional institutions, failed states, corruption, clientelism, patronage, civil war, betrayal, persistent inequality, discrimination, and other treacherous behavior. I was carried away by what I found and simply lost control of my own intellectual agenda. Research is full of surprises, and this voyage from light to darkness has been—believe it or not—incredibly fun. It has been by far the most challenging, interesting, engaging, fascinating, and in many cases bewildering intellectual problem I have come across.

This book is an outcome of a research program titled the Quality of Government Institute, at the University of Gothenburg, which Sören Holmberg and I started in 2004. I am deeply indebted to Sören for his companionship, humor, and creativity, but especially for letting me share his very special insights into the art and craft of political science. It is simply a privilege to work with him and to have him as a friend and colleague.

Since the start in 2004, the Quality of Government (QoG) Institute has become a fairly large operation and now engages about twenty-five colleagues and research assistants. It would not have been possible to create this wonderfully vibrant research community without Jan Teorell, Mette Anthonsen, and Andreas Bågenholm. They have, in sequence, served in the crucial position of program manager for the Institute, and I am as grateful as I am impressed by their creativity in both intellectual and organizational matters. Thanks to them, it has been a sheer joy building the QoG Institute.

The QoG Institute has been very fortunate to be able to recruit a number of exceptionally talented and committed research assistants. I thank Rasmus Broms, Mathias A. Färdigh, Naghmeh Nasiritousi, Petra Olsson, and Marcus Samanni for having carried out both intellectually challenging and administratively burdensome tasks with so much energy and enthusiasm. In addition, Marcus Samanni has been responsible for managing our two large data sets and has provided invaluable research assistance with the statistical work for this book.

I am fortunate to have had the chance to work and write with a number of inspiring and talented "youngish" colleagues during this project. Carl Dahlström, Daniel Eek, Staffan Kumlin, Victor Lapuente, Johannes Lindvall, Eleonora Pasotti, Anna Persson, Dietlind Stolle, and Jan Teorell have made me optimistic about the future of the social sciences. And since I have learned that nowadays age should be understood as a "social construct," Eric Uslaner should be counted in this group as well. Ric's advice and comments on early versions of this book have been particularly valuable, and over the years we have shared many thoughts and ideas about social trust and corruption.

I have been fortunate to be invited to serve as visiting fellow or to present early versions of chapters of this book at other universities, and some of these sessions have been particularly important for carrying out this project. Peter Hall made it possible for me to spend the spring semester 2006 at the Center for European Studies at Harvard. I cannot imagine a more intellectually stimulating place than the CES under Peter's directorship. I owe him a debt of gratitude for his interest in my work and for sharing his thoughts on how to understand the difficult problem of institutional change. I also want to thank the wonderful group of Harvard students in my class Corruption, Poverty, and Development in a Comparative Perspective during that semester. I was also fortunate then to get the chance to discuss my research with Vivien Schmidt, who generously shared her ideas on how to understand political discourse about policies and institutional change.

Elinor Ostrom invited me to spend a couple of days at the Workshop in Political Theory and Policy Analysis at Indiana University–Bloomington, where I presented a first version of what became the central theme of this book. Her encouragement for this project from its very start has been tremendously important for me. She was the first person to persuade me to dig deep into the historical dimension of this problem, a piece of advice that turned out to be crucial.

Michael Freeden and, at a later stage, Amir Paz-Fuchs invited me to their workshops at the University of Oxford. Although they had very different audiences, both occasions proved to be turning points for my thinking about several aspects of how to understand what should count as "quality of government."

At the early stages of this project, Dietlind Stolle arranged for me to spend a very stimulating week at the Department of Political Science at McGill University. In addition to our long conversations about how to understand the relation between social capital and political institutions, we co-organized what turned out to be a very inspiring workshop on this theme that took place in 2006 at the European Consortium for Political Research in Helsinki.

Bruce Ackerman and Susan Rose-Ackerman kindly asked me to present an early version of chapter 1 at the Legal Theory Workshop at Yale. Getting feedback from them and this group of distinguished legal scholars was a very rewarding as well as challenging intellectual experience.

First Claus Offe and, on another occasion, Alina Mungiu-Pippidi gave me the opportunity to get valuable comments from seminars at the Hertie School of Governance in Berlin, and both generously shared their ideas on how to understand corruption. Jens Alber invited me to present an early version of chapter 6 at his seminar at the Wissenschaftzentrum in Berlin. Carsten Schneider gave me the opportunity to present what became chapter 6 at the inauguration of the Center for the Study of Imperfections in Democracies at the Central European University in Budapest.

Pierre Cahuc and Yann Algan invited me to a workshop at Science Po in Paris, where I was asked to present my ideas to a group of economists interested in the relation between political institutions and social trust. I have also been able to discuss my research with Arne Bigsten, Ola Olsson, and their group of development economists at the Department of Economics at the University of Gothenburg. Magnus Henrekson invited me to present what became the final chapter of this book at the Research Institute of Industrial Economics in Stockholm, where I was surprised to get support for my line of argument from Assar Lindbeck, something I never thought I would experience. To get feedback from economists on occasions like these has been very important for developing some of the arguments in this book.

A number of colleagues have taken time to serve as visiting fellows at the QoG Institute and have generously shared their insights and knowledge. In particular, I thank Apostolis Papakostas, Michael Johnston, Michael Hechter, Strom Thacker, and Luis de Sousa.

Late in this project, I was invited to serve as visiting fellow at the Research School of Social Sciences at the Australian National University. This turned out to be the perfect place to discuss a number of outstanding issues when I was finishing the book, and I thank Keith Dowding, Lina Eriksson, and visiting fellow Jacques Thomassen for making this such a pleasant and intellectually stimulating experience.

Last, but absolutely not least, I thank a number of dear friends and colleagues whom for many years I have been able to count on for all sorts of advice and support (and some very good laughs): Sheri Berman, Carina Gunnarsson, Jörgen Hermansson, Sven Hort, Desmond King, Margaret Levi, Cathie Jo Martin, Gunnar Olofsson, Jonas Pontusson, Stefan Svallfors, and Sven Steinmo. Friends like these make academic life like sailing (on the rare occasions, at least on the Swedish west coast) when the sun is shining and winds are perfect.

I dedicate this book to my two incredible children—Jonathan Rothstein, now twenty-four, and Isabelle Rothstein, who is now eighteen. And since my time for trying to do it for them is now definitively over, may they always be blessed with other sources of "good governance." Also, I have been fortunate that my coproducer in this project, AnnChristin Rothstein, has been so successful in cajoling me away from work to do more important things in life with her.

*   *   *

The QoG Institute has received especially generous funding from the Bank of Sweden Tercentenary Foundation (Riksbankens Jubileumsfond) as well as grants from the Swedish Science Council and the Swedish Council for Working Life and Social Research. The Institute has been hosted by the Department of Political Science in Gothenburg, and

I thank Ulf Bjereld, who has been chair of the department during this period, for his support and "good governance" for this project. I also thank Marianne Ednell-Persson and Eva Mueller for providing the QoG Institute with skillful administrative support, something that has turned out to be of great importance, not least when it comes to handling the complicated economics of a large research program.

*   *   *

Parts of this book consist of revised versions of published articles or working papers, in several cases written with colleagues at the QoG Institute. I hereby gratefully acknowledge the publishers' and my coauthors' permission to publish revised versions of these articles and working papers in this book.

Chapter 1: "What Is Quality of Government: A Theory of Impartial Institutions." *Governance* 28 (2008): 2–165–90 (with Jan Teorell).

Chapter 2: "Quality of Government: What You Get." *Annual Review of Political Science* 13 (2009): 135–61 (with Sören Holmberg and Naghmeh Nasiritousi).

Chapter 3: "Corruption Kills." Working Paper 16, Quality of Government Institute, University of Gothenburg, 2009 (with Sören Holmberg).

Chapter 4: "Creating Political Legitimacy: Representative Democracy versus Quality of Government." *American Behavioral Scientist* 53 (2009): 311–30.

Chapter 6: "Quality of Government, Political Power and the Welfare State." Working Paper 6, Quality of Government Institute, University of Gothenburg, 2010 (with Jan Teorell and Marcus Samanni).

Chapter 8: "Political Corruption: An Experimental Approach." *Rationality and Society* 21 (2009): 81–112 (with Daniel Eek).

What Is Quality of Government?

Drinking Water in Luanda

O n June 16, 2006, the *New York Times* published a front-page article about Angola. The article is introduced by a large photograph showing two boys and a girl—a fair guess is they are about ten years old—fetching water from a stream that runs through what looks like an incredibly large garbage dump. The article starts this way: "In a nation whose multibillion dollar oil boom should arguably make its people rich enough to drink Evian, the water that many in this capital depend on goes by a less fancy name: Bengo. The Bengo River passes north of here, its waters dark with grit, its banks strewn with garbage." The article continues to describe how poor Angolans living in the slums of the capital, Luanda, have no option other than to use the polluted water from the Bengo River. This is the reason for one of the worst cholera epidemics to strike Africa, sickening over 43,000 people and killing more than 1,600 from February to June of 2006. Cholera is typically spread through contact with contaminated water, and according to the article, it exists everywhere in Luanda's slums. As the picture shows, "Children stripped to their underwear dance through sewage-clogged creeks and slide down garbage dumps on sleds made of sheet metal into excrement-fouled puddles." The article goes on to state that economists say the oil boom has given the Angolan government a huge budget surplus and more money than it can spend, yet it seems unable to provide the population with such basic things as the safe water and sanitation that would prevent cholera epidemics. The article concludes by citing experts from various international organizations who argue that the situation is caused by two factors—by the lack of infrastructure, exacerbated by the huge influx of people to the capital owing to the civil war that ended in 2002, and by the high level of corruption.

When the leading international anticorruption organization Transparency International published its annual Global Corruption report for 2008, the specific focus of the report, as well as its title, was "Corruption in the Water Sector." The report contains no fewer than twenty-three chapters covering more than one hundred pages analyzing this specific connection between corruption and safe water. In addition, a semipublic international organization called the Water Integrity Network, concerned with this specific problem, was established in 2006, funded by grants from the international development authorities in Germany, the Netherlands, Sweden, and Switzerland.[1] In addition to presenting policy initiatives, this network brings together anticorruption civil society movements and water professionals. Thus, both in the media and in leading policy and advocate organizations, there is an increasing agreement that lack of safe water is a major obstacle to health and well-being in the world's population and that this problem is to a large extent caused by factors that can be defined as the quality of government (henceforth QoG).

The magnitude of the QoG problem regarding the specific issue of access to safe water can be illustrated by the following example. According to a conservative estimation by the World Health Organization, 1.2 billion people lack access to sufficient quantities of safe water, and 2.6 billion are without adequate sanitation. Consequently, 80 percent of all illnesses in the developing world are estimated to be the result of waterborne diseases, claiming the lives of 1.8 million children every year (UNDP 2006). A conservative estimate is that 12,000 people die every day from water- and sanitation-related illnesses (Cunningham and Cunningham 2008; Postel and Mastny 2005; Stålgren 2006a). An increasing number of experts who study the provision of safe water no longer see this enormous problem as one of engineering. That is, it is not the lack of technical solutions (pumps, reservoirs, dams, etc.) that is the main obstacle explaining why such large numbers of mainly poor people in developing countries lack access to safe water. Neither do they see the problem as the lack of a natural supply of clean water. Instead, the problem seems to be related to dysfunction in the structure of the legal and administrative institutions. More precisely, they see it as caused by a lack of adequate institutions for the maintenance, pricing, and distribution of

1. See http://www.waterintegritynetwork.net/.

rights to land and water (Anbarci, Escaleras, and Register 2009; Krause 2009; Bruns and Meinzen-Dick 2000; Meinzen-Dick 2007; Sjöstedt 2008).

According to the report by Transparency International, there are an almost infinite number of reasons that corruption and other forms of "bad governance" can be detrimental to the provision of safe water. Among these are private companies that illegally pollute natural water resources, destroying the ecological system, and that pay bribes to avoid being prosecuted and punished by the justice system. Water resources management, not least in dealing with delicate ecosystems, is often complicated both technically and conceptually and is therefore an area where different interests may collude (cf. Stålgren 2006b). In the struggle over the use of natural water resources, kickbacks as well as patronage and clientelist politics may play a large role. Similarly, ordinary people's lack of legally documented and guaranteed property rights to the land they use may prevent them from investing in necessary technical equipment (Sjöstedt 2008).

Providing safe water often requires huge investments in dams, water cleaning equipment, and sewage systems that are carried out by private contractors. Public procurement for big contracts is a well-known source of large-scale corruption, resulting in inflated costs and low quality of the construction that is eventually put in place. Many of these installations are technically very complicated, working against transparency in the procurement process. In addition, petty corruption at the point of service delivery may deter people from using safe water or make them reluctant to pay for water at all, since they may suspect the money will be stolen instead of being used to maintain the safe water equipment. Water managers may then have far too little money to keep the installations running. In some countries this is a huge problem. For example, one study from India showed that, during the previous six months, 40 percent of water customers had been making small payments to falsify meter readings and lower their water bills (Davis 2004). Similarly, a national survey in Guatemala showed that more than 15 percent of the population reported paying a bribe to get a water connection. In Bangladesh and Ecuador, "private vendors, cartels and even water mafias have been known to collude with public water officials to prevent network extension" (Sohail and Cavill 2008, 44). In subsidies for irrigation systems, many cases are also known when large and strongly organized interest groups with substantial economic resources have heavily influenced pol-

icy at the expense of "the common good" and of agents less easily organized or economically strong. For example, a study of Mexico shows that
the richest 20 percent of farmers get more than 70 percent of government
subsidies for irrigation (Rijsberman 2008).

Food Stands on a Caribbean Island

Lack of access to safe water is of course not the only social ill related
to low quality of government. Poverty is another case, as illustrated by
the following "true story": Just across the street from Vigie Airport on
Saint Lucia—a captivating and stunningly beautiful island in the Caribbean, but also a relatively poor country with a per capita GDP of about
US$9,000—are two run-down sheds from which coffee and food are
served. Like many other local buildings on this island, the sheds, easily
seen from the airport entrance, are in a really bad state. Outside, where
customers eat and drink, there are no real tables or chairs, just broken
stools and pallets that have been thrown over. This sad appearance guarantees that tourists hardly ever venture to these places, although they
may have plenty of time (and money) to spend while waiting for their
planes to leave. If you dare to use their services, you will find the local food they serve cheap and excellent. The women running these small
businesses are friendly and talkative, and the location, just along the
beach with a postcard view of the ocean, is absolutely stunning. A lot
of tourists from the United States and Europe travel through this airport, but hardly any frequent these two small places to get a cup of coffee, a snack, or a meal, probably because they look so shabby. Instead,
most tourists go to the restaurant inside the airport building, run by a
global fast-food company, which is expensive and crowded, does not offer a view of the beach, and provides lousy service and really bad food.

If you ask the two women who run the coffee shops why they don't
make better use of their perfect location—for example, by repairing their
run-down sheds, investing in a porch, and putting out some chairs and tables to attract more business from the tourist crowd, they answer: "Great
idea. I've thought about it, but there are two problems. First, although
I have been here for twenty years, I don't own this piece of land. I'm a
squatter, so I can be forced away by the authorities at any time. Second,
if I did invest and opened a real coffee shop, I could probably never afford to pay off the health inspectors." Further conversation reveals that

the women do not know if it is even possible to buy the property or get a permanent lease, and they do not know how much they would have to bribe the health inspectors.

Reading the literature about the lack of economic growth in developing countries shows that there are probably thousands of stories like this from poor or semipoor countries like Saint Lucia. The lack of predictable legal institutions that can secure property rights and curb corruption hinders many "micro businesspeople" from making investments that in all likelihood would vastly improve their (and their country's) economic situation. In the bigger picture this reflects a key theme in current political economy: the crucial role of the quality of government. Since the late 1990s, economists and political scientists alike have started to argue that dysfunctional government institutions play a central part in many of the world's most pressing economic and social problems. This is a change from many earlier theories that focused on the lack of things like technology, skills, and infrastructure. Two prominent scholars in this field, Daron Acemoglu and James Robinson, have argued that factors like technology, skills, and physical capital are just "proximate" causes behind the lack of economic development. In order to move from proximate to fundamental causes, they argue, we must ask the next question, Why do some countries have less human capital, physical capital, and technology and make worse use of their factors and opportunities? Their answer is institutions—that is, the quality of government (Acemoglu and Robinson 2008, 28). This central place for institutions and "good governance" is also different from the earlier focus on deregulation, privatization, and liberalization known as "the Washington Consensus," which dominated much of the discussion about policies for developing and former communist countries during the 1990s (Rodrik 2008).

An issue not addressed in this literature, however, is more exactly what makes some government institutions better than others, or What is quality of government? Although a number of empirical indexes and measures have been developed and used heavily by many prominent international organizations as well as by researchers, there is a troubling lack of conceptual precision in this approach (Thomas 2009; Andrews 2008). Most troubling is that it is detached from normative political theories about justice, the proper role of the state, and democracy. It should be obvious that as soon as one puts terms like "good" or "quality" into a definition, it is impossible to refrain from discussing the normative issues about what should count as "good" that have been raised in political philosophy.[2] The same argument can be made for the concept of corruption that is usually defined as the "misuse" or "abuse" of public power for private gain. It goes without saying that one cannot understand what should count as "misuse" or "abuse" of a public position without referring to a normative standard for the proper role of the state and what type of moral standards citizens have the right to expect when public power is exercised (Lundquist 1999; Thompson 2005). I want to emphasize that this is not a question about internal academic civilities. Without a foundation in a set of universal ethical standards, translating an approach like the "good governance" agenda into policies risks ending up in mindless utilitarianism where basic human rights of (often poor) people are sacrificed in the name of some overall utility (Talbott 2005).

A central aim of this book is to propose that a key feature of quality of government, based on a specific normative and behavioral criterion, is impartiality in the exercise of public authority. The argument is that democracy, which concerns access to government power, cannot be a sufficient criterion of quality of government. If QoG merely equaled democracy, the importance of the way power is exercised by government authorities would be left out.

Conceptualizing Quality of Government: A Critique

The story from Saint Lucia highlights that it is not necessarily the lack of entrepreneurship or resources in human or physical capital that hinders economic development, but the low quality of the government institutions that implement laws and policies (Helpman 2008; Clague et al. 1999; Easterly 2001; Easterly and Levine 2003; Evans and Rauch 1999; Hall and Jones 1999; Knack and Keefer 1997; Kornai and Rose-Ackerman 2004; Rodrik, Subramanian, and Trebbi 2004; North, Wallis, and Weingast 2009). Not being able to predict government action when it reaches you and the lack of accurate information about what government bureaucrats can and cannot do to you are central ingredients of this problem (cf. Evans 2005; Lange 2005).

But the rapid growth in research on "good governance" in recent

2. On the other hand, the problem with much political theory is that "those who write about justice often see little need to say much about the institutions required to deliver the form of justice they favour" (Dowding, Goodin, and Pateman 2004, 5).

years has not been concerned only with growth and economic development. The "quality of government" factor has also been argued to have substantial effects on a number of important noneconomic phenomena, both at the individual level—such as subjective happiness (Frey and Stutzer 2000; Helliwell and Huang 2008) and citizen support for government (Anderson and Tverdova 2003)—and at the societal level, such as the incidence of civil war (Fearon and Laitin 2003; Öberg and Melander 2010) and democratic stability (Mungiu-Pippidi 2006; Rose and Shin 2001; Zakaria 2003). This emphasis on the quality of government institutions also stands in stark contrast to neoclassical economics that focused primarily on deregulation and "getting prices right" by establishing free markets. The problem with this approach has been captured poignantly by Dani Rodrik in a report presented to the International Monetary Fund in 1999:

> The encounter between neo-classical economics and developing societies served to reveal the institutional underpinnings of market economies. A clearly delineated system of property rights, a regulatory apparatus curbing the worst forms of fraud, anti-competitive behavior, and moral hazard, a moderately cohesive society exhibiting trust and social cooperation, social and political institutions that mitigate risk and manage social conflicts, the rule of law and clean government—these are social arrangements that economists usually take for granted, but which are conspicuous by their absence in poor countries. . . . Hence it became clear that incentives would not work or generate perverse results in the absence of adequate institutions. (Rodrik 2007, 153)

The emphasis on good governance is also different from some previous studies that point to long-term cultural traits as being related to the importance of social capital (Putnam 1993). Social capital, defined as access to beneficial social networks and having generalized trust in other people, seems to be determined by the quality of government institutions rather than the other way around (Delhey and Newton 2005; Rothstein and Stolle 2008).

As I said above, this research agenda has largely failed to address a key issue: how quality of government should be defined conceptually. At least five problems may be identified with existing definitions: either they are extremely broad and cover too much, or they suffer from a functionalist slant, or they do not distinguish between substantial and procedural definitions, or they deal only with one part of the problem of corruption. An additional problem is that in some approaches there is a clear ideological slant that trades accuracy for political ideals.

To illustrate the problem with definitions that are too broad, consider Daniel Kaufmann and his associates at the World Bank Research Institute, responsible for providing the most widely used empirical governance indicators. They define governance as "the traditions and institutions by which authority in a country is exercised." More specifically, this includes: "(1) the process by which governments are selected, monitored and replaced, (2) the capacity of the government to effectively formulate and implement sound policies, and (3) the respect of citizens and the state for the institutions that govern economic and social interactions among them" (Kaufmann, Kraay, and Mastruzzi 2004, 3).

The problem is that such a definition is just about as broad as any definition of "politics." For example, it does not distinguish between issues that concern the access to power and those related to the exercise of power. Moreover, in including "sound policies" in the definition, it fails to distinguish between the content of specific policy programs (political substance) on the one hand and the governing procedures on the other. In the words of Philip Keefer (2004, 5), "If the study of governance extends to all questions related to how groups of people govern themselves . . . , then there are few subjects in all of political science and political economy that do not fall within the governance domain." Or put differently, if quality of government is everything, then maybe it is nothing.

Yet some political institutions or aspects of "politics" clearly must matter more than others for what should count as quality of government. I thus agree with the critique launched by Marilyn Grindle (2004, 530) that "the good governance agenda is overwhelming" and, in particular, with her argument that it fails to distinguish between various institutional particularities and more basic principles. In the long discussion of how democracy should be defined, the distinction between procedural and substantive definitions is a central theme (cf. Dowding, Goodin, and Pateman 2004). Since I am striving for a universal and procedural definition of QoG that could be acceptable to groups in a democracy with, to quote John Rawls (2005, xvi), "a pluralism of incompatible yet reasonable," comprehensive religious, philosophical, and moral doctrines, including substantial policies in the definition is a very risky business and not likely to achieve broad-based legitimacy. This is also why I prefer the term "quality of government" to the World Bank term "good governance," whose connotations are too broad.

The functionalist problem is amply illustrated by other economists who have tried to be more specific by defining "good governance" as what can be shown to be "good for economic development" (La Porta et al. 1999, 223). One problem with this definition is that it leaves out many important noneconomic consequences of QoG referred to above, such as high social trust, subjective well-being, and population health. Another problem is that, as with all functionalist definitions, it comes at the expense of being able to define a country's level of QoG without first having to measure the effects of QoG. This makes it impossible at the conceptual level to generalize what QoG is, because the institutional arrangements that cause growth in one country may be very different from those of other countries. The functionalist approach thus makes it impossible to work out a general and universal theory of QoG and would render all comparisons invalid. As is well known, functionalist approaches also border on tautologies. As argued by the *Economist* (June 4, 2005), defining "good governance" as "good for economic development" may generate the following infinite regress: "What is required for growth? Good governance. And what counts as good governance? That which promotes growth. And what is required for growth . . ." Just as war seems too important a subject to be left solely to the generals, the conceptualization of QoG ought not to be left entirely in the hands of economists.

Although it avoids omitting noneconomic outcomes, the same criticism can be launched at the definition provided by Jeff Huther and Anwar Shah (2005, 40): "Governance is a multifaceted concept encompassing all aspects of the exercise of authority through formal and informal institutions in the management of the resource endowment of a state. The quality of governance is thus determined by the impact of this exercise of power on the quality of life enjoyed by its citizens."

To paraphrase: "What is required for the quality of life enjoyed by citizens? Quality of governance. What is quality of governance? That which promotes the quality of life."

A fourth point of criticism is that QoG should not be defined solely as the absence of corruption. While a high degree of corruption is clearly antithetical to QoG, the latter encompasses more than merely the absence of corruption. Many other practices that are not usually seen as corruption, such as clientelism, nepotism, cronyism, patronage, discrimination, and "capturing" of administrative agencies by the interest groups they are set up to regulate and control should obviously be included (Pasotti 2010; Rose-Ackerman 2004a). In addition, "corruption" can have very wide connotations (Johnston 2005), and as I will argue below, the standard definitions of this concept are not very helpful.

The problem with ideological definitions of QoG is readily seen in the all too common "small is beautiful" idea put forward by quite a number of neoclassical economists. A case in point is Alberto Alesina and George-Marios Angeletos, who from a strict deductive logic conclude that "a large government increases corruption and rent-seeking" (2005, 1234). The clear policy implication of this statement is that if one wants to improve QoG, one should lower governments' policy ambitions, especially when it comes to redistributive and interventionist policies. My first argument against this idea is that in most studies where QoG, or corruption, or both has been measured, the four Nordic countries rank at the top (they have very low levels of corruption and high QoG).[3] One can say many things about these countries, but not that they are characterized by low levels of public spending or small ambitions when it comes to government intervention (cf. Lindert 2004; Rothstein 1996).

That the size of government or the extensiveness of its policies is positively related to high levels of QoG was actually discovered in one of the first articles in this line of research. Using a wealth of data from between 49 and 212 countries in their search for what determines QoG, Rafael La Porta and his colleagues arrived at this conclusion: "Finally, we have consistently found that the better performing governments are larger and collect higher taxes. Poorly performing governments, in contrast, are smaller and collect fewer taxes" (La Porta et al. 1999, 266). However, I cannot help pointing out that the authors of this article were quick to add that "this result does not of course imply that it is often, or ever, socially desirable to expand a government of a given quality, but it tells us that identifying big government with bad government can be highly misleading" (ibid.).

I agree with Alesina and Angeletos that governments sometimes enact policies counterproductive to economic growth, but that is not related to size. However, defining exactly which policies benefit economic

3. For example, in the 2009 Global Competitiveness report issued by the World Economic Forum, the four Nordic countries were ranked 4, 5, 6, and 14. In the 2009 Corruption Perceptions Index issued by Transparency International they were ranked 2, 3, 6, and 11.

growth turns out to be a difficult task. I am far from convinced that present-day economics can give clear answers to what "sound policies" are, not least since Nobel laureate in economics Paul Krugman (2009) recently declared that the past thirty years of macroeconomic research have been "useless at best and harmful at worst." I am thus not fully persuaded that present-day economics can give good answers to such questions as Should pensions, health care, or education be a private or a public matter or a mix thereof? Should the government be engaged in helping small firms grow? Is an active labor market policy a "sound policy" or not? The Nordic cases indicate that there is very little that speaks for the notion that governments characterized by high levels of public spending and intervention have low QoG. As North, Wallis, and Weingast (2009) argue, rich countries have much larger governments than poor countries, and the authors explain this by arguing that not only are infrastructure and the rule of law to be understood as public goods, and thus to be financed by the state, but so are public education, research, and many social insurance programs.

A further argument for reserving the definition of QoG to procedures and not to substance is what could be called the "Platonist-Leninist" risk in this discussion: that the democratic process will be emptied of most substantial issues if experts from various international organizations such as the World Bank[4] prescribe almost all public policies. After all, what should political parties do, and what is the point of having an ideological debate and elections if the content of most of the important policies has been decided beforehand by international economic experts? If QoG becomes a way for experts to define what are to be understood as "sound policies" (the term used by the World Bank), there is not much left for political parties and politicians to decide on the representational side of the democratic system. The argument against this "Platonist-Leninist" alternative to democracy has been eloquently put forward by Robert Dahl, and I support his conclusion that "its extraordinary demands on the knowledge and virtue of the guardians are all but impossible to satisfy in practice" (Dahl 1989, 65).

I admit there is a political science bias in this argument. Following the works of Robert Dahl and John Rawls, the idea in rights-based political theory is that social scientists should limit their normative ambitions to constructing fair procedures, such as representative democracy and

4. Or those with superior knowledge in scientific Marxism.

equal protection under the law, for which there can be an "overlapping consensus." The hope is that human agents active in such fair procedural systems will also produce substantively good outcomes in terms of policies, which is different from having experts and scientists deciding the content and substance of the policies. Following this, we should strive for a definition of QoG that is procedural instead of substantive.

A major problem in the literature is that the efforts by most researchers to define what should count as quality of government have been detached from the analysis of modern political philosophy, especially work carried out on democratic theory and theories of justice. My argument is that what should count as "quality" concerning how public policies and institutions are designed and operate should primarily be treated as a normative problem and thus cannot be solved without taking into account the questions raised in political philosophy. The justification of most modern political theory is that specifying political procedures that can be motivated by norms of justice will give policy outcomes a greater chance of being beneficial and morally just (Rawls 2005, lx). The implication is that a definition of QoG based on such a normative perspective should not be at odds with features shown empirically to have beneficial social and economic consequences. In what follows, I will present a conceptualization of QoG incorporating insights from political philosophy, accompanied (in this chapter) with some preliminary examples about the effects of different institutional arrangements. The chapter that follows will present a broader picture of the effects of variations in QoG.

Quality of Government as Impartiality

A state regulates relations with its citizens along two dimensions. One is the "input" side, which relates to access to public authority. This is where we find rules about elections, party financing, the right to stand for office, and the formation of cabinets. The "output" side refers to the way political authority is exercised. On the input side, where the access to power and thus the content of policies is determined, the most widely accepted basic regulatory principle has been formulated by Robert Dahl (1989) as that of political equality. This is also John Rawls's (2005) basic idea on how to construct a nonutilitarian society based on his well-known principles of justice. As I will stress further in a subsequent section, political equality certainly implies impartial treatment on the input side of the system, and this makes political equality and impartiality partially overlapping concepts (Rawls 2005; cf. Goodin 2004, 97). My argument for a more precise definition of QoG, however, is based on the idea that democracy in the form of political equality on the input side has been shown to sometimes generate very low QoG (Charron and Lapuente 2010). It is not difficult to find examples where a majority of voters support corrupt politicians, clientelism, and outright discrimination against ethnic minorities (Pasotti 2010, 28–33). As formulated by Robert Goodin: "Outcomes that are undeniably democratic can be palpably unjust" (2004, 98). The conclusion is that impartiality on the output side of the political system, that is, in the exercise of public authority, should be the basis for what should count as QoG.

Such a definition of impartiality in the exercise of public power reads like this: When implementing laws and policies, government officials shall not take into consideration anything about the citizen/case that is not stipulated beforehand in the policy or the law (Strömberg 2000).[5] As Cupit writes: "To act impartially is to be unmoved by certain sorts of considerations—such as special relationships and personal preferences. It is to treat people alike irrespective of personal relationships and personal likes and dislikes" (Cupit 2000; cf. Barry 1995, 11). The connection to "good" or "quality" is motivated by the fact that impartiality is the driving notion behind Rawls's theory of justice. As Goodin argues: "Certainly, the antithesis of justice is favouritism" (2004, 100). In this context, impartiality is not a demand on actors on the input side of the political system but is first and foremost an attribute of the actions taken by civil servants, professional bodies in public service, law enforcement personnel, and the like. To effectuate this ideal, it may also be necessary to inscribe impartiality as an ideal into the mind-set of these actors, an issue I shall return to in the following chapters.

To see why this definition of QoG is universal, it is useful to compare it with Dahl's idea of political equality as a basic norm for democracy. Every particular democratic state is different in its institutional configuration. It should suffice to point to the extreme variation in the electoral

5. That this definition does not imply that no concerns other than those stipulated beforehand by law should be taken into consideration when settling a case. Time or budget constraints would, for example, be perfectly legitimate concerns, even though they are rarely mentioned in laws or specific policies. Rather, this definition implies that no characteristic of the *citizen* or the *case* to be dealt with—other than those stipulated in the policy or law—should be taken into consideration.

systems in, for example, the Swiss, the Danish, and the British democracies. There are in fact innumerable ways to organize a national democracy (presidentialism versus parliamentarianism, unicameralism versus bicameralism, proportional versus majoritarian electoral systems, variation in the power of the courts, federalism versus unitarianism, the role of referenda, the strength of local governments, etc.). As long as the principle of equality in the access to power is not violated (for example, by giving one specific political party the right to rule or by refusing to give some specific group of citizens the right to stand for office or take part in the public debate), we consider such differing political systems as those in Finland and in the United States to be democracies. In a representative democracy it should be possible to justify all institutional arrangements on the input side as "political equality."

Impartiality as the parallel legitimatizing and defining principle for the "output" side can in a similar way encompass various administrative practices. For example, impartiality applied to decisions about recruitment to the civil service implies that selection should be based on the merits and qualifications stated beforehand as necessary for the position, but exactly which merits or qualifications should count can vary significantly. However, if recruitment were to be based on clientelist personal contacts, political leanings, bribes, or belonging to a certain ethnic group, the impartiality principle would be violated. In accordance with Dahl's basic norm for democracy, QoG as impartiality is procedural, which means it can encompass very different policies and does not rule out support for specific groups or interests. One example is social policies—for example, support for poor families with children. Enacting such policies would not break the principle of impartiality, but denying such allowances to families from a certain ethnic group or parents with a certain sexual orientation would.

How does QoG as impartiality relate to established definitions of corruption? The established view defines corruption as the "abuse (or misuse) of public office for private gain," or some close variant along those lines (see, e.g., Alt and Dreyer Lassen 2003, 345; Treisman 2000, 399). This definition has some virtues compared with earlier alternatives such as the "public opinion" (corruption is what the public perceives as corrupt) and "public interest" (corruption is what violates the public interest) conceptions of corruption. Yet it suffers from a crucial weakness: it makes no reference to what kinds of acts constitute the "misuse" or "abuse" of public office, which makes the definition of corruption relativistic. Without a basic norm (such as impartiality), these definitions simply avoid the question of what should count as corruption or, to be more precise, what is the norm of practice that is being "abused."

I therefore concur with Oscar Kurer (2005, 230) in stating that "corruption involves a holder of public office violating the impartiality principle in order to achieve private gain." As Kurer argues, this definition of corruption has the advantage that what counts as a breach of impartiality is fairly universally understood and thus not related to how things like "abuse" or "misuse" of public power are viewed in different cultures. As I will show below, most people in highly corrupt settings do not internalize corruption as something morally acceptable. On the contrary, even if they have to take part in corrupt practices to get by or even to survive, they usually identify the practices as morally wrong. The norm that is violated when corruption occurs is the impartiality principle governing the exercise of public power, whose core component is the notion of nondiscrimination, whether for money, race, religion, or sex/gender. The advantage of this definition of QoG is that impartiality rules out not only all forms of corruption but also practices such as clientelism, patronage, nepotism, political favoritism, discrimination, and other "particularisms" (Mungiu-Pippidi 2006; Pasotti 2010). In other words, whereas impartiality implies the absence of corruption, the reverse is not necessarily true: the absence of corruption does not preclude all forms of partiality in the exercise of government power.

Equally important, however, are the things the norm of impartiality does not rule out. Since QoG as impartiality is a procedural norm confined to the exercise of public power, one important field that is not affected by this conception is the substance of the policies. This builds on the idea that noncorruption implies that "a state ought to treat equally those who deserve equally" (Kurer 2005, 223). This is in line with the argument that the content of public policies should not be included in the definition of QoG. Instead, it is impartiality in the exercise of power (the "ought to treat equally" principle) that is the central component of QoG.[6] To treat equally, of course, does not imply that everyone should

6. This is supported by empirical research in social policy showing that people who perceive themselves to have been treated even-handedly by the authorities also believe that the political system in general is more legitimate (see Kumlin 2004, chaps. 8 and 9).

get the same. Only people in need of a kidney transplant should get one. Instead, this follows the idea of "equal concern and respect" launched by Ronald Dworkin (1977).

In political philosophy, this distinction between which norms should guide the content versus the procedural sides of the political system is readily seen in Brian Barry's important book *Justice as Impartiality*. Barry argues that impartiality should be a normative criterion in the exercise of political power: "Like cases should be treated alike" (Barry 1995, 126). His idea of "second order impartiality" implies that the input side of the political system should be arranged so that it gives no special favor to any conception of "the good." However, as Barry readily admits, his theory "accepts that a demand of neutrality cannot be imposed on the outcomes" (Barry 1998, 238). Accordingly, when it comes to decisions about the content of the policies governments should pursue, it is not neutrality or impartiality but "reasonableness" that is his main criterion (Barry 1998, 238; cf. Hardin 1998). By this he means that people engaged in the political process should give sound arguments based on a secular understanding of knowledge for why they prefer certain policies over others. In Barry's words, "What is required is as far as possible a polity in which arguments are weighed and the best arguments win, rather than one in which all that can be said is that votes are counted and the side with the most votes wins" (Barry 1995, 103).

The implication is the one I argue for here, that impartiality cannot be a moral basis for the content of policies that individuals, interest groups, and political parties pursue on the input side of the political system, since reasonableness is not the same as impartiality. For example, in a given situation there may be good reasons for lowering pensions and for increasing support to families with children. But this is not the same as being impartial between these two groups, because there is no such thing as an impartial way to decide in a case like this (Arneson 1998). This is particularly problematic when it comes to conflicts over which public goods a state should provide, since such goods often cannot be divided into minor parts (like money), something that often makes reasonable compromises easier to reach. Either the airport or dam is built or nothing is built (Miller 2004).

What is presented here is not a form of the grand ambition that Barry, Rawls, and other political philosophers have pursued—to construct a universal theory of social and political justice. My ambition is more modest—to construct a theory of what should count as quality of government. The implication is that when a policy has been decided on by the representative democratic system, be it deemed just or unjust according to whatever universal theory of justice one would apply, QoG implies that it has to be implemented in accordance with the principle of impartiality. The following section will illustrate the definition of impartiality as QoG by responding to four types of criticism that have been leveled against this concept.

The Scope of Impartiality

Contrary to my previous belief, the concept of impartiality has not been high on the agenda in research on bureaucracy and public administration. For example, the widely used 664-page *Handbook of Public Administration* has no index entry for "impartiality" (Peters and Pierre 2002). A search in the *Social Science Citation Index* also gives surprisingly meager results.[7] This lack of interest is all the more surprising since the idea of the impartial civil servant goes back to the most central figure in bureaucratic theory, Max Weber. Moreover, it seems as if most research in public administration has argued either that the impartial mode of operating the state machinery is ineffective or that impartiality is an impossible ideal (cf. du Gay 2000). The bureaucratic mode of operation has been said to be too rigid for the active modern, policy-oriented state, which requires flexibility and commitment from its officials. In this line of reasoning, the ideal of the impartial civil servant has been accused of being insensitive to the complexities and the special needs of different cases (Olsen 2006).

Another critique has come from the public choice approach. According to this theory, civil servants are motivated more by a drive to promote their own interests than by ethics related to some public interest such as impartiality (Dunleavy 1991). This critique is in line with a more general idea that politics is to be seen foremost as a partisan interest struggle, in which case there would be no room within the state for impartial agents

7. The *Social Science Citation Index* (Web of Science) lists a total of three published articles with the keyword impartiality combined with any of the following keywords: bureaucracy, public administration, civil service, public service. The database searches for keywords given in the title, in the keywords provided by the authors, or in the abstract, and covers about 2.6 million scholarly articles published since 1986.

such as judges or civil servants. Although there is not much that speaks for this theory from empirical research, it is still an important approach.

A third critique has come from within the field of political philosophy, not least the various multiculturalist and feminist approaches.[8] The argument has been that impartiality is in fact impossible to achieve because individuals, whether civil servants or otherwise, cannot step outside their particularistic personalities. Instead, their actions will always be impregnated by things like ideological commitments, sex/gender, cultural/ethnic identity, class background, and such.

Moreover, it has been stated that partiality is the idea of life itself: to be deeply attached to other persons and causes is what life is really about. Impartiality is thus an offense against this inner meaning of life (Mendus 2002, 2–3). According to this line of critique the idea of "justice as impartiality" launched by Brian Barry (1995) is a nonstarter simply because impartiality is both an impossible and an undesirable ideal. As the feminist political philosopher Iris Marion Young states, "No one can adopt a point of view that is completely impersonal and dispassionate, completely separated from any particular context and commitments" (Young 1993, 127–28).

To summarize, impartiality is a truly contested concept. Several intellectual discourses argue that it is either an impossible or an unwanted ideal. To address these objections, I draw on an idea launched by Michael Walzer (1983), that society consists of different spheres with different modes of domination that normatively should not be transferable, and that impartiality as a moral virtue does not apply generally but only in one of the spheres I will outline below.

Impartiality's Sphere

My starting point is that one need not accept the underlying communitarian philosophy of Michael Walzer's (1983) theory in order to acknowledge that there is something genuinely correct about his idea that what is acceptable in one social sphere—for example, the family—is not morally acceptable in another sphere such as the state. In organizational

---

8. The debate within political and moral philosophy between impartialists and their critics is vast, and I cannot give it the attention it deserves here. See Mendus (2002) for an overview.

theory, this has been labeled as different logics of "appropriateness" (Olsen 2006). In short, we have different normative ideas about what should count as fairness and justice (or behavior deemed appropriate) in different societal spheres. For example, while it is normatively fair to use money to get one's way in market transactions, it is not so in politics (for instance, we do not allow the buying and selling of votes). What is important in Walzer's approach is not only the idea that norms should be different in different societal spheres, but that we should recognize that the same individuals often operate simultaneously in different spheres and are carriers of different norms about what is appropriate in these different spheres. For example, an impartial and incorruptible judge can also be a devoted (and thus very partial) mother, a person who operates on the housing market guided by the logic of pure self-interested utility maximization, and an activist in an animal rights group. This simultaneity has two very important implications. First, QoG as impartiality implies that those who exercise public power need to know and acknowledge the boundaries between what norms apply in different moral spheres. Second, they need to know which norms are appropriate (and inappropriate) in the "state" sphere and how they differ from what is considered legitimate in the other spheres. The argument is thus not that impartiality is a general moral virtue that should be applied universally in all social spheres, but instead that it is restricted to when public power is exercised.

One problem with Walzer's theory is that the number of moral spheres seems to be both infinite and arbitrary. He readily acknowledges that his theory is not meant to be universal but is historically and culturally particularistic. Second, there is no basic concept or theory behind his idea of the historical existence of different moral spheres that explains why he ends up with the ones he presents. Walzer's moral spheres are thus defined by reference only to historical particularities (1983, 20). The lack of universality in his theory of "spheres" is a problem because, as I argued above, a theory of how QoG should be defined ought to be universal. Otherwise, we may very well end up in a relativistic morass with one theory of QoG per country, religion, gender, ethnicity, or socioeconomic class. Following such logic in the area of human rights implies that we would have one definition of human rights per culture or country. Such a lack of universality implies that not only a comparative approach but also the search for a common theory becomes futile.

My solution to these problems starts from an idea of the two dimen-

Type of interest

	Other-regarding	Self-regarding
"All"	**The State**	**The Market**
"Few"	**The Family** **The Clan**	**The Interest** **Organization**

Scope of interest

FIGURE 1.1. Dimensions of interests and moral spheres.

sions of interests. One is the type of interest, the other is its scope. Type refers to the distinction between self-regarding and other-regarding interests. Scope refers to the "demos" question: how many are to be included in our sphere of interest. Here, the question is whether the type of interest that dominates is meant to be for "everyone" or is restricted to one's friends, family, clan, tribe, party affiliates, subdivision in an academic discipline, or other such groups. If we combine these two dimensions, we get the following four spheres of conduct that relate to impartiality (see fig. 1.1).

The logic of this model is as follows: In the "state" sphere, the norm is that the exercise of power should be in accordance with the enacted laws and polices and that they should apply equally to "all," as stated in the two principles of political equality and equality before the law. In the "market" sphere, the accepted norm is that behavior according to self-interest is justifiable, but the scope dimension "all" implies that everyone should have equal access to the market (exemplified in, for example, laws against monopolies/trusts and equal access to the protection of property rights/contracts). We should simply sell to and buy from anyone if the price is right, regardless of family background, ethnicity, or religion. However, the accepted norm in the private sphere is that we should not behave according to self-interest against our family (or clan) members or friends but should pursue what we, from some other-regarding notion, deem good for all members of this small group. The point here is that such groups do not, as with the market, have free entrance but are restricted to their "members." Last, interest groups are driven by the idea of making things better for their members (self-interest), and they are also restricted to members. In general, members or leaders of such groups cannot be expected to act according to some "public" interest, and their claims are generally not impartial but, on the contrary, are very partial. This goes also for most political parties. One should recognize that most people who become engaged in politics are not craving impartiality. They want to further an often very partial cause, and this is usually seen as a perfectly legitimate reason. This also reflects why impartiality does not work well as a basic norm for legitimacy on the input side of the political system. Interest organizations, for example, often do not adhere to impartiality when dealing with the state but instead act according to "logic of exchange" in negotiations. This is where we find policies and practices related to what usually is labeled "neocorporatist" or "interest-group" politics (for a somewhat related idea, see Lange 2005; Brand 1988).

The point to take from this application of Walzer's theory, which is also my response to the critics of impartiality as a basic norm for the exercise of public power, is that social science should not be based on the idea that society is dominated by agents with only one script of human behavior or a single set of moral norms, be it self-interest, the principle of care, rent seeking, bureaucratic ethics, feelings of community, altruism, or for that matter impartiality. According to this model, humans have a greater repertoire than being only self-regarding, and they understand that what is appropriate in one sphere is fundamentally wrong in another (March and Olsen 1989). From a normative perspective, we can also see that while self-interest is justifiable in some spheres, it is unacceptable in others. For example, agents on a market who used "other-regarding interest" as their main template of behavior would simply be deemed stupid and probably would soon go out of business, while civil servants or parents who acted according to pure self-interest would be seen by most people as morally deplorable. In this respect, a large part of the discussion of Brian Barry's "justice as impartiality" appears to be misguided, because this distinction between "spheres of behavior" has been left out. While, for many, increased justice implies policies that contain more partiality (for example, extra resources to underprivileged groups), they usually do not want these policies, once enacted, to be implemented in a partial way where bureaucrats are given total discretion in every case (Tebble 2002; Young 1990). For example, it may be perfectly legitimate to argue for the government to establish academic positions that only women (or some other disadvantaged group) could apply for, given the gender inequality that exists in higher academic positions. But once such a position is announced and a number of women apply, the impartiality norm takes over, since those who have argued for such a quota system usually want the most qualified among the preferred group to get the position. Thus, while impartiality is a norm to be followed in one sphere, it would be dysfunctional and also unethical in other spheres.

This conditionality in the application of impartiality as a justice principle in fact goes all the way back to John Stuart Mill: "Impartiality, in short, as an obligation of justice, may be said to mean being exclusively influenced by the considerations which it is supposed ought to influence the particular case in hand, and resisting the solicitations of any motives which prompt to conduct different from what those considerations would dictate" (Mill 1861/1992, 154).

I am not arguing that impartiality is equivalent to "objectivity." Terminology is a tricky business (especially if you trade in a language that is not your own). Still, I would say that, as a concept, objectivity has an absolute and perfectionist ring that implies humans can have full knowledge of a case, weigh all things equally, and come down with a decision as if the outcome were decided by some law of nature. I argue that impartiality implies somewhat more human and realistic demands. First, it is about a "matter-of-factness," implying that things the policy or law says should not affect the decision are to be left out. Second, it requires that the public official not be a party to the case, neither directly nor indirectly. Moreover, the idea of QoG as impartiality stands in sharp contrast to the public choice idea of public officials' maximizing their self-interest. For example, the impartial civil servant should not be susceptible to bribery, should not decide in cases where friends and relatives are involved, and should not favor any special interest (ethnically, economically, or otherwise organized) when applying laws and rules.

Thus, in "the state" sphere we are concerned with the typical civil servant's or professional's acting according to the impartiality principle, implying that he or she should be guided by the public interest instead of by self-interest or loyalty to any group, party, or "special interest." Decisions should be made according to what is stipulated and intended in the law or policy, disregarding the bureaucrats' own interests. The special interests that are acceptable in other spheres (money from the market, loyalties to family and friends, and adherence to different special interests) should not be allowed to influence decisions. However, we have no moral objection when the very same persons leave the courtroom or public office, go to the "market," and try to get the very best deal when selling a house or buying a new car. Likewise, we do not object if in their private dealings these persons take special care for their family and friends (cf. Barry 1995, 205).[9] On the contrary, being loyal to family, friends, and community is often regarded as a virtue. However, we object strongly if civil servants in their professional life do not refrain from handling cases that concern friends or members of their own families.

Moreover, as private individuals we would argue that these persons have the same rights as every other citizen to support whatever special interests or political causes they like. But again, if they are strongly involved or engaged in a certain cause or interest organization, they should declare a conflict of interest and abstain from handling a case that may influence the outcome of this cause or be of importance to this organization. Likewise, a civil servant who handles public contracts cannot have economic interests in any of the potential bidders. Thus, the demand for impartiality from civil servants is not absolute objectivity, and the idea of QoG as impartiality is not based on the presumption that certain persons have it "in their nature" to be disinterested in all areas of life. What QoG demands is that people employed to exercise government powers recognize clear boundaries between this sphere and other societal spheres that put severe restrictions on what types of behavior and decisions are acceptable.

The point of separating the spheres can be illustrated by referring to the fact that the common language uses different words for different kinds of transgressions. When norms from the market are imported to the state sphere, such transactions are usually referred to as bribes. When norms from the family/clan sphere enter the state sphere, the word used is nepotism or patronage. Last, when norms from the interest-group sphere are employed in the state sphere, the problem is usually called corporatism, clientelism, or influence peddling (as in "the military-industrial complex").

9. The judge or civil servant is allowed to read his own children as many pedagogically advanced bedtime stories as he likes, for example, without being blamed for not respecting the ideal of impartiality. (I spent almost a week in an academic workshop on "equality of opportunity," learning that not all children are being read enough bedtime stories, which of course is inimical to equality of opportunity. The policy proposals for how to remedy this launched by my dear colleagues in political philosophy could at best be described as fanciful.)

The Feminist Challenge:
Commitment, Flexibility, and Impartiality

Feminist scholars have pointed to the possibility of a conflict between the principle of impartiality and the capacity of the state to deliver the kind of social services required of public sector employees in the welfare state who must perform curative and caring work. Following Joan Tronto, Helena Stensöta has argued that we expect, for example, preschool teachers, medical professionals, and social workers to demonstrate empathy and compassion and not be governed by some general and abstract logic of justice as impartiality (Stensöta 2010). According to this approach, the "logic of care" leads to a more context-dependent ethic than the impartial application of universal rules. In specific terms, we do not want nurses in a public hospital to treat all patients alike. They should give more care and attention to those who need it. In this and many similar policy areas, legitimacy in implementation requires that public employees be committed, engaged, and dedicated to their tasks instead of being impartial or, worse, indifferent.

The feminist discussion about "the logic of care" casts light on an important dimension of this theory about QoG as impartiality. Impartiality is not to be understood as implying that the implementation of public policies equals an old-style Weberian rigid, indifferent rule following, or personal detachment, or a lack of creativity and flexibility by the people working in the public sector. Certainly most of us want children who attend a public preschool to be approached with empathy and concern rather than by dry-as-dust rules. Obviously, different children need different degrees of attention, comfort, and support in different situations. However, most people would be morally upset if preschool staff deliberately directed their care and concern toward children from families who had bribed them, or who belonged to a certain ethnic group, and thus in practice discriminated against the other children. As this case shows, there is no conflict between professionally distributed care and the principle of impartiality. As defined here, a traditional rule-based Weberian bureaucracy may in some areas be an incarnation of the impartiality principle, but so may professional standards that are based on strong commitment to the policy goals while implementing these goals with a high degree of flexibility, be they the reduction of poverty, the preservation of forests (Kaufman 1960), or an active labor market policy (Rothstein 1996).

Competing Conceptions of Quality of Government

As I argued above, impartiality could hardly be considered the sole normative yardstick for assessing all aspects of a political system. Self-evidently, normatively despicable policies, such as an apartheid system, can in theory be implemented impartially. However, QoG as impartiality shares this problem with representative democracy, since there is no guarantee that democracy will equal justice (Dowding, Goodin, and Pateman 2004). To get a broader picture of the problem of how QoG should be defined, I relate this theory of impartiality to a set of three competing conceptions of what constitutes quality of government. First, I will argue that representative democracy is probably not a necessary condition for QoG. Second, I will show that the impartiality principle implies and encompasses the rule of law, while the opposite is not true. Efficiency/effectiveness, finally, lacks an independent normative justification and is therefore always secondary to impartiality. Nevertheless, there are reasons to believe that impartiality should enhance effectiveness/efficiency.

Democracy

The reasons democracy as majoritarian rule alone does not suffice as a definition of QoG are both theoretical and empirical. The theoretical reason is well known: there are simply no guarantees that a majority will respect the impartiality principle when government power is to be exercised. For example, in an ethnically divided society, the political party representing the ethnic majority, after being elected, may decide that all citizens from the minority working as civil servants should be fired or that citizens from the minority will not get public contracts. This would clearly be a breach of the impartiality principle in the exercise of government authority, albeit stemming from democratic principles in the access to authority.

Empirically, there is no straightforward relation between democracy in the access to public power and impartiality in the exercise of public power. On the contrary, democracy seems to be related curvilinearly to the level of corruption (Montinola and Jackman 2002; Sung 2004). Moreover, there are countries (such as Jamaica) that have been democracies for five decades but that score very low on measures of QoG. And some countries (such as Singapore) that have not been democracies dur-

ing this period score high on QoG (Werlin 2007). Empirical research indicates that initially democratization may lower levels of QoG. For example, some of the worst cases of corruption have appeared in newly
democratized countries, such as Peru under its former president Alberto
Fujimori (McMillan and Zoido 2004). Conversely, some undemocratic
countries have shown impressive results in curbing corruption and establishing fairly impartial bureaucracies, prime examples being Hong Kong
and Singapore (Root 1996).

Moreover, as I will show in the next chapter, in terms of producing
valued social outcomes, the track record of democracy is surprisingly
uneven. The inherently ambiguous results on whether democracy matters for economic growth perhaps constitute the most prominent example (see, e.g., Kurzman, Werum, and Burkhart 2002; Przeworski
and Limongi 1993). In addition, some have raised questions about the
presumed positive effects of democracy on human development, arguing that this relation is either extremely slow and evolving over decades
(Gerring, Thacker, and Alfaro 2005) or, even worse, vanishes completely
once we correct for missing data bias (Ross 2006). Simply put, knowing
how far a country is democratic (or not) cannot help explain the multi-
tude of highly valued economic and social consequences of QoG documented in the literature.

This said, democracy and impartiality do overlap at the conceptual
level in two very important areas. First, this is apparent with respect to
the "bundle of political rights" required to uphold a democratic system.
Democracy, in Guillermo O'Donnell's words (2001, 18), presupposes "a
legal system that enacts and backs the universalistic and inclusive assignment of these rights." Democratic legitimacy requires that political
rights, such as freedom of association and of expression, must be secured
within a legal framework, and this framework must in turn be impartially applied to all its subjects (Bratton and Chang 2006). As a consequence, democracy as political equality entails impartial government institutions, especially in the regulation of access to political power.

Second, this overlap is also readily seen if we consider the idea of
"free and fair elections." Elections have to be administered by the existing government, but if they are to be considered free and, in particular,
fair, the ruling party must refrain from organizing them in a manner that
undermines the possibility for the opposition to obtain power. That is,
free and fair elections must be administered by impartial government institutions (Schedler 2002, 44; Choe 1997). But again, the impartial orga-

nization of elections does not imply that their content or outcome is impartial. On the contrary, the reason many people take part in elections (and politics in general) is that they are motivated by very partial interests. This issue is becoming increasingly relevant in research about democratization. One of the best-known scholars in this field of research, Larry Diamond, has expressed this:

> There is a specter haunting democracy in the world today. It is bad governance—governance that serves only the interests of a narrow ruling elite. Governance that is drenched in corruption, patronage, favoritism, and abuse of power. Governance that is not responding to the massive and long-deferred social agenda of reducing inequality and unemployment and fighting against dehumanizing poverty. Governance that is not delivering broad improvement in people's lives because it is stealing, squandering, or skewing the available resources. (Diamond 2007, 119)

The joint condition of the legal system enforcing political rights and the election process itself being impartially administered means that when democracy, in its basic sense, has been accomplished, certain spheres of government action must be regulated by the impartiality principle—even on the input side. In other words, democracy and impartial government institutions are partially overlapping concepts. They are only partially overlapping, however, since democracy can threaten impartiality in the exercise of government power, and democracy is related to many things other than impartiality, especially when it comes to the content of policies.

The Rule of Law

Establishing the rule of law is usually placed high on the agenda for reforming developing and transitional countries. But what does "the rule of law" mean? Although unequivocally embraced as a virtue of any political system, the concept is rarely defined. One reason may of course be that the concept is inherently ambiguous. As a recent review article makes clear, even legal scholars argue over its exact meaning (Rose 2004).

To begin with, they dispute whether the rule of law should be given a purely procedural interpretation, bearing no implications for the actual substance of promulgated laws. Defenders of a procedural notion claim that the rule of law must be distinguished from the rule of "good" law. Critics argue that this distinction would allow morally detested regimes, such as Nazi Germany, to be classified as abiding by the rule of law. Against the procedural view, these critics seek to inscribe into the rule of law various substantive moral values of liberal democracy. Yet even among proceduralists, who adhere to a narrower conception, ambiguities remain. Usually they pay more attention to listing the internal qualities of the laws themselves—such as the need for the law to be clear, understandable, general, internally consistent, prospective, stable, and so on—rather than to defining the core principles a political system must abide by to be in accordance with the rule of law.

Searching for these core principles, one may instead turn to conceptions developed within political science. Barry Weingast (1997, 245) defines the rule of law as "a set of stable political rules and rights applied impartially to all citizens." Similarly, Guillermo O'Donnell (2004, 33) offers a minimal definition of the rule of law as "that whatever law exists is written down and publicly promulgated by an appropriate authority before the events meant to be regulated by it, and is fairly applied by relevant state institutions including the judiciary." As these definitions should make clear, the rule of law is perfectly compatible with the principle of impartial government institutions. This connection is most explicitly recognized by O'Donnell:

> By "fairly applied" I mean that the administrative application or judicial adjudication of legal rules is consistent across equivalent cases; is made without taking into consideration the class, status, or relative amounts of power held by the parties in such cases; and applies procedures that are preestablished, knowable, and allow a fair chance for the views and interests at stake in each case to be properly voiced. (ibid.)
>
> The rule of law thus embodies the principle "equality [of all] before the law." It entails "a crucial principle of fairness—that like cases be treated alike." (ibid., 33–34)

The connection between the two concepts may be stated even more strongly: impartiality implies the rule of law. Procedural impartiality, to be accomplished in practice, requires a set of rules that regulate proper conduct—such as distinguishing which are "like" cases, and what specific concerns are legitimate in specific cases. The most general set of such rules for governing a society is its laws. These laws must be consistently applied to everyone—including those who promulgate the laws themselves. No one is above the law. Thus, a corollary of impartial government institutions is the notion of an impartially applied legal system—the rule of law.

Impartiality, however, also applies to spheres of state action other than those directly governed by law. When public policy is to be enacted in "human processing" areas, such as education, health care, welfare benefits, and active labor-market programs, wide discretionary powers usually need to be transferred to lower-level government officials responsible for implementing policy. The reason is that they have to adapt action to the specific circumstances in each case, and it has turned out to be administratively impossible to enact precise laws and regulations that can guide this. One can think of examples such as deciding when the social problem in a family reaches a level where the children must be taken into custody, or what type of work an unemployed person should be obliged to accept without risking the loss of unemployment benefits, or just when unruliness at a bar or restaurant reaches a level where its license to sell alcohol should be withdrawn (Rothstein 1998a, chap. 4). According to our theory, of course, impartial behavior on behalf of these policy enactments is a key virtue for reaching legitimacy in the exercise of public power. But it falls outside the sphere of government activity that can be precisely regulated by rule of law measures. This is not a novel insight: Aristotle himself observed that written laws cannot be applied precisely in every situation, since the legislators, "being unable to define for all cases . . . are obliged to make universal statements, which are not applicable to all but only to most cases" (quoted in Brand 1988, 46). In other words, the impartiality principle not only entails but encompasses the rule of law.

Effectiveness/Efficiency

It would certainly be strange to argue that a government that is very inefficient or ineffective can have a high QoG. Economists often treat the state's capacity for action as a core element of their governance concept. Anwar Shah (2005, xxiii), for one, considers two features of government performance: responsiveness ("whether the public manager is doing the right things—that is, delivering services consistent with citizen preferences") and efficiency ("whether the public manager is doing them right—that is, providing services of a given quality in the least-costly manner"). Similarly, Rafael La Porta and his colleagues (1999) include "efficiency"—"successful provision of essential public goods"—

and "effective spending" among their operational quality of government indicators. As these examples suggest, there are (at least) two dimensions of state capacity: the degree of successful policy implementation—effectiveness—and the amount of government output delivered relative to input efficiency. I shall, however, treat these two dimensions jointly.

The argument presented here on this point is, first, that impartiality is always preferable to efficiency/effectiveness. This rests on the Rawlsian antiutilitarian theory of justice, which implies that utility always comes second to rights (Rawls 1984). In Ronald Dworkin's extension of this theory, the implication for the exercise of power is that the state should treat every citizen with "equal concern and respect" (1977, 180–81), which in my terminology equals impartiality. Issues about effectiveness and efficiency simply do not have as strong a theoretical and normative underpinning as does impartiality.

Second, there is a case for arguing that impartiality may enhance effectiveness/efficiency. One of the organizational structures arguably underpinning impartiality is meritocratic recruitment to the civil service. Impartiality would thus imply recruitment based on merit and competence rather than political connections or being a member of a clientelist network. As James Rauch and Peter Evans have shown (2000), in developing countries, meritocratic principles of recruitment and promotion turn out to be strongly positively related to the subjective ratings of corruption and bureaucratic efficiency as well as to economic growth.

Can Impartiality Be Measured?

From positive theory as well as from a policy perspective, one could argue that a theoretical and conceptual operation like this is of little use if it is not possible to operationalize and measure impartiality. Together with my collaborators at the Quality of Government Institute at the University of Gothenburg, I have launched a web-based country expert survey on this specific topic. The first round of this survey, sent out in 2008, produced answers from 529 public administration experts (mainly professors in public administration) from fifty-eight countries.[10] The survey was fairly short (seven web pages) and took about ten minutes to complete. Our research strategy has been to construct questions from the

---

10. The survey is currently being extended to cover about 140 countries.

theoretical construction of impartiality in the exercise of public power as defined above. For example:

Q: By a common definition, impartiality implies that when implementing policies, public sector employees should not take anything about the citizen/case into consideration that is not stipulated in the policy. Generally speaking, how often would you say that public sector employees today, in your chosen country, act impartially when deciding how to implement a policy in an individual case?[11]

The second measurement strategy in this survey has been to use a couple of scenario questions, for example, the case of a cash transfer program to the "needy poor." This question was formulated as follows:

Q: Hypothetically, let's say that a typical public employee was given the task to distribute an amount equivalent to 1000 USD per capita to the needy poor in your country. According to your judgment, please state the percentage that would reach:

The question is then followed by six predetermined response categories for which the respondents could fill in numbers from 0 to 100 (provided they summed to 100 percent). The percentage reaching the "needy poor" is supposed to be a gauge of how impartially this particular policy would be implemented.

The third measurement strategy in this survey has been to provide examples of government behavior that clearly breach the impartiality principle. Three such examples were provided and, again, the response categories ranged from 1, "Hardly ever," to 7, "Almost always."

Q: Thinking about the country you have chosen, how often would you say the following occurs today?

a. Firms that provide the most favorable kickbacks to senior officials are awarded public procurement contracts in favor of firms making the lowest bid.

b. When deciding how to implement policies in individual cases, public sector employees treat some groups in society unfairly.

---

11. Respondents were asked to answer on a scale ranging from 1, "hardly ever," to 7, "almost always."

c. When granting licenses to start up private firms, public sector employees favor applicants with which they have strong personal contacts.

The preliminary results have been presented in Teorell (2009). First, although answers from the experts for each country vary, so far they are within a range that makes comparisons between the countries possible. Second, the variation between the countries in the degree of QoG as impartiality looks much as can be predicted from other measures such as the World Governance Indicators produced by the World Bank Research Institute or the Corruption Perception Index from Transparency International. The countries perceived by the experts as having the least impartial public administrations are South Africa, Russia, Ukraine, Kazakhstan, and Kyrgyzstan, while the ones with most impartial public administrations are Denmark, Switzerland, Austria, Norway, and New Zealand. Jan Teorell has used this measure of QoG to see how well it predicts a number of standard factors used in this type of research, such as the level of social trust, confidence in government institutions, economic growth, and life satisfaction. The main result that comes out of the QoG as impartiality measure is that the QoG survey is a better predictor of institutional trust, economic growth, and life satisfaction than the World Bank's World Government Indicators (WGI). Teorell summarizes the results as follows:

> only in the case of subjective well-being did the benchmark measures from WGI systematically outperform the impartiality index in terms of predictive fit (the other partial exception is the correlation between control of corruption and trust in the police). A low-cost web survey with public administration scholars . . . thus produced a gauge of quality of government that could well compete with the hoards of data sources and sophisticated estimation techniques employed by the World Bank Institute. Although this of course involves a comparison of not only the measurement strategy but also the underlying theory, it is encouraging news for our survey. (Teorell 2009)

Thus the answer to whether quality of government as impartiality can be measured is yes. It is possible to construct questions that tap into this concept in a meaningful way. Country experts in public administrations do answer questions about this issue intelligibly, and they do not argue that they are meaningless, impossible to answer, or uninteresting. Moreover, even though we so far only have fifty-eight countries, mainly from the industrialized Western world (the survey is currently being expanded), the results show that QoG as impartiality in the exercise of public power has not only theoretical justification but also empirical clout.

CHAPTER TWO

Quality of Government: What You Get

Quality of Government and Quality of Life

As I argued in the previous chapter, international organizations such as the World Bank and the United Nations have for about a decade emphasized the importance of *good governance* and *sound institutions* from a development perspective. In this chapter I will present a review of the empirical research, together with some benchmark empirical analyses of the bivariate relations between three widely used measures of QoG (the World Bank's Government Effectiveness Index, its Rule of Law Index, and Transparency International's Corruption Perceptions Index) and different measures of important societal outcomes in four areas: the economy, environmental sustainability, social policy, and life satisfaction. Since population health is such an important issue in itself, it will get a chapter of its own (chapter 3). The empirical analysis employs data from the Quality of Government Institute's data bank (Teorell et al. 2010). The central question for this chapter is simple and straightforward: *Does quality of government translate into quality of life?* As I argued in the previous chapter, this is the hope not only of empirical researchers but also of political theorists in the sense that just (in this case, impartial) institutions will result in increased social justice.

The 2000 United Nations Millennium Declaration identifies *good governance* as a requirement for countries to foster economic development and reduce poverty (United Nations 2000, sec. 13). In addition, the 2002 United Nations Human Development Report singles out democracy as a particularly important feature of good governance. The report states: "For politics and political institutions to promote human development and safeguard the freedom and dignity of all people, democracy must widen and deepen" (UNDP 2002, 1). However, the report also warns: "The links between democracy and human development are not automatic: when a small elite dominates economic and political decisions, the link between democracy and equity can be broken" (UNDP 2002, 3). This warning was later expanded in the 2003 United Nations Human Development Report. Although still championing good governance and the importance of democratic institutions, the 2003 report states that reforms in this area are not sufficient on their own for fostering economic growth and equitable development (UNDP 2003, 76). A closer look at the data from the Human Development Index (HDI) shows that in the 1990s, a time of democratization and reform, twenty-one countries saw a fall in their HDI ranking (measuring health, education, and standards of living). This can be compared with the 1980s, before the big push for good governance had begun, when only four countries saw their HDI ranking decline (Years of Plenty? 2003).

The complex conceptual and empirical relation between QoG and economic and social development is manifest in discussions about whether the effects of good governance are in fact as important as has been stated by the international policy community. Critics have claimed that the benefits of good governance have been overstated. The lack of objective data and the absence of a universal definition of "good governance" have implied that empirical results in different studies support both sides of the debate. For example, while some studies show that a high QoG leads to greater income inequality (Lopez 2004), other studies show the reverse (Gupta, Davoodi, and Alonso-Terme 1998). The differences in these results stem partly from the authors' measuring different aspects of good governance. While the first study uses the International Country Risk Guide (ICRG) index of good governance as a measure of its governance variable, the latter study uses six indexes of corruption (one of which is the ICRG index). Thus, because "good governance" is such a broad concept and encompasses a range of issues, empirical analyses hinge greatly on the definition of the term.

However, the measurement problem may not be as difficult as this discussion suggests, since three of the most widely used indexes of QoG correlate at the 0.90 level. These three indexes are the World Bank's Government Effectiveness Index, Transparency International's Corruption Perceptions Index, and the Rule of Law Index, also from the World

Bank. For a few countries there are interesting differences, but the general impression is that these variables go hand in hand.

Quality of Government and the Economic Growth Debate

The argument about the relation between QoG and economic growth comes from a variety of sources. One is what has been called "the institutional revolution," whose foremost proponent has been the Nobel laureate economic historian Douglass North (North 1990; cf. Helpman 2008). It should be stressed, however, that North has not focused exclusively on the importance of legal or semilegal institutions for economic growth. On the contrary, there is a strong "cultural" line in his argument, which includes things like "shared mental models" and "the belief system of societies." In many of his writings, North actually gives more weight to the informal (cultural) institutions for economic growth than to the formal ones. For example, he argues that to make impersonal productive economic exchange generally possible, societies need a certain set of institutional frameworks. However, "while formal rules can help in creating such frameworks, it is the informal constraints embodied in norms of behavior, conventions, and internally imposed codes of conduct that are critical" (North 1998b; see also North, Wallis, and Weingast 2009). Thus North's arguments are closely related to theories stressing the role of the basic social norms in a society, such as social capital and generalized trust, that can be seen as informal institutions.

Development scholars in political science and economics have also contributed significantly to the institutional revolution. The idea that efficient markets can be created only by deregulation or privatization has not fared well. Shock therapy capitalism has, to put it mildly, run into a number of problems because its proponents did not pay adequate attention to the need for institutions to hinder fraudulent, anticompetitive, and similar types of behavior (Kornai, Rothstein, and Rose-Ackerman 2004). If, for example, public contracts are given only to economic agents that are "well connected," belong to a specific ethnic majority, or have paid bribes, the economy is likely to suffer. Similarly, if workers threatened by unemployment have no social safety nets (unemployment benefits, vocational training, etc.), they or their unions may prevent rationalization and structural change of the economy.

As part of this discussion, a large number of studies in the good governance field have focused on the economic effects of institutions. For example, Kaufmann, Kraay, and Zoido-Lobatón find that "a one standard deviation improvement in governance leads to between a 2.5-fold (in the case of voice and accountability) and a 4-fold (in the case of political instability and violence) increase in per capita income" (1999, 15). Similarly, Kaufmann finds that

> an improvement in rule of law by one standard deviation from the low levels in Ukraine to those "middling" levels prevailing in South Africa would lead to a fourfold increase in per capita income in the long run. A larger increase in the quality of rule of law (by two standard deviations) in Ukraine (or in other countries in the former Soviet Union), to the much higher level in Slovenia or Spain, would further multiply this income per capita increase.(Kaufmann 2004, 15)

According to Kaufmann, similar economic improvements would follow from changes in the level of corruption or protection of civil liberties. Criticisms of such findings, however, come from two directions. The first comes from those who point to the issue of reverse causality. For example, Goldsmith states that "counter to optimistic claims about how much 'institutions matter,' . . . greater transparency, accountability, and participation are often a result, rather than a direct cause of faster development" (Goldsmith 2007, 165). He arrives at this conclusion by analyzing the history of specific governance reforms and the economic development of the United States, Argentina, Mauritius, and Jamaica. He shows that in the United States and Argentina, economic growth took off before major governance reforms had been adopted. Moreover, he argues that although Mauritius and Jamaica have similar sets of institutions, their development paths have been very different (Goldsmith 2007, 170–81). These observations lead him to conclude that "meritocratic bureaucracies, independent judiciaries, and honest elections are worthy goals in their own right, but setting them up need not give a perceptible jolt to development" (181). He further argues that if other conditions are favorable, economic growth can be accomplished even in countries with low-quality government institutions. Moreover, Goldsmith maintains that high-quality institutions are more likely to be established as an effect of an increase in production and income, but that governance reforms may be needed in the long run to sustain development (ibid.).

According to this view, then, industrialization has a tendency to give rise to better institutions. Similar conclusions are drawn by other researchers, who point to an endogeneity problem that is inherent when linking good governance and economic growth. These methodological problems in the research, they claim, have contributed to an overestimation of the effects of good governance (Przeworski 2004; Glaeser et al. 2004). Nevertheless, seen from a nineteenth-century European perspective, the historical record can be interpreted as supporting both cases. The English case seems to give evidence for the importance of the "QoG causes economic growth" hypothesis (North 1990). The Swedish case also seems to indicate that a large number of institutional reforms in the "good governance" direction were implemented just before the start of industrialization that put the country on a path of economic growth (Myhrman 2003; Rothstein 1998b).

I should underline that one is not likely to encounter a straightforward sequential logic here. It is very unlikely that a country can first set up a full-blown set of good governance institutions, then start to develop as an effect of this. First, as Grindle (2004) has argued, the "full set" is a very tall order. It includes not only independent courts and the rule of law, but also institutions for effective taxation, auditing, patents, an effective police force, an enforcement service, a bureau for land rights, inheritance law, a companies act, and so on. Second, from what we now think we know about how social causation works, we should expect to find things like "feedback mechanisms," "autocorrelation," and "path dependency," making the "independent" and "dependent" variables in this story very difficult to sort out (Hall 2003). To this one should add that we are not likely to find effects of just the formal establishment of institutions; instead, results will be influenced by how people in general come to perceive the credibility of such institutions.

Despite these criticisms, there are those who support the idea that good governance leads to economic growth but who still criticize the good governance agenda. Their criticism focuses on how this economic growth translates into reduced poverty and income inequality. For example, some argue that the policy implications of QoG tend to emphasize small governments, which could be viewed as being anti-poor (Shepherd 2000, 270). Shepherd, for example, argues that while reforms of the civil service have been successful in reducing the number of government employees, the reforms have failed to fix the problem of low pay. This has resulted in the continuation of "informal payment systems and other forms of corruption," which drain public sector employees of motivation to fulfill their duties (282). He further argues that the problem is that civil service reforms have not been coordinated with other policies such as universal primary education or basic health care, implying that the "output" side (service delivery outcomes) has suffered as a result of cuts on the "input" side. His conclusion is that even though good governance reforms may be necessary, in themselves they are not sufficient to reduce poverty. Rather, universal policies need to be launched, particularly in sectors such as education and health care (283).

On the other hand, the supporters of the good governance agenda argue that the poor suffer most under bad governments; thus reforms toward good governance will benefit the poor. According to this view, taking action to reduce corruption, increase access to legal services for the poor, improve ethics among the police to reduce discrimination against the poor, promote democratic institutions, increase the quality and efficiency of public good services, and manage the economy well will benefit poor people in the long term (Shepherd 2000, 270). In their cross-country study for 1960 to 1990, Chong and Calderón find support for this view. Their findings show a negative and significant relation between institutional quality and poverty. They state that "the more efficient a country's institutions, the lower the level, incidence, and severity of poverty" (Chong and Calderón 2000, 130). The risk of expropriation and the quality of the bureaucracy are shown to matter most for poverty levels, while corruption and law and order play a less significant role. Chong and Calderón theorize that this is because the poor usually live in rural areas, where the central government's hold is weaker. Therefore what matters most is to affect those things that have a direct bearing on the poor, such as the insecurity of expropriations and the inefficiencies of service delivery (130–31). They also put forth the notion that institutional reform may at first increase poverty in a country because of high initial transaction costs until the new system has started to function efficiently (125).

These views are in line with the argument made by development economist Hernando de Soto (2000) about what can be called *the social construction of capital*. To give a short recapitulation of de Soto's well-known argument: Capital is not the same as assets or even property. For assets/property to become capital, there must be a universally accepted legal construction by which ownership is generally respected. Through such a normative/legal institutional invention, assets/property that become capital can be used, for example, as security for loans for investing in small enterprises. The point is that de Soto shows that in the Western world this took a long and very complex process of legal institution building, in some cases several hundred years. The feudal idea of what constituted property was very different from the modern/capitalist idea. According to de Soto, assets cannot be transformed to and used as capital until recognized by "all" others. This in turn demands not only a strong legal "good governance" framework but also the type of general change in belief systems that, for example, Douglass North has argued is necessary. Perceptions about the trustworthiness of those to be entrusted with responsibilities for securing property rights are perhaps particularly important to change in this regard.

The general impression from this research is that there appears to be a consensus that a link exists between good governance and economic outcome, although the causality and the benefits to the poor are somewhat contested. Several commentators point to a need for more rigorous theoretical frameworks on how the good governance agenda can lead to pro-poor growth (economic growth that reduces absolute or relative levels of poverty) (Grindle 2004; Resnick and Birner 2006).

Quality of Government and the Corruption Debate

As I argued in the previous chapter, QoG cannot be defined solely as the absence of corruption. Although a high degree of corruption is clearly antithetical to QoG, the latter encompasses more than merely its absence. Still, for many, achieving QoG is closely connected to anticorruption policies. The opening pages of the United Nations report *Global Programme Against Corruption* state that "the most significant achievement in governance during the 1990s was the shattering of the taboo that barred discussion of corruption, particularly in diplomatic circles and intergovernmental institutions." It is difficult to say why this taboo existed for such a long time—one idea is that pointing out the "C" problem in developing countries could be seen as "blaming the victim." Another is that exposing corruption in developing countries would have decreased political support for international aid. Until the mid-1990s, the World Bank also saw corruption as an internal political problem, and since the Bank was forbidden to interfere in a country's internal politics, corruption was deemed outside its scope. This all changed when former World Bank president James D. Wolfensohn simply redefined corruption as an economic problem. In an interview in 2005, he stated: "Ten years ago, when I came here, the Bank never talked about corruption, and now we are doing programs in more than a hundred countries, and it is a regular subject for discussion" (World Bank 2005).

This reluctance to engage with corruption also prevailed in much of the social sciences. For example, the *Handbook of Development Economics*, published in four volumes between 1988 and 1995, has no index entry for "corruption." Moreover, most undergraduate-level textbooks in political science and economics hardly give corruption any attention (cf. Johnston 2006). During the past decade, however, corruption and other problems of dysfunctional governance have received increasing attention in the social sciences, not least as a result of the "institutional revolution" in economics and political science (Levi 2006).

Today there exists a vast literature on the effects of corruption. While some authors argue that particular types of corruption can have a positive effect on economic development (Nye 1967; Khan 1996, 1998), most studies point to its negative consequences (Mauro 1995; Akçay 2006; Transparency International 2008b; Gupta, Davoodi, and Alonso-Terme 1998). According to the first view, corruption can take different forms, of which some are efficiency enhancing and some are efficiency reducing. Hence a cost-benefit analysis must be carried out to establish the overall effect of corruption (Nye 1967; Khan 1996, 1998). According to the opposing view, corruption has negative effects on GDP growth (Mo 2001), income inequality and poverty (Gupta, Davoodi, and Alonso-Terme 1998), and health outcomes (Transparency International 2006). The mechanism here is that corruption acts like an illegal tax that distorts decision making and economic processes.

Several studies show that corruption influences what the government spends on education and health care and lowers human development as measured by life expectancy, educational attainment, and standard of living (Zhang, Cao, and Vaughn 2009; Mauro 1995; Gupta, Davoodi, and Alonso-Terme 1998). Kaufmann similarly finds that an improvement of one standard deviation in control of corruption would reduce child mortality by 75 percent, as well as lead to significant gains in literacy (Kaufmann 2004, 15–16). Moreover, as Rose-Ackerman has argued, "Corruption also tends to distort the allocation of economic benefits, favoring the haves over the have-nots—leading to a less equitable income distribution. A share of the country's wealth is distributed to insiders and corrupt bidders, contributing to inequalities in wealth" (cited in Akçay

2006, 33–34). Thus we can conclude that corruption generally has negative consequences for human development because it reduces economic
growth and diverts money from social services.

Quality of Government and the Rule of Law Debate

At the opening of the seventeenth session of the United Nations Commission on Crime Prevention and Criminal Justice, Antonio Maria
Costa, the executive director of the United Nations Office on Drugs and
Crime, delivered a speech titled "Rule of Law: A (Missing) Millennium
Development Goal That Can Help Reach the Other MDGs." In the
speech he emphasized the need for stronger rule of law to meet the Millennium Development Goals:

> Economic analysis has consistently shown the clear correlation between
> weak rule of law and weak socio-economic performance. Clear correlation,
> I said, though some people actually see strong causality: in countries ravaged
> by crime and corruption, and where governments lost control of their land,
> the poor suffer the most, and the services provided to them get delayed, or
> never arrive. They—the so-called "bottom billion"—have no access to justice,
> health care and education and face rising food prices: how can such countries
> meet the MDGs? (Costa 2008)

Empirical studies often support the view that the rule of law is important for economic development. Kaufmann and Kraay, for instance,
show that an improvement of one standard deviation in the rule of law
indicator "raises per capita income nearly fourfold in the very long run"
(Kaufmann and Kraay 2002, 181). Moreover, poor countries do not score
well on the rule of law indicator, whereas all rich countries do (except for
more poorly scoring Italy and Greece) (Economics and the Rule of Law
2008). On the other hand, critics point to the example of China, which
has witnessed unprecedented growth without scoring well on the rule of
law indicator. In this view, rule of law cannot be seen as a universal economic recipe, since it may not be a prerequisite for growth (ibid.). Messick (1999) also offers a warning against viewing rule of law as a pan-
acea. He argues that cross-sectional regressions do not satisfactorily
answer the question of causality. First, developed countries can spend
more on their judicial systems. Second, it may be that the same under-

lying variables that foster economic development also make the legal system work better. On this point, Messick makes a connection to the debate about the importance of "social capital," which has often been defined as historically established social norms of generalized trust and honest reciprocity. One can argue that social capital understood in this way is equivalent to the type of informal institutions put forward by North and by Mungiu-Pippidi, as presented in chapter 1. However, as has been shown by the work I have carried out with Daniel Eek, Staffan Kumlin, and Dietlind Stolle, there are relatively strong empirical indicators showing that precisely the opposite may be the case—that social trust is caused by high-quality legal institutions and administrative authorities (see chap. 6 in this book; Rothstein and Stolle 2008; Kumlin and Rothstein 2010).

The Policy Outcomes of Quality of Government

As the preceding discussion has shown, QoG is a broad topic that in recent years has been the focus of much research. Nevertheless, many of the debates in this field are still in question owing to the lack of strong and robust empirical indicators—for example, on the topic of whether good governance promotes economic growth and social well-being. Besley and Kudamatsu (2006, 313) argue that "in spite of the inexorable march of democracy around the globe, just how democratic institutions affect human well-being is open to debate. The evidence that democracy promotes prosperity is neither strong nor robust." A recent study by Schiffbauer and Shen (2010) shows that poor but large and politically stable dictatorships exhibit a higher growth rate than comparable (equally poor) democracies. The results from the QoG Institute's data set that covers between 18 and 180 countries, presented in tables 2.1 (correlations) and 2.2 (regression coefficients), as well as in figures 2.4 and 2.5, show that the three QoG variables (rule of law, corruption perception, and government effectiveness) have positive effects on a number of important social outcomes such as (various measures of) *population health, subjective well-being, environmental outcomes*, and *social policy outcomes*. Simply put, this first and admittedly crude overview of available data shows that the higher the level of QoG in a given country, the fewer babies die, the longer people live, the greater people's life satisfaction, the better the environment, and the fewer people unemployed

TABLE 2.1. **Correlates of three interrelated QoG variables with outcomes in the fields of health, ecology, economy, social welfare, and subjective well-being (r)**

Societal outcome variables	Correlation (r)						Effect of the QoG variables
	Rule of law	n	Government effectiveness	n	Corruption Perceptions Index	n	
Health outcomes							
Subjective health	+.37	45	+.44	45	+.37	39	Positive
Life expectancy at birth	+.62	180	+.62	180	+.53	98	Positive
Infant mortality rate	−.66	178	−.66	180	−.55	94	Positive
Mortality rate children <5 years	−.62	186	−.62	188	−.51	100	Positive
Prevalence of HIV	−.17	148	−.17	148	−.10	95	Positive
Environmental outcomes							
Environmental Sustainability Index	+.50	146	+.51	146	+.54	98	Positive
Air quality	+.37	146	+.33	146	+.39	98	Positive
Water quality	+.47	146	+.47	146	+.47	98	Positive
Improved drinking water source	+.57	165	+.57	165	+.58	86	Positive
Carbon emissions	+.49	178	+.48	180	+.70	100	Negative
Forest cover change	+.42	172	+.39	172	+.41	92	Positive
Economic outcomes							
GDP per capita	+.88	131	+.87	131	+.87	93	Positive
GDP growth	+.10	130	±.00	130	+.20	93	Positive
Gini Index	−.44	149	−.44	149	−.46	99	Positive[a]
Unemployment	−.47	30	−.46	30	−.48	30	Positive[a]
Societal outcomes/outputs							
Social security laws	+.52	84	+.51	84	+.51	77	Positive
Benefit generosity index	+.17	18	+.14	18	+.17	18	Positive
Relative poverty rate	−.47	30	−.39	30	−.33	30	Positive
Human Development Index	+.71	175	+.73	175	+.70	100	Positive
Subjective well−being							
Happiness	+.41	77	+.44	77	+.45	70	Positive
Life satisfaction	+.65	78	+.66	78	+.66	71	Positive
Good society index	+.83	71	+.84	71	+.83	64	Positive

[a]Less inequality and less unemployment.

Comments: The three QoG variables are highly intercorrelated (about .90). Their separate effects on the outcome variables are always the same. The effects column indicates whether the QoG variables are positively or negatively related to a "good" outcome in the societal variables. n = number of countries. The good society index includes measures of life expectancy, infant mortality, and life satisfaction and is presented in Holmberg (2007).

TABLE 2.2. **Effects of QoG (government effectiveness) on some twenty societal outcomes (regression coefficients)**

Societal outcome variables	b	p	Unit for the dependent variable	Effect of QoG: government effectiveness
Health outcomes				
Subjective health	0.12	.003	1–5; very poor–very good	Positive
Life expectancy at birth	7.82	.000	Years	Positive
Infant mortality rate	−27.6	.000	Deaths per 1,000 live births	Positive
Mortality rate children <5 years	−41.4	.000	Deaths per 1,000 live births	Positive
Prevalence of HIV	−0.98	.044	% of population aged 15–49	Positive
Ecological outcomes				
Environmental Sustainability Index	4.3	.000	Composite index (29.2–75.1)[a]	Positive
Air quality	0.20	.000	Composite index (−1.6–2.17)[a]	Positive
Water quality	0.30	.000	Composite index (−1.93–1.64)[a]	Positive
Improved drinking water source	11.3	.000	% of population with access	Positive
Carbon emissions	3.44	.000	Tons of carbon per capita	Negative
Forest cover change	0.56	.000	% (average annual rate of change)	Positive
Economic outcomes				
GDP per capita	7.8	.000	US$1,000 in 1996 constant prices	Positive
GDP growth	0.47	.511	% (real GDP per capita)	Not significant
Gini Index	−4.7	.000	Index (theoretically 0–100)	Positive[b]
Unemployment	−2.8	.011	% of civilian labor force	Positive[b]
Societal outcomes/outputs				
Social security laws	0.12	.000	Composite index (0–0.87)[a]	Positive
Benefit generosity index	2.8	.556	Composite index (18.6–41.7)[a]	Not significant
Relative poverty rate	−2.3	.032	% of population below 50% of median income	Positive
Human development index	0.13	.000	Composite index (theoretically 0–1)	Positive
Subjective well-being				
Happiness	0.12	.000	1–4; not at all happy–very happy	Positive
Life satisfaction	0.74	.000	1–10; dissatisfied–satisfied	Positive
The good society index	14.9	.000	Composite index (theoretically 1–71)	Positive

[a]Minimum and maximum value in the QoG data set.

[b]Less inequality and less unemployment.

Comments: The QoG variable (government effectiveness) is defined as the independent factor in a series of regression analyses with some twenty societal outcome variables as dependent factors. The source for the government effectiveness variable is the World Bank. Higher effectiveness scores signify more effective government. The effect of QoG column indicates whether government effectiveness is positively or negatively related to a "good" outcome in the societal outcome variables.

or defined as living in poverty. However, correlations with economic growth are surprisingly weak, while the correlation with GDP per capita is very strong.

One interpretation of this result could be that the causality between economic growth and QoG is more like a "virtuous circle" where "feedback mechanisms" play an important role. Dani Rodrik has stressed, "I am not aware of any strong econometric evidence that relates standard governance criteria to *growth* (all the evidence is about *income levels*)" (Rodrik 2008, 146). Recently this has been challenged by Aidt (2009, 271), who argues from a new and refined set of data that there is "a strong negative correlation between growth in genuine wealth per capita . . . and corruption." These results are central to the wider question of the policy outcomes of QoG. As will be evident in the following section, a country's GDP is one of its major determinants of policy outcomes in fields such as social well-being, public health, and the environment.

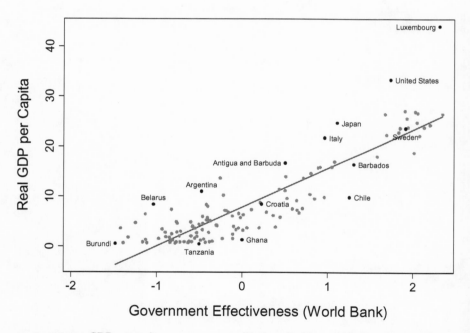

FIGURE 2.1. GDP per capita vs. government effectiveness. R^2 = .76. *Sources*: QoG data bank (Teorell et al. 2010); Heston, Summers, and Aten 2002 (GDP per capita data pertain to the year 2000); World Bank Governance Indicators, 2002.

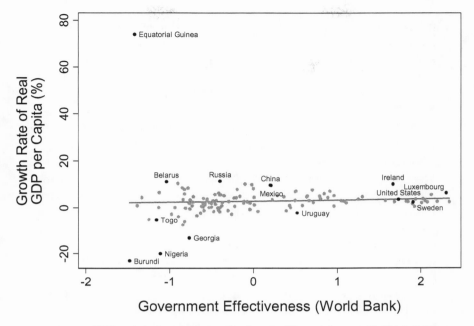

FIGURE 2.2. GDP growth vs. government effectiveness. $R^2 = .00$. *Sources*: QoG data bank (Teorell et al. 2010); Heston, Summers, and Aten 2002 (GDP growth data pertain to the year 2000); World Bank Governance Indicators, 2002.

Building on the discussions in the previous section, I will therefore explore in greater detail the effects of QoG on these policy areas.

Quality of Government and Social Well-Being

Within the topic of *social well-being*, indicators such as poverty, economic inequality, the existence of effective social insurance systems, subjective measures of life satisfaction, and the United Nations' measure of human development (HDI) are included. As I mentioned above, there is a debate about whether QoG necessarily leads to pro-poor growth. Kraay (2004) explores this using household survey data on average incomes from eighty developing countries, mainly from the 1990s. He shows that what matters the most for poverty reduction is growth in average incomes. However, poverty reduction is also affected by distributional changes. Using the World Bank's rule of law indicator as a proxy for institutional quality, he finds that "poverty increasing distributional change is more likely to occur in countries with better institutional quality." Nevertheless, he argues that this negative distributional effect on poverty in countries with high QoG is outweighed by the positive effect of institutional quality on economic growth (Kraay 2004, 20). Using a different method, Blaydes and Kayser (2007) arrive at the opposite conclusion when examining the link between democracy and propoor growth. They argue that even though democracy may not promote economic growth, democratic countries are more likely than autocratic states to promote economic redistribution that is beneficial to the poor. Blaydes and Kayser credit this to democratic countries' investments in human capital development and the benefits of competitive elections to poor voters, who are often marginalized in autocracies. The corruption literature makes similar inferences on the link between QoG and poverty. Research shows that corruption affects poverty through its consequences for economic and governance factors, such as through lower quality of public infrastructure, decreases in tax revenue, and poorer targeting of social programs (Chetwynd, Chetwynd, and Spector 2003).

Other studies focus more directly on the empirical link between governance and inequality. For example, Chong and Gradstein (2004) find that better ranking on the political stability and the rule of law measures, as well as the ICRG index, leads to a decrease in inequality. Lopez (2004), on the other hand, finds the opposite result using the ICRG index (Resnick and Birner 2006, 19). However, Chong and Calderón (2000) find a nonlinear relation: for richer countries, quality of institutions and income equality have a positive relation, while in poorer countries the relation is negative. They argue that this may be because institutional reforms first increase income inequality before decreasing it when institutional efficiency improves. Borrowing from Olson's (1996) theories on economic development and institutions, they theorize that bad governance often entails capture of the state by specific groups who prosper at the expense of the poor. Thus, in the long run governance reform will reduce inequality by removing discrimination against the marginalized section of the population (Chong and Calderón 2000, 124–25; Uslaner 2008). As shown in tables 2.1 and 2.2, the relation between the QoG variables and measures of inequality (unemployment and the relative poverty rate; see fig. 2.3) are reasonably strong. Tables 2.1 and 2.2 also show positive correlations between the QoG variables and policy

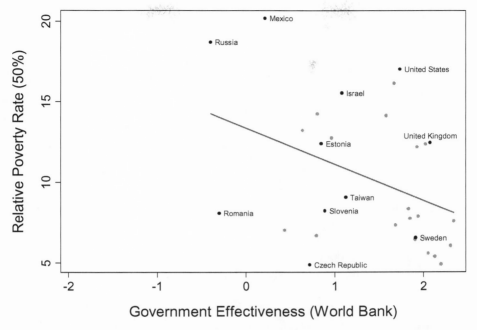

FIGURE 2.3. Relative poverty rate vs. government effectiveness. $R^2 = .15$. *Sources*: QoG data bank (Teorell et al. 2010); Luxembourg Income Study, 1996–2004; World Bank Governance Indicators, 2002. *Comment*: Percentage of population earning less than 50 percent of the median income. Mostly OECD countries.

measures for reducing inequality such as the "benefit generosity index" and the measure of social security laws.

*   *   *

Thus, a high QoG appears to have positive effects on social well-being. This result echoes that of Sacks and Levi (2007), who show a link between QoG and social welfare and social well-being, measured by the level of food security of households. Other measures of social well-being show similar results. For instance, Helliwell (2006), Helliwell and Huang (2008), Samanni and Holmberg (2010), Ott (2010), and Pacek and Radcliff (2008) have observed positive links between QoG and subjective well-being (a measure of an individual's evaluation of their quality of life in total). Helliwell (2006) reports that QoG-as measured by the averages of six main World Bank indicators-accounts for a large part of the international differences in subjective well-being found through surveys. Using measures of the degree of life satisfaction instead of degrees of happiness and adding more countries, Ott shows that QoG has a strong impact on subjective well-being and that the effect is stronger than for measures of democracy. As Ott writes, it makes a great difference "if citizens are treated carefully and respectfully" and that how the state does so is more important than what and how much it produces in terms of policies and the size of government (Ott 2010, 365).

Finally, Pacek and Radcliff (2008) find a positive link between welfare state generosity and subjective well-being when examining survey data from eighteen industrial democracies from 1981 to 2000. They conclude that the higher the "quality of welfare policy" (as measured by the comprehensiveness of social security programs, including pensions, sickness compensation, and unemployment support), the more satisfied individuals are with their lives. One reason for this, they believe, is that welfare states better protect their citizens from the insecurities produced by the market, thereby improving their quality of life. To capture this, Holmberg has constructed a "good society index" from three variables:

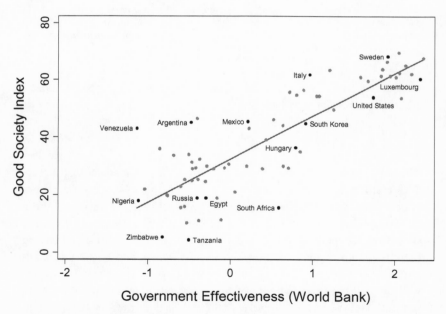

FIGURE 2.4. The good society index vs. government effectiveness. $R^2 = .71$. *Sources*: QoG data bank (Teorell et al. 2010); Holmberg 2007; World Bank Governance Indicators, 2002.

World Health Organization measures on infant mortality and life expectancy and subjective well-being from the World Value Survey, thereby combining both objective and subjective measures. In Holmberg's words: "In the good society newborn infants should survive, people should grow old before they die and in between people should be satisfied with their lives." This index is elegant precisely because it is so simple. Leaving out many other measures of what could constitute a good life (democracy, economic prosperity, access to culture, education, etc.), it makes it possible to analyze the impact of such items on "the good society" as defined by Holmberg (2007). As shown in figure 2.4, there is a strong correlation between this measure of what constitutes a "good society" and QoG.

Nevertheless, we should expect that the effect of QoG variables on social well-being goes through a complex pattern of causality that is affected by intermediaries such as economic and institutional factors. Nevertheless, most evidence—including the empirical results presented here—points to positive outcomes of QoG on policy areas, such as reduced poverty and greater life satisfaction.

Quality of Government and Environmental Issues

While most studies find a causal relation between QoG, economic standard, and social well-being, the same cannot be said for the effects of QoG variables on *environmental outcomes*. Here the debate is complicated because we lack an unambiguous definition of environmental sustainability. Because it is a broad concept that encompasses a range of issues, a plethora of competing sustainability indexes have been created (Böhringer and Jochem 2007). Consequently, empirical results are largely determined by the choice of the sustainability index used. For instance, while Morse (2006) finds that corruption is negatively correlated with environmental sustainability (as measured by the Environmental Sustainability Index [ESI]), Ewers and Smith (2007) obtain an opposite result using the Ecological Footprint index. The differences arise because the Ecological Footprint emphasizes the measurement of a country's impact on the planet through its consumption patterns, in contrast to the ESI's broader measurements, which include a country's pollution levels, environmental management, capacity to improve environmental performance, and so forth. The question therefore appears to be whether one should assign greater significance to ratifications of environmental agreements, technological advances, and reductions in pollution levels or to a country's total impact on the planet. In other words: "If sustainability is viewed in terms of capacity and global stewardship, then the richer countries do well relative to the poorer ones, while if sustainability is seen in terms of the stress placed on the environment, then the richer countries come out worse" (Morse and Fraser 2005, 633).

Nevertheless, if one focuses on a country's level of water and air pollution, then empirical studies have revealed a number of mechanisms through which QoG variables affect environmental outcomes. The so-called environmental Kuznets curve has been shown to hold for some pollutants, particularly those that have local impacts; pollution increases as countries develop from a low level of GDP per capita and subsequently falls at higher levels of income when people's preferences change in favor of preserving the environment. This means that corruption can have a direct and an indirect effect on pollution levels. The direct effect takes place by increased pollution at any given income level through, for example, bribing officials to bypass pollution laws. Another example is

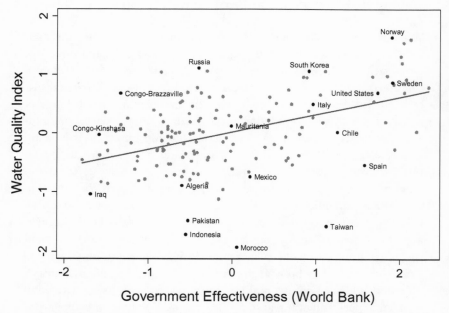

FIGURE 2.5. Water quality vs. government effectiveness. $R^2 = .22$. *Sources*: QoG data bank (Teorell et al. 2010); Esty and Porter 2005.

the *Global Corruption Report 2008*, emphasizing the link between corruption and water pollution, which has been associated with the degradation of wetlands and other important ecosystems and with desertification, as well as having negative consequences for wildlife preservation. The indirect effect of corruption, on the other hand, can be either positive or negative, depending on how pollution interacts with economic development at a certain level of per capita income (Welsch 2004; Lopez and Mitra 2000). Empirical investigations are thus required to determine which effect plays a larger role in the equation.

Welsch (2004) uses different indicators of ambient air and water pollution for 106 countries and finds that corruption enhances pollution at all income levels. He argues that low-income countries have the most to gain in terms of less air and water pollution by reducing corruption. Damania, Fredriksson, and List (2003) similarly find that lower corruption is correlated with tougher environmental regulations by investigating allowable lead content per gallon of gasoline. Nevertheless, their study shows that developing countries have conditionally lower levels of lead per gallon of gasoline than developed countries if per capita income is taken into consideration.

Fredriksson and Mani (2002) explore the interaction of the rule of law with corruption and demonstrate that environmental policy stringency is lowest in countries with a low degree of rule of law and a high level of corruption. They also show that with a high degree of rule of law, the negative effect of corruption on environmental stringency grows, owing to the increased incentive to bribe officials and circumvent environmental laws. Fredriksson and Mani therefore conclude that greater policy stringency must go hand in hand with efforts to reduce corruption if environmental policies are to have the intended effects. Esty and Porter (2005) also find that institutional factors play a role in explaining environmental performance in terms of urban particulates and energy efficiency, although income levels appear to be the dominant factor in determining environmental outcome. They therefore conclude that environmental policy makers should prioritize poverty alleviation.

Other studies have focused on the link between democracy and environmental policy. Neumayer (2002), for example, finds evidence of a positive association between democracy and environmental commitment, in terms of the ratification of environmental agreements, participation in international environmental organizations, assigning protection status to a greater percentage of their land area, and so on. He warns, however, that this does not necessarily translate into better environmental outcomes:

> The link between democracy and environmental outcomes is likely to be weaker the more factors outside a government's control impact upon outcomes, the longer the time-span between environmental commitment and its effect on environmental outcomes is and the more difficult environmental outcomes are to monitor. If these conditions hold true, then the electorate in a democracy will appreciate the difficulty of holding governments accountable for environmental outcomes rather than commitment and will look for commitment instead. (Neumayer 2002, 145)

Barrett and Graddy (2000) look at the link between civil and political freedoms and environmental quality and find that some of the pollutants that have the most adverse effects on human health are lower in countries with greater civil and political freedoms. In a different study, Fredriksson and Wollscheid look at environmental policy stringency and democracy and show that democracies have stricter environmental policies than autocracies. However, they argue that this result appears to be driven primarily by parliamentary democracies, whereas presidential-congressional systems often do not set environmental policies that are significantly different from those of nondemocracies. They credit this to less separation of powers and greater legislative cohesion in parliamentary systems (Fredriksson and Wollscheid 2007, 390). In addition, there appears to be some evidence that the transition from autocracy to democracy may result in widespread environmental degradation if the period is marked by political instability. Examples of this could be seen in Indonesia after the fall of Suharto in 1998, when deforestation increased (Matthews and Mock 2003, 32).

Tables 2.1 and 2.2 show that environmental outcomes correlate positively with QoG, which confirms some of the associations found in the previous literature. On the other hand, as shown in figure 2.6 below, the QoG variables can be seen to have a negative effect on carbon emissions, which is also in line with previous studies finding that the less local a particular type of pollution is and the more externalities it has, the less likely governments are to tackle it. Overall, therefore, although significant relations can be found between QoG and environmental outcomes, care should be taken in interpreting these results. As many studies point out, this is due to the broadness of the concept of environmental

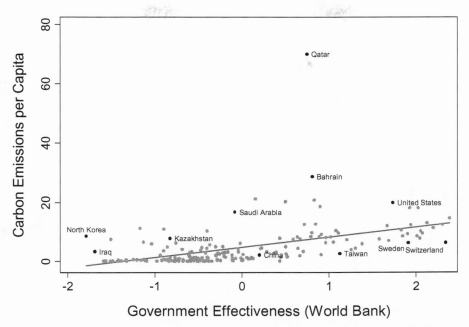

FIGURE 2.6. Carbon emissions vs. government effectiveness. R^2 = .23. *Sources*: QoG data bank (Teorell et al. 2010); Esty and Porter 2005; (carbon emissions data pertain to the year 2001); World Bank Governance Indicators, 2002.

sustainability, the weakness of some of the data, and the difficulties in assigning cause and effect because of the many interactions with economic performance and other contextual factors.

Quality of Government and Development Policy

This research review merely presents a small section of the now vast literature on QoG. Nevertheless, I can make some general observations. First, while QoG appears to be a worthy cause to pursue, the research on the topic remains thin in a number of areas. For example, Resnick and Birner (2006, 18) mention that cross-national studies focusing on the political process as an interaction variable are absent from the literature. Others point to the weakness in theoretical foundation in some areas, such as the interdependent nature of institutions. Goldsmith, for instance, seeks greater efforts in "capturing nonlinear and lagged relationships in governance" (Goldsmith 2007, 182). A related point of criticism is that the research on good governance does not easily translate into simply executed policies. To start with, there is little agreement, for example, on *what type* of rule of law or *what form* of democracy is required for a country to reap the full effects of QoG. Some authors employ a "thick" definition of rule of law, while others use a more formal "thin" definition. The former considers states as being ruled by law only "if the state's power is constrained and if basic freedoms, such as those of speech and association, are guaranteed." The latter narrows its focus to "property rights and the efficient administration of justice" (Economics and the Rule of Law 2008). Similarly, Welzel and Inglehart (2008) stress the importance of distinguishing between effective and ineffective democracies. The narrow definition of democracy focuses on holding regular elections that can be considered free and fair, and this type is known as "electoral democracy." The broader definition, "liberal democracy," maintains that competitive elections in themselves do not lead to genuine democracy. Rather, they argue, effective democracy relies on "the wide distribution of participatory resources and a trusting, tolerant public that prizes free choice" (Welzel and Inglehart 2008, 126–27).

In addition, Helliwell and Huang argue that different countries may require different institutional structures at different points in time. Through examining life satisfaction in relation to various aspects of good governance in a large cross-national study, they find that "honest and efficient governments are of especial salience for poorer countries, while voice, accountability, and political stability are of greater relative importance for the richer countries." They therefore argue that "even if at some more fundamental level all individuals have the same basic preference structures, the relative costs and benefits of different sorts of institutional structure vary with circumstances" (Helliwell and Huang 2008, 603).

A healthy reminder of the consequences of this institutional heterogeneity is that in the 1960s, donors such as USAID and the Ford Foundation set out on an ambitious task of reforming the judicial systems in a number of developing countries. After a few years, however, some of the key individuals involved in the project (known as the "law and development" movement) admitted the program had failed (Messick 1999, 125). The failure has been analyzed in a number of studies, and some key criticisms have emerged. For one thing, this approach did not have a clear theory of how law affected development. This left practitioners with little or no guidance on what type of reforms should be prioritized, and they were also not able to predict the effects of the various changes in the legal systems. A second problem was the lack of participation by lawyers and other legal practitioners in the developing countries, who were to implement the reforms and who were going to be affected by them. Third, too much weight was given to changing the formal legal institutions "to the exclusion of customary law and the other informal ways in which many people in developing nations order their lives" (Messick 1999, 126).

However, as Trubek and Galanter had already pointed out in 1974, maybe the most important reason for the failure was the rather "naive belief that the American legal system (and its legal culture generally) . . . could be easily transplanted to developing countries" (Messik 1999, 126). Perhaps the good governance agenda will fall into the same traps as the "law and development" movement did, unless more attention is paid to forming rigorous theories about how good governance works and can be established in practice.

CHAPTER THREE

Corruption: The Killing Fields

Quality of Government and the Health Sector

Immediately after she had given birth to her first child at one of the public hospitals in the city of Bangalore in India, Nasam Velankanni wanted the midwife to put the crying baby on her chest. However, before she had even a glimpse of her newborn, a nurse whisked the infant away and an attendant asked for a bribe. Nasam Velankanni was told that the customary price if she wanted to hold her child directly after birth was US$12 for a boy and US$7 for a girl. The attendant demanded the money immediately, because the doctors were leaving for the day and wanted their share before going home. For Nasam Velankanni and her family, twelve dollars was a substantial amount of money, since her husband was working for less than one dollar a day. Eventually the poor woman's mother-in-law promised to pawn her gold earrings, so Nasam Velankanni got to hold her newborn. Even though the government of India has established fierce measures to combat such petty corruption and extortion in the health care sector, the custom remains, partly because many poor people are afraid their babies will receive bad treatment from angry health care workers if they do not pay (Dugger 2005).

This story, told in the *New York Times* on August 30, 2005, is only one of innumerable descriptions of corruption and similar dysfunctional government practices in many countries. Survey data about perceptions of corruption from twenty-three developing countries shows that the health care sector is ranked number one in corruption among nine sectors in three countries,[1] number two in three other countries,[2] and within the top four most corrupt sectors in four more countries.[3] In many of these countries, over 80 percent of the population have experienced corrupt practices in the health care sector. A survey of deaths caused by malaria in rural Tanzania reported that nearly 80 percent of the children who died of this usually curable disease had been to modern health facilities. That they were not cured can to a large extent be explained by such corrupt practices as drug pilfering, provider absenteeism, stolen equipment, and very low levels of diagnostic effort (World Bank 2010, 2).

Another survey from former communist countries in Central and Eastern Europe has shown that in most of these countries, well over 50 percent of the population think corruption among doctors is widespread (Lewis 2006). Even in such relatively developed European Union countries as Hungary, the practice is to leave an envelope at the doctor's desk with a sum that is quite substantial for an ordinary Hungarian family (Kornai 2000). Another example is the very high level of absenteeism among health personnel in many national health care systems in developing countries. For various reasons (low pay, bad control, low sense of public duty, greed), they simply do not show up for work. Instead, they decide to earn extra money by working "on the side" (Lewis and Lloyd-Sherlock 2009; Widmalm 2008).

In 2006, Transparency International published a special report about the devastating effects that corruption has on people's access to health care and on health in general. The report documents the existence of corruption and similar practices in many areas of the health care sector, such as the administration of hospitals, "under the table" payments to doctors in many Eastern European countries, the existence of counterfeit drugs in Nicaragua, and overbilling of insurance companies in the United States. The report indicates that while the type of corruption illustrated by the Bangalore case above is unusual in the OECD (Organisation for Economic Co-operation and Development) countries, other corrupt practices in the health care sector plague many developed countries. Recently the *New York Review of Books*, one of the world's most influential literary magazines, published a lengthy article

---

1. Moldova, Slovakia, and Tajikistan.
2. Bangladesh, India, and Sri Lanka.
3. Kazakhstan, Kyrgyzstan, Madagascar, and Morocco.

(and a following "exchange") titled "Drug Companies and Doctors: A Story of Corruption," in which Marcia Angell claims that medical doctors in the United States are evaluating the effects of new drugs manufactured by companies in which they have an economic interest. An interesting part of this "exchange" is that the author of the article does not equate corruption with criminal behavior. Instead, she argues that corruption should be understood as "undermining the impartiality that is essential both to medical research and clinical practices." As Angell argues, "Judges do not hear cases in which they have a financial interest. Reporters do not write stories about companies in which they have a financial interest. By the same token, doctors should not have a financial interest in treatments they are evaluating" (Angell 2009, 6).

With this definition of corruption, Angell is in line with the former World Bank economist Daniel Kaufmann, who introduced the concept of "legal corruption" to mean agents' acting to "collude and purchase, or unduly influence the rules of the game, shape the institutions, the policies and regulations and the laws for their own private benefits."[4] According to Kaufmann, legal corruption is closely connected to activities that undermine collective action (Kaufmann and Vicente 2005). The concept of "legal corruption" is especially important in the health care sector, where hospitals, insurers, or pharmaceutical companies that act dishonestly to enrich themselves instead of putting the patients' medical needs first may not be doing anything formally illegal. But as Savedoff and Hussman have argued, "They are abusing the public's trust in the sense that people and organisations engaged in health care delivery are held to a higher standard in the interest of protecting people's health" (2006, 146). Since the medical profession usually is given broad discretion, they are assumed to act in their patients' best interests.

Studying the Relation between the Quality of Government and Good Health

To start with the conclusion, low QoG has a significant negative impact on population health. Gupta, Davoodi, and Tiongson (2000), as well as Doces and Sanjian (2009), have demonstrated that corruption indicators are negatively associated with, for instance, high levels of child and

4. http://info.worldbank.org/etools/bspan/PresentationView.asp?PID=2363&EID=1056.

maternal mortality. In this chapter I will give a preliminary overview of the relation between variables that measure the *quality of government* (QoG) and a number of standard measures of population health in the light of how much money and what type (private or public) is spent on health care in different countries (Bloom and Canning 2000). In addition to the academic interest a study like this will have, such an analysis may be important to policy makers in both the health care sector and the development sector. Simply put, if you want to improve population health (measured as infant mortality and expected life time at birth), what works? More precisely, is it better to simply increase spending on health care (and if so, should this be public or private money?), or is it better to improve the overall quality of the countries' government institutions?

I should add that indicators of population health such as the ones used here can be interpreted as telling us more about a society than just how healthy its population is. As argued by Hall and Lamont, there are good arguments for taking population health as a measure of how successful different societies are. Based on the idea of "capabilities" launched by Amartya Sen, and criticizing various strands of "post-enlightenment thought for leading to a balkanization within (and between) the social science disciplines," they argue that, all else being equal, health enhances individuals' abilities "to pursue the goals important to their lives, whether through individual or collective action," and this is what they believe defines a successful society (Hall and Lamont 2009, 2). Obviously, I agree.

The empirical case studies and illustrations noted above are important for increasing our knowledge about the great variety of corrupt practices that can take place in the health care sector. They are also very valuable for laying bare the "microlevel" logic of these practices, and they give insights into how the agents' behavior can be understood. However, like all case studies, they can be questioned because of the difficulty of generalizing from the data. One reason many health economists have refrained from studying the influence of QoG on the performance of the health care sector in their countries has been the lack of data for intracountry comparisons. However, by using available measures of indicators of the quality of government institutions in a large number of countries, a small group of scholars has started to analyze this problem at a more generalizable level. The general finding, which I will refer to below, is that the "quality of government factor" is positively related statistically to standard measures of population health such as infant mortality and life expectancy at birth. Moreover, in some studies it has been shown to be more important than the level of public spending on health care. Before I summarize this literature, I must make a few arguments for why the health care sector may be especially prone to corruption and similar dysfunctional government practices.

Ways of Causality

There are several reasons population health should be related to the quality of government. The indirect links are that since a country's QoG is positively related to economic performance, high QoG should result in more economic growth, implying better food, better housing, access to safe water and sanitation, less strenuous working conditions, fewer destitute people, and so forth (Bloom and Canning 2000). However, the link between a country's economic prosperity and population health is by no means clear-cut. The "wealthier is healthier" proposition has problems with the fact that there is great variation in, for example, infant mortality and life expectancy between equally poor and (albeit to a lesser extent) equally rich countries (Evans 2009).

How an institutional factor like QoG indirectly affects population health can be illustrated by illnesses caused by lack of access to safe water, as I mentioned in chapter 1. To repeat, about 1.2 billion people lack access to enough safe water and nearly 3 billion are without adequate sanitation; and the World Health Organization (WHO) estimates that 80 percent of all illnesses in the developing world are the result of waterborne pathogens. An increasing number of experts argue that this is not mainly an engineering problem that can be solved by more investment in dams, sewerage, water cleaning stations, and such. Instead, the problem is seen as caused by a lack of adequate government institutions (Bruns and Meinzen-Dick 2000; Transparency International 2008a; Sjöstedt 2008).

Other such indirect causal chains demonstrate that QoG is positively related to social capital (a combination of extended social networks and generalized trust), which in turn has been shown to have a positive effect on health (Lindstrom and Mohseni 2009; Rothstein and Stolle 2008; Schultz, O'Brien, and Tadesse 2008). Hall and Taylor argue that not being able to cope with various life challenges often leads to problems with

emotional as well as physiological health. Lacking networks and relations based on mutual trust is one important factor in why people cannot handle various challenges (Hall and Taylor 2009). As will be shown
in chapter 8, an experimental approach shows that experiencing corruption in public authorities diminishes not only people's trust in these authorities, but also their trust in "people in general." Thus, one can argue
for a causal chain that goes from corruption to low trust/low social capital to health problems (Hall and Taylor 2009). Moreover, as shown in the
previous chapter, studies based on comparative survey data show that
living under corrupt, unreliable, and untrustworthy government institutions is a very important explanation for low subjective well-being (unhappiness), especially in poorer countries (Helliwell and Huang 2008).
Since low life satisfaction can cause health problems, there could thus
also be a causal chain running from corruption to unhappiness to low
population health.

High levels of QoG should also make people more willing to pay
taxes, since they would feel more confident that their tax money will
be used well by various government agencies (Scholz and Lubell 1998).
Since there is a positive correlation between *public* spending on health
care and the standard measures of population health, high QoG should
result in more public spending on health care and thus better population
health.

Furthermore, as shown by research in social epidemiology, there
is a strong causal link between social and economic inequality, on the
one hand, and low levels of population health on the other. For example, Wilkinson and Picket show that this relation between equality and
well-being exists both when they compare Western OECD countries and
when they compare the fifty states of the United States. What is striking
about their findings is that mental illness, physical health problems, and
shorter life expectancy are not hitting only poor people in unequal societies. Instead, they show, for example, that "across whole populations,
mental illness is five times higher in the most unequal compared to the
least unequal societies" (Wilkinson and Pickett 2009, 181). The same
goes for problems like obesity, lower life expectancy, and various physical illnesses. As they point out, the Nordic countries and Japan are doing the best in their sample. This shows that low levels of inequality (and
the following higher level of population health) can be reached without
an encompassing, high-spending welfare state (Japan). However, as they
also point out, most of the countries with high levels of population health

are encompassing welfare states (the Nordic countries). Thus there may be another indirect causal link between QoG and population health because in countries with low QoG, people will not trust the government with enough money (taxes), and without economic resources, there will be a shortage of social policies that ameliorate a high level of inequality, which this type of research considers a major cause of low population health (Marmot 2004; Siegrist and Marmot 2006; Wilkinson and Pickett 2009; cf. Fritzell and Lundberg 2007).

As is indicated by the empirical illustrations I mentioned above, one could also hypothesize a number of more direct causal mechanisms between QoG and population health. The health care sector produces a type of service in which what economists call "problems of asymmetric information" are common. The source of the funding for medical treatment, whether the patient herself, a government agency, or a private insurance agency, cannot have anything close to "perfect information" about whether the treatment doctors suggest is motivated by medical reasons or by a desire for personal enrichment. Moreover, when a "third party" pays, something that is common in most developed countries, patient and doctor can collaborate to use treatments that cost more than is medically necessary. The health care sector is special, since the provider of the service usually determines what the "customers" should buy (Savedoff and Hussmann 2006). Thus the health care service is a classic case for "market failures," implying that governments usually have to be involved to avoid massive inefficiency (Barr 2004). This implies that an efficient health care sector often involves a complex mix of public, semiprivate, and private providers as well as regulatory agencies. Taken together, the economic magnitude of the health care sector in many countries, the complex mix of actors, and the information problems may make this sector especially prone to corruption (legal or illegal) as well as to other forms of low QoG.

State of the Art

Surprisingly, there are only a handful of studies in the health and governance literature that have systematically analyzed the relation between population health, health care, and QoG.

Employing data from ninety-one countries, Rajkumar and Swaroop analyzed the effect of public health spending on child mortality by modeling the interaction between public spending and QoG variables such as "quality of bureaucracy" and "control of corruption." Controlling for a number of other variables, such as income inequality and ethnolinguistic division, they conclude that QoG is central in determining the effectiveness of public spending on health care. The empirical analysis reveals that a one percentage point increase in public health spending's share of GDP lowers the child mortality rate by 0.32 percent in countries with high QoG and by 0.20 percent in countries with average QoG, but has no effect in countries with low QoG (Rajkumar and Swaroop 2008).

One of the few meta-analyses of the relation between QoG and health has been carried out by Maureen Lewis for the Center for Global Development. The main finding is that "good governance" is a critical factor in making national health care systems work, and that public spending on health care is inefficient in countries with low QoG. Unless governments shift their attention to the institutional factors that affect performance in the health sector, it is doubtful that mortality rates will decline (Lewis and Lloyd-Sherlock 2009). Wagstaff and Claeson (2004) have shown that an increase in the levels of public health funding in countries that have received a medium or low score on CPIA (Country Policy and Institutional Assessment, which measures the quality of policies and institutions) from the World Bank would not by itself necessarily lead to a reduction in child mortality. Conversely, they demonstrate that in countries with high levels of QoG, an increase in government health budgets would reduce mortality rates for children and mothers based on the assumption that the additional funding is distributed to programs and institutions according to the same ratio as current allocations. A similar result is reached by a study with data from 118 developing countries (Baldacci et al. 2008). Regarding the specific question of HIV, an analysis of 149 countries shows that the prevalence of HIV is significantly related to low QoG (Menon-Johansson 2005). Last, Klomp and de Haan (2008), who have undertaken the most advanced study so far in this area in terms of data and methods, criticize the type of studies mentioned above for taking into account only a few control variables, casting doubt on their conclusions about the positive effect of QoG on population health. They nevertheless argue that the relation between governance and (the quality of) the health care sector is arguably a key variable in explaining differences in health outcome across countries. In addition to a wealth of data from 101 countries for measuring QoG, Klomp and de Haan use sixteen indicators for measuring health. To the standard indicators above, they add, for instance, the prevalence of a number of diseases such as HIV, polio, and tuberculosis. Moreover, they measure the standard of the health care sector by using ten indicators such as number of health care personnel per thousand inhabitants and immunization rates for four illnesses (hepatitis, diphtheria, measles, and tuberculosis).

Klomp and de Haan's main finding is that governance influences health through its indirect positive effects on the standard of the health care sector and on income. They estimate that a 1 percent improvement in governance leads to an improvement of 0.55 percent in the quality of the health care sector and 3.54 percent in the health of individuals. Moreover, the study shows that it is through the indirect positive effects on income that governance can contribute most to an improvement in health. However, the authors also argue that the significance of these indirect effects varies between country groups. For countries with relatively healthy populations, QoG will have a positive indirect effect through the quality of the health care sector, but not through income. On the other hand, for countries with poor population health, the case will be the opposite; QoG will have a positive indirect effect through income, but not through the quality of the health care sector (Klomp and de Haan 2008). Lazarova and Mosca (2008) use a similar argument when they make the case that absolute income is what matters most in improving health indicators in countries below a certain threshold (5,000 PPP [purchasing power parity] international dollars per capita), whereas in the countries above this threshold QoG is the most important determinant of health.

One conclusion from this study is that the influence of QoG on the health care sector may be explained in that only in countries with a relatively high level of general QoG are people willing to pay taxes at the level needed to have a high standard of health care. However, the causality may also run in the opposite direction. In countries where people perceive that the quality of health care is low (for example, because they experience various forms of corruption by the health care staff), they will not be willing to pay enough in taxes to increase the general QoG. Another conclusion is that the small amount of research in this area and the variation in the results point to the need for more research.

Charting Basic Relationships

In this section I will provide some basic statistics to show the relation between QoG and population health, using the data from the Quality of
Government Institute's open source data set (Teorell et al. 2010). Aided
by some of the meta-analyses cited above, I will analyze three QoG variables and five indicators of population health. Since money always matters, not least in this policy sector, I will also include some spending variables and hence incorporate four measures of health spending as well. A
pivotal question is to what extent quality of government matters besides,
or on top of, spending on health care. A related but largely overlooked
question in the literature is whether public or private health spending
is better at creating good health. And if one type of health spending is
better than the other, does the same still hold in combination with good
government?

The three QoG variables are the World Bank's Rule of Law Index,
the World Bank's Government Effectiveness Index, and Transparency
International's Corruption Perceptions Index. In theory they measure
different things, but in practice, as I argued earlier, all three are highly
interrelated, with correlation coefficients of about .93. However, for in-
formational purposes all three are included in the analysis.

Four of the five health variables are also highly internally correlated
across the sample of some 180 countries. The internal correlations vary
between .85 and .97. The four variables are life expectancy at birth, mortality rate for children under five, maternal mortality rate, and healthy
life expectancy—all taken from WHO. The fifth health variable is much
less closely correlated with the other four (about .10). It is the subjective health measure taken from the World Value Survey, available for
only about forty-five countries in the Quality of Government Institute's
data set. The money variables measure total health spending (percentage of GDP), government spending on health (percentage of GDP), private spending on health (percentage of GDP), and private share of total
health spending (percentage). All spending measures have been put together by WHO.

It should be observed that all the spending variables are relative in the
sense that they measure money spent as a percentage of GDP (or in one
case, total health spending as a percentage of GDP). This means they
are priority or policy variables, indicating which kinds of health spend-

ing different countries have opted for. What they do not measure is how *much* money different countries spend on health in an absolute sense.

In the figure appendix to this chapter, which is presented in full on the QoG Institute's web page, thirty-five bivariate scatter plots with regression lines are included for all of our five health variables, and they have been run against the three QoG variables and the four health-spending measures.[5] Browsing through all these very informative scatter plots gives an excellent overview of bivariate relations around the world between, on the one hand, health spending and QoG and, on the other, health spending and good health. Five of these instructive plots can be found at the end of this chapter. Added to this, twenty-four more scatter plots have been included that demonstrate the connections between two health indicators (healthy life expectancy and mortality rate for children under five) and three measures of health care spending and three QoG variables in OECD countries as well as non-OECD countries (see the QoG Institute's web page).[6] This addition was in order to compare hands-on the relations among more developed and richer countries with those of less developed and poorer countries. In the health literature, the degree of economic development is often included as an intervening or interacting variable ultimately affecting population health. The hypothesis is that a better economy leads to better health for the population. The OECD versus non-OECD classification of countries is used as a proxy for the level of economic development and wealth.

The results are summarized in a set of tables in the table appendix at the end of this chapter. All QoG variables reveal strong and positive bivariate relations with all five health indicators. Here a positive relation indicates that *more* of a QoG variable is positively associated with *higher* levels of life expectancy, *lower* levels of mortality rates for children and mothers, *higher* levels of healthy life expectancy, and *higher* levels of subjective health feelings. The positive relation with QoG is most pronounced for healthy life expectancy and least noticeable for subjective health.

In contrast to the strong relations between the QoG variables and the health indicators, the relation between the health care spending measures and population health is rather weak most of the time and occasionally is nonexistent. The connection is positive for health levels but

5. http://www.qog.pol.gu.se,—Working Paper 2009, 16.
6. http://www.qog.pol.gu.se,—Working Paper 2009, 16.

weak for total health care spending and government health care spending. However, for private health care spending as well as for private share of total health care spending, the relation to good population health is close to zero or slightly negative. A negative relation in this context means that *more* private health care spending (as a percentage of GDP) is coupled with *lower* life expectancy, *higher* mortality rates among children and mothers, *lower* healthy life expectancy, and *lower* subjective health assessments.

Controlling for being an OECD (rich) or a non-OECD (not so rich or even poor) country does not change any of the relations. The QoG variables are all positively related to good health among OECD as well as non-OECD countries. However, if anything, the relations are somewhat stronger among OECD countries. Notwithstanding, it is worth emphasizing that the connection between QoG and good health remains rather strong and positive among the less economically developed non-OECD countries. The conclusion is that quality of government matters for good population health among poor as well as rich countries.

Even the relations between health care spending and level of population health stay the same after taking OECD membership into consideration. All correlations are weak if they exist at all. But the relation between total health care spending and good health as well as the relation between government health care spending and good health is positive among OECD and non-OECD countries. For private health care spending there is no relation, or a negative one, with health indicators like the mortality rate of children under five and healthy life expectancy. Thus, money matters for good population health, but only to a limited extent. And preferably it should be public money, not private.

Testing the results for overlapping or confounding effects in multivariate analyses further strengthens these conclusions. For example, as in table 3.5, regressing a health indicator (healthy life expectancy) on a QoG variable (government effectiveness) and two health care spending variables (government as well as private expenditure on health care) underscores the previous finding that both quality of government and public health care spending—independent of each other—are strongly and positively connected to high levels of population health.[7] Private expenditure on health care, however, is not associated with good health.

7. The results remain unchanged when interaction terms are included in the regression analyses. There are no significant interaction effects from government effectiveness and

If there is any connection it tends to be negative, not positive.[8] The regression model in table 3.5 has also been run with another QoG variable (the World Bank Corruption Perceptions Index, covering 185 countries) showing that all the results stay the same.

Consequently, the policy recommendations coming out of this study to improve health levels around the world, in rich countries as well as in poor countries, are to improve the quality of government—corruption kills—and to finance health care with public, not private, money.

Some Further Thoughts on Why Quality of Government Affects Population Health

As I said above, there are many reasons for variations in the level of quality of government to have an effect on population health. Some are what have been called the direct factors, such as absenteeism because health workers want to earn more money illegally on the side. Demands of extra "under the table" fees may deter some of those most need of health care from visiting clinics. Corruption in the procurement of contracts and the supply of pharmaceuticals may be other such direct factors. However, as in the cases of safe water and policies that ameliorate the worst forms of inequality, there may also be strong indirect effects between QoG and population health. The finding that it is public and not private spending that has a positive effect on population health demands further investigation. One way to understand this surprising effect might be the following. According to a recent study by Anirudh Krishna (2010), what drives people into poverty in many developing countries (and also the uninsured in the United States) is that they, or someone in their families, are hit by an illness that requires extensive medical treatment. Without

---

the health spending variables on levels of healthy life expectancy. The independent linear effect of government effectiveness is the most important.

8. Regressions have been run separately for testing among OECD countries and non-OECD countries. The QoG variable has a strong and significant positive effect on healthy life expectancy in both analyses, among OECD and non-OECD countries. Government health care spending also has a positive effect in both cases, but among the few OECD countries the regression coefficient is not significant. Private health care spending has a nonsignificant but negative effect on good health among OECD as well as non-OECD countries.

health insurance, the medical bills become so great a financial burden that they often have to sell land, cattle, or other assets they have used to accumulate income. The lack of publicly funded health insurance results in severe poverty for many, which in turn may be the reason they are hit by the inequality-bad health effect that the social epidemiologists have analyzed, or they may simply lack resources for even basic preventive health care.

Figure and Table Appendix

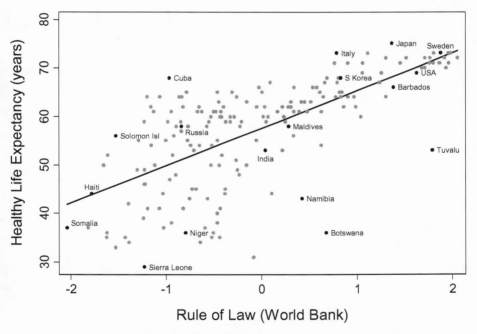

FIGURE 3.1. Healthy life expectancy vs. rule of law. R^2 = .47. *Source*: World Health Organization (2003); World Bank Governance Indicators, 2002.

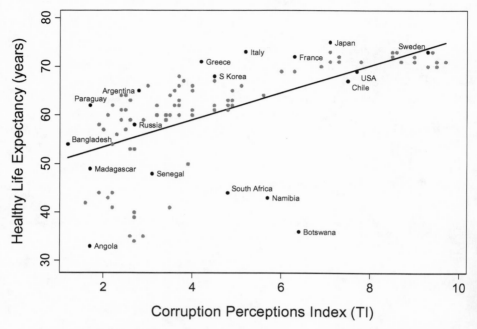

FIGURE 3.2. Healthy life expectancy vs. corruption. $R^2 = .71$. *Source*: World Health Organization (2003); Transparency International (2002).

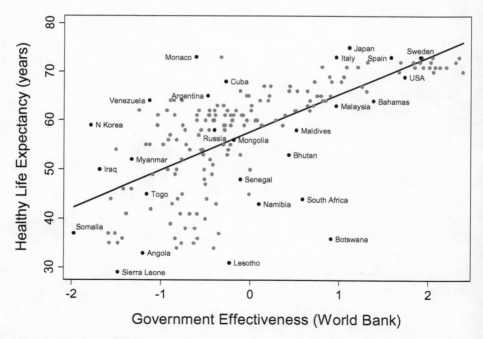

FIGURE 3.3. Healthy life expectancy vs. government effectiveness. $R^2 = .47$. *Source*: World Health Organization (2003); World Bank Governance Indicators, 2002.

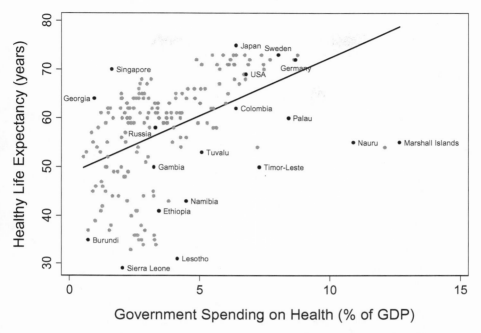

FIGURE 3.4. Healthy life expectancy vs. government spending on health care (percentage of GDP). $R^2 = .23$. *Source*: World Health Organization (2003).

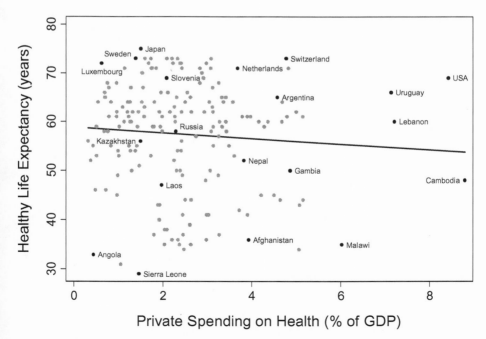

FIGURE 3.5. Healthy life expectancy vs. private spending on health care (percentage of GDP). $R^2 = .01$. *Source*: World Health Organization (2003).

TABLE 3.1. **Relation between three quality of government variables and five indicators of health**

Health indicator	Rule of law		Corruption Perception Index		Government effectiveness	
	R^2	Relation	R^2	Relation	R^2	Relation
Life expectancy at birth	.38	Positive	.28	Positive	.38	Positive
Mortality rate children <5	.38	Positive	.26	Positive	.38	Positive
Maternal mortality rate	.32	Positive	.24	Positive	.33	Positive
Healthy life expectancy	.47	Positive	.38	Positive	.47	Positive
Subjective health (World Value Survey)	.14	Positive	.20	Positive	.19	Positive

Source: The data come from the QoG Institute data bank.
Comment: A positive relation indicates that more of the QoG variable is positively associated with *higher* life expectancy, *lower* mortality rates for children and mothers, *higher* healthy life expectancies, and *higher* levels of subjective healthy. A negative relation indicates the opposite on all accounts. The data come from the QoG Institute data bank. All variables are specified in the figures.

TABLE 3.2. **Relation between four measures of health care spending and five indicators of health**

Health indicator	Total health care spending (% of GDP)		Government spending on health care (% of GDP)		Private spending on health care (% of GDP)		Private share of total health care spending (%)	
	R^2	Relation	R^2	Relation	R^2	Relation	R^2	Relation
Life expectancy at birth	.13	Positive	.23	Positive	.01	Negative	.14	Negative
Mortality rate children < 5	.14	Positive	.20	Positive	.00	Negative	.13	Negative
Maternal mortality rate	.11	Positive	.19	Positive	.00	Negative	.10	Negative
Healthy life expectancy	.16	Positive	.23	Positive	.01	Negative	.14	Negative
Subjective health (World Value Survey)	.20	Positive	.10	Positive	.09	Positive	.01	Negative

Source: The data come from the QoG Institute data bank.
Comment: A negative relation means that more private spending on health care as a percentage of GDP or as a percentage of total health spending is associated with *lower* life expectancy, *higher* mortality rates among children and mothers, *lower* healthy life expectancy, and *lower* levels of subjective health assessment.

TABLE 3.3. **Relation between three quality of government variables and two indicators of health levels among OECD and non-OECD countries**

Corruption Perception Index

Health indicator	OECD countries		Non-OECD countries	
	R^2	Relation	R^2	Relation
Mortality rate children <5	.24	Positive	.17	Positive
Healthy life expectancy	.49	Positive	.13	Positive

Government effectiveness

Health indicator	OECD countries		Non-OECD countries	
	R^2	Relation	R^2	Relation
Mortality rate children <5	.37	Positive	.34	Positive
Healthy life expectancy	.55	Positive	.30	Positive

Rule of law

Health indicator	OECD countries		Non-OECD countries	
	R^2	Relation	R^2	Relation
Mortality rate children <5	.44	Positive	.33	Positive
Healthy life expectancy	.55	Positive	.30	Positive

Source: The data come from the QoG Institute data bank.
Comment: A positive relation indicates that more of the QoG variable is positively related to *higher* levels of healthy life expectancy and to *lower* levels of child mortality.

TABLE 3.4. **Relation between three measures of spending on health care and two indicators of health levels among OECD and non-OECD countries**

Total health care spending (% of GDP)

Health indicator	OECD countries		Non-OECD countries	
	R^2	Relation	R^2	Relation
Mortality rate children <5	.06	Positive	.08	Positive
Healthy life expectancy	.13	Positive	.04	Positive

Government spending on health care (% of GDP)

Health indicator	OECD countries		Non-OECD countries	
	R^2	Relation	R^2	Relation
Mortality rate children <5	.19	Positive	.12	Positive
Healthy life expectancy	.28	Positive	.09	Positive

Private spending on health care (% of GDP)

Health indicator	OECD countries		Non-OECD countries	
	R^2	Relation	R^2	Relation
Mortality rate children <5	.01	Negative	.00	Negative
Healthy life expectancy	.00	Negative	.01	Negative

Comment: See table 3.2. A positive relation indicates that more of the health care spending variable is associated with *higher* levels of health. A negative relation means that more health care spending is related to *lower* levels of health.

TABLE 3.5. **Regressing healthy life expectancy on government effectiveness and government and private expenditures on health care**

	Coefficient	t-value
Constant	54.3***	30.1
Government effectiveness	6.60***	9.6
Government expenditure on health care (% of GDP)	0.96***	3.0
Private expenditure on health care (% of GDP)	−0.10	−0.2

Adj. R^2 = .48; *** $p < 0.001$.
Comment: The dependent variable (healthy life expectancy) is measured in years. The expenditure variables are measured as a percentage of GDP. The World Bank's Government Effectiveness variable is standardized and varies in most cases between −2.5 (low effectiveness) and +2.5 (high effectiveness).

CHAPTER FOUR

Creating Political Legitimacy: Representative Democracy versus Quality of Government

BE NICE TO AMERICA . . . or we'll bring democracy to your country!

D riving around my hometown of Gothenburg in western Sweden, one can occasionally spot cars sporting a red bumper sticker with this sentence.[1] Behind this amusing slogan is the now widespread recognition that the Bush administration's efforts to create a legitimate political authority in Iraq by introducing mass electoral democracy have failed. Even though the Iraqi people have cast their votes several times in surprisingly large numbers, and even though the elections were carried out in a reasonably orderly and—at least for this part of the world—surprisingly fair manner, the Iraqi government has been unable to establish itself as the legitimate political authority. In his address to the nation on December 18, 2005, former U.S. president George W. Bush made a prediction: "Three days ago, in large numbers, Iraqis went to the polls to choose their own leaders—a landmark day in the history of liberty. In the coming weeks, the ballots will be counted, a new government formed, and a people who suffered in tyranny for so long will become full members of the free world."[2]

To put it mildly, things did not develop as the Bush administration and its intellectual entourage had predicted (Plesch 2005). Enabling the

---

1. See http://www.stickergiant.com/; click on "social-political," "progressive," and "anti-Bush."

2. http://www.whitehouse.gov/news/releases/2005/12/20051218–2.html.

Iraqi people to vote and thereby to choose who is going to wield political authority over them has hardly created political legitimacy (Rangwala 2005). Yet this failure seems to have come as a big surprise (cf. Frum and Perle 2003). Why should people turn to violent protests when they have ousted a brutal dictator and now have a government they have elected? In a so-called fact sheet titled "Democracy in Iraq," issued on December 12, 2005, the White House stated: "Two and a half years ago, Iraq was in the grip of a cruel dictator. Since then, Iraqis have assumed sovereignty of their country, held free elections, drafted a democratic constitution, and approved that constitution in a nationwide referendum. In three days, they will go to the polls for the third time this year and choose a new government under their new constitution. Difficult work remains, but 2005 will be recorded as a turning point in the history of Iraq, the Middle East, and freedom."[3]

The Bush administration was hardly alone in thinking that democratic elections resulting in majority rule would create political legitimacy. Indeed, this idea seems to be taken for granted in the scholarly literature as well as by leading international organizations (Goodwin-Gill 2006). The former liberal Danish prime minister, Anders Fogh Rasmussen (now head of NATO), made the following comment when the Danish troops returned home from Iraq:

> What we aimed at, the Iraqi people also got. We were successful in carrying out referenda about a new constitution and a democratic election for a government that everyone has recognized as free and fair. But I honestly have to admit that I underestimated the strength of religious fanaticism that fights against freedom and democracy. Like many other Westerners, I believed the demand for democracy and freedom was so universal and strong among all kinds of people that the foreign troops would be received with open arms as liberators.[4]

The view that democratic elections are an effective way of creating political legitimacy not only has been criticized in the aftermath of the Iraq war, it has also been questioned in other conflict-ridden areas such as the Balkans (Ragaru 2003).

Like most central concepts in social science, political legitimacy is

---

3. http://www.whitehouse.gov/news/releases/2005/12/20051212-1.html.
4. Danish daily newspaper *Politiken*, August 9, 2007; my translation.

important, problematic, and difficult to define. Four distinct views about the attainment of legitimacy are found in the literature. People may accept the political authority of leaders in their country owing to tradition, the leaders' personal appeal (charisma), the government's production of goods and services, or belief in the fairness of the procedural mechanisms responsible for selecting leaders (Beetham 1991).

I will have nothing to say in this chapter about the first two points. The third point is interesting because it comes in two forms. One is that a government can achieve political legitimacy because it serves some notion of the common interest in coordinating citizens' activities in a socially beneficial way. This enables it to gain acceptance for its policies from a large proportion of the population (Przeworski, Stokes, and Manin 1999). Alternatively, it can obtain legitimacy by receiving support from a just large enough part of the population (e.g., a narrow majority) or a segment of powerful interest groups, by giving these groups special favor at the expense of the common good (Zakaria 2003; cf. Miller 2004). The problem here is that many other groups in society are unable to press for their own interests because they cannot overcome obstacles to collective action (e.g., consumers, the unemployed). This latter type of legitimacy is usually considered a result of patronage or neocorporatism; it will not feature strongly in the following analysis.

The last and—for present purposes—most important point is usually understood as a process in which legitimacy is attained by enacting procedural constitutional representative democracy. According to this view, people will accept a political authority because they have been given the right to take part in free and fair elections, resulting in a government that represents the majority of citizens. This constitutes "the essence of democracy: rule of the people by the people" (Lindberg 2006, 1). As formulated by Bernhard Manin (1997, 33), "Identity between the will of the representatives and the will of the people is secured through formal legal provisions" constituting some variant of representative democracy. Those who are not part of the majority will still perceive the system as legitimate because they stand a fair chance of becoming the majority in the next election. This procedural package comes with a bundle of other rights for articulating interests, such as the right to stand for office, the right to organize, freedom of expression, and so forth (Dahl 1989).

This chapter will challenge this widely held idea that electoral democracy is the key to creating political legitimacy and presents an alternative. Needless to say, this is not a critique of electoral democracy as such, which I accept as an indispensable part of a legitimate political system, but is an argument against the idea that it can serve as the main pillar for creating political legitimacy (cf. Lindberg 2009). My central argument is simple: electoral democracy is overrated when it comes to creating political legitimacy. Instead, political legitimacy is created, maintained, and destroyed not so much by the input side of the political system as by the output side. In brief, political legitimacy depends more on the quality of government and less on the quality of elections or political representation. Formulated another way, if you have QoG, you will get political legitimacy.

Does Electoral Democracy Promote Political Legitimacy?

As I stated above, the idea that electoral democracy is the key to political legitimacy is usually taken for granted (Goodwin-Gill 2006), not only in political science but also by international aid organizations. For example, when Guillermo O'Donnell (one of the most prominent scholars in this field of research) received the first Lifetime Achievement Award for the advancement of political science from the International Political Science Association in 2006, he stated in his keynote speech that "across most of the globe today, the ultimate claim of a political regime to be legitimate—or at least acceptable—rests on the kind of popular consent that purportedly finds expression in the act of free voting" (O'Donnell 2007, 6). Likewise, as the political philosopher Allen Buchanan puts it, "According to what may be the most plausible versions of democratic theory, the inequality that political power inevitably involves is justifiable if every citizen has 'an equal say' in determining who will wield the power and how it will be wielded" (Buchanan 2002, 699; see also Barry 1995).

There seem to be three ideas behind this claim. One is that free voting is based on the principle of political equality, which is the basic norm that renders a political authority legitimate (Dahl 2006). While most democracies place restrictions on the right to vote (young people, prisoners, and the mentally ill may be excluded), and quite a few ban certain types of (extremist) parties and political expressions (Issacharoff 2007), political equality that translates into "one citizen, one vote" can be seen as a signal that the state treats all citizens with equal concern and respect (Dworkin 1977). This sign of respect may of course in itself create a form of legitimacy.

The second argument is that numbers count, and at the end of the day the majority should have its way in decisions about public policies. Third, electoral democracy provides losers with the hope that the next time around they may stand a new chance of becoming winners (O'Donnell 2007). All three arguments rest on the view that legitimacy is created on the input side of the political system—that is, that it results from an effective form of interest articulation. Electoral democracy offers at least some approximation of the realization of the will of the people (Esaiasson 2003). Article 21 in the United Nations Declaration of Human Rights, states this as follows: "The will of the people shall be the basis of the authority of government; this will shall be expressed in periodic and genuine elections which shall be by universal and equal suffrage and shall be held by secret vote or by equivalent free voting procedures."

A central question in this debate is of course whether something like "the will of the people" can be said to exist. How can we distinguish between sudden changes of popular opinion and the long-term interest of the people? Consider a society dominated by strong clan-based loyalties, where it is customary for officials to appropriate public funds for the well-being of their clan. If most citizens believed that members of the other clans would refrain from such practices when they were in office, then they would be willing to scrap this clan-based system and replace it with a more universal alternative (cf. Mungiu-Pippidi 2006). Since most clan leaders and members do not believe the other clans would honor such an agreement, the system is stuck in a corrupt equilibrium. Determining the will of the people in a situation like this is impossible.

Let me offer another example. In 1955 a referendum was held in Sweden to determine if driving should be on the left or right side of the road. All neighboring countries had already changed, or decided to change, to right-hand driving (and Volvo and Saab produced cars only for right-hand driving!), so the argument for a change was pretty straightforward. Nevertheless, 82.9 percent voted in favor of keeping left-hand driving, and only 15.3 percent voted for a change. However, in 1963 the Swedish Parliament decided the country should switch. Once the change had taken place, it received massive popular support. I would guess that, if asked, 99 percent of Swedes would say this was one of the wisest decisions their political representatives had ever made. In cases like this (and they are many) it is very hard to determine what the will of the people consists of. Although the Swedish universal day care/preschool system is very much the pride of the nation for strengthening gender equality today, it had very little popular support when it was launched in the early 1970s (Westerståhl and Johansson 1985). Although the evidence is mixed on whether citizens' initiatives and referenda create good or bad policy outcomes, a recent study using survey data from American states shows that frequent use of referenda tends to increase distrust in government (Dyck 2009).

Another common critique of the "will of the people" theory is that even in a well-established democracy, political leaders or other elites often have the resources required to manufacture whatever "will of the people" they happen to desire—for example, by manipulating the agenda (Esaiasson 2003). While I agree with Gerry Mackie (2003) and Donald Wittman (1995) that the social choice critique of electoral democracy is one of the most overblown discussions ever to have taken place in the social sciences, arguments for electoral democracy have other weaknesses as well.

A Closer Look at Norway

A particularly interesting example of these weaknesses can be found in present-day Norway. In the 1990s the Norwegian government, like its Scandinavian counterparts, organized a mega–social science research project designed to analyze how well the country's democracy functions. This research program was led by prominent scholars—three political scientists, one sociologist, and a specialist in cultural studies—and engaged over a hundred scholars from many other disciplines including law and the humanities. Studies on almost every aspect of Norwegian democracy were carried out between 1998 and 2003 and culminated in a final report. To put it mildly, this report gives a very bleak picture of the present quality of democracy in Norway. The report concludes, "The parliamentary chain of government is weakened in every link; parties and elections are less mobilizing; minority governments imply that the connection between election results and policy formation is broken; and elected assemblies have been suffering a notable loss of domain" (Selle and Østerud 2006, 31).

The report also points to other ways Norwegian representative democracy had eroded over the course of the study: the parliament had lost power to market forces, the mass media had become more dominated by the logic of the market, parties and major nationwide interest organizations functioned less well and recruited fewer members and activists (Selle and Østerud 2006).

The entire research program was premised on the belief that electoral democracy creates legitimacy (Tranvik and Selle 2003). The program's empirical studies—on almost every conceivable aspect of the workings of Norwegian democracy—were evaluated against this normative ideal (described as the "parliamentary chain of government," starting with the voters and ending with the political decisions that are actually implemented (Christiansen and Togeby 2006).

In his thoughtful (and positive) review of this report, Stein Ringen (2004) made a poignant comment. While he did not disagree with the report's many criticisms of the workings of Norwegian democracy, he pointed out an intriguing irony. Norway is an extremely rich country with a highly educated electorate. The income from North Sea oil creates an almost unmanageable budget surplus for the government. For many years the country has been peaceful, lacking major social conflicts. Norway has a long popular democratic tradition, going back to at least 1814 when the constitution was created. Further, this is a country with a very generous welfare system, few industrial conflicts, an ethnically homogeneous population with a high level of social trust, a vibrant civil society, and a political culture built on compromise, full respect of minority rights, and no known violations of human rights or liberties. Together with the other Nordic countries, Norway ranks at the very top in the United Nations Development Program's measure of human development. By standard measures, corruption is among the lowest in the world, and politicians are for the most part seen as honest and benevolent. Ringen's most interesting remark was that if it is not possible to get a system of electoral (read "will of the people") democracy to work reasonably well in a country like this, then where on earth is such a system going to work? If this is what empirical reality looks like in rich, peaceful, and homogeneous Norway, then what are the chances that this system of democratic representation will create legitimacy in countries like Iraq, Nigeria, or Bosnia-Herzegovina?

Electoral Democracy: What Can We Expect?

Norway's problems with democracy are not unique—the paradox is that while electoral democracy is hugely successful on the global level, especially considering the number of countries that have introduced some variant of this system, and (not least) as a normative ideal, the citizens who actually live in countries that practice the system are less and less satisfied with its actual workings. Trust in central political institutions of electoral/representative democracy (parties, parliaments, politicians, local governments) appears to be decreasing in most established democracies (Dogan 2005; Holmberg 1999b; Pharr and Putnam 2000). There are also important problems in the central institutions of the democratic chain of command in the other Scandinavian countries (Esaiasson and Holmberg 1996; Teorell 1998). In Sweden, also a peaceful, rich, and well-established democracy, the congruence in political opinions between the members of Parliament and the majority of the electorate on a number of specific issues has been measured since the late 1960s. The result is not good news for those who believe in the "will of the people" idea. In fact, the congruence is far lower than a lottery would have produced (Holmberg 1999c). The results from similar studies of Germany, France, and the United States are no better (Holmberg 1999a).

Moreover, survey research in Sweden fails to show a positive correlation between citizens' political trust and congruence of their opinions with those of their elected representatives on a number of political issues (Holmberg 2000). From twenty yearly survey studies on the confidence Swedish citizens have in various political institutions comes a truly puzzling result. Institutions whose leaders are elected (political parties, unions, the European Union Parliament, the Swedish Parliament, and the city councils) generate less confidence than those in which citizens have no direct voice in selecting leaders, such as the public health care system, universities, the courts, the police, the social service, the Central Bank, and the royal family (Holmberg and Weibull 2007). Overall, Swedish citizens have greater confidence in appointed power holders (doctors, professors, judges, policemen, central bank leaders, social workers) than in elected ones.

The shortcomings of the established representative system for producing an unbiased or reasonably well-informed will of the people has resulted in some pretty radical suggestions for alternative models, such as the adoption of a "deliberation day" (Ackerman and Fishkin 2004) and other forms to tap the "will of the people" outside the electoral-representative system.[5] Still, most observers would argue that proclaiming that the Scandinavian democracies (or other established Western-

---

5. See, for example, the interesting experiments carried out at the Centre for Delibera-

style democracies) are in a state of deep crisis and on the verge of collapsing would be crying wolf. True, political parties are not always havens for democratic procedures. True, Rupert Murdoch–style mass media offer no ideal for unbiased political information. True, private money plays a troubling role in many democracies. True, voter turnout is lower than we would hope for. True, interest and lobby groups often play a dubious role. True, powerful bureaucracies have been known for derailing policy intentions during implementation. The list can go on and on. In fact if, as Dahl (2006) states, political equality is the norm that underpins electoral democracy, and if this is to be understood as providing this system with legitimacy by ensuring that every citizen has the same chance of influencing public policies, then every known national democracy is (and will always be) light-years away from realizing this ideal. At the end of the day, all this evidence about the failings of actual Western-style democracies leads us to ask if something other than the will of the people renders these governments legitimate.

Minorities, Electoral Democracy, and Legitimacy

Up to this point I have discussed the ample empirical research showing that even for citizens who are in majority, electoral democracy does not work very well to articulate their interests and transform them into appropriate public policies. Beyond this, the notion that electoral democracy in and of itself can serve as a vehicle for creating legitimacy appears to be mistaken. In all known democracies there are minority groups who know they are never destined to become the majority, no matter how many elections are held. For these minorities, legitimacy cannot derive from the belief that they will prevail in some future election (Przeworski 1991, 10–33). Even so, many of these perpetual minorities do not rebel against their political systems. In some cases they seem to thrive. To take a few examples, Finland has a spatially concentrated Swedish-speaking minority with a distinct culture that constitutes about 6 percent of the population. This minority has higher levels of trust in Finnish political parties and is more satisfied with the performance of the Finnish government than the Finnish-speaking majority (Bengtsson and Grönlund

tive Democracy and Global Governance at the Australian National University and led by John Dryzek; www.deliberativedemocracy.anu.edu.au/.

2005).[6] German-speaking minorities in Denmark, Belgium, France, and Italy appear to be doing equally well (Wolff 2001).

Other kinds of minorities are in a similar situation. Scandinavian voters who would prefer to live in a society with considerably lower levels of public spending (such as Germany or the United Kingdom) have no chance of becoming a majority. In a recent analysis based on survey data from thirty-eight national election studies, Peter Esaiasson shows there is surprisingly little evidence that those on the losing side of a national election decrease their support for the political system. In fact, in many cases the losers actually become more supportive (Esaiasson 2007). This casts further doubt on the "will of the people" theory of legitimacy, as well as on the Schumpeterian view that the main function of elections is to provide accountability.

Thus, in many cases it appears that the "will of the people" electoral representative democracy is not the main vehicle for creating political legitimacy for minorities. In the cases I know best (Denmark and Finland), there is little support for the idea that ethnic and linguistic minorities regard the political system as illegitimate even though they can never hope to attain a majority and consequently determine public policy.[7] If so, what other feature of the political system is responsible for that attainment of political legitimacy? Obvious candidates include factors like minority rights and the rule of law, but I argue that these concepts do not go to the heart of the matter. To shed light on this, I will discuss a recent example when legitimacy completely broke down: the outbreak of civil war in the former Yugoslavia.

The Counterpoint to Legitimacy: Civil War

The complexity of the concept of legitimacy makes it very difficult to operationalize and measure it in empirical research. Surveys are often

6. There are certainly cases where things have turned out to be more complicated (the Quebecois, the Catholics in Northern Ireland, the Basques).

7. I am focusing on ethnic minorities here. There are of course other types of minorities based on, for example, sexual orientation, social class, and opinions. People who think that abortion is murder and therefore should not be allowed will in all likelihood always constitute a minority in the Nordic countries. What makes the minorities mentioned above interesting is that they also live in distinct parts of the country, which should make collective action easier, according to what Russell Hardin (1995) has labeled the logic of coordination.

used, but person's stating that she does not have confidence in a political institution is not necessarily a good measure of lack of political legitimacy. Low confidence in a parliament, for example, may be due to a healthy skepticism of authorities that we often conceive of as a democratic virtue; dislike of the current majority but not necessarily of the democratic system as a whole; or disdain for some recent policy or scandal despite support for the system.

Another window on the causes of legitimacy can be provided by historical case studies of its breakdown. What counts as a breakdown of legitimacy is of course debatable, but most people would agree that when large groups of citizens take up guns and start a civil war, this is a clear-cut indicator that something has gone astray with the democratic system's legitimacy.[8] By studying these events, we may discover the causal mechanism responsible for the breakdown of legitimacy. When it comes to newly established democracies, recent empirical research presents us with a fascinating finding: the process of establishing electoral democracy generates considerable political violence (Mann 2005). When citizens get the right to participate in reasonably free and fair elections and choose representatives who in due time will adopt policies mandated by the will of the people, things ought to go well. But this seems not necessarily to be the case. Often, the resulting political representatives are "elected to fight" (Mansfield and Snyder 2005).

The civil war in the former Yugoslavia is a case in point. There are certainly numerous explanations for the outbreak of this war, ranging from ancient hatreds to the ambition of specific political leaders and the failure of the international community to intervene in time. Other explanations cite particular decisions (or miscalculations) by certain political leaders. Some point to historical and cultural forces that appear to have made the war inevitable. The number of explanations is overwhelming, and sometimes it seems as if each writer on the subject has a distinct one.

In the following discussion I try to sort out the sequence of events that led to the outbreak of violence. The analysis is very simple and inspired by noncooperative evolutionary game theory. In such situations, people react to recent actions by the other agents, and their behavior—peaceful cooperation or defection by engaging in violence—depends on

---

8. Or as Torbjörn Vallinder, one of my first teachers in political science, used to say: "Democracy is a simple thing. You count the heads instead of chopping them off."

their beliefs about others' behavior (Aumann and Dreze 2005). People base these decisions not on perfect information (which is virtually impossible to get in a case like this) but on whatever information they can obtain. Moreover, they constantly "adjust their behavior based on what they think other agents are going to do, and these expectations are generated endogenously by information about what other agents have done in the past" (Young 1998, 29). A central part of this theory is that behavior is disentangled from basic beliefs. The agents' behavior evolves dynamically as they learn what the other side is doing, while their normative beliefs about the world (e.g., that it is best to live in peace with one's neighbors in different ethnic communities) are not necessarily revised.

This is not the place to give a thorough background of this tragic conflict. What I want to underline is an argument put forward by Michael Ignatieff (1993, 13), that in many respects this conflict was unexpected. First, this is because Tito's policy from the 1960s to replace the various national identities with a Yugoslav identity was relatively successful. Second, since Serbs and Croats had similar languages and habits, they were "neighbours, friends and spouses, not inhabitants of different planets" (Ignatieff 1993, 15). Several analyses of specific ethnically mixed villages substantiate this argument (Gagnon 2004; Oberschall 2000). This is in line with Fearon and Laitin's (2003) quantitative analysis lending support to the argument that ethnic diversity is not a primary cause of civil wars. Third, Ignatieff argues convincingly that the conflict cannot be traced back to some uniquely Balkan viciousness. The nationalist ethnic cleansing and murderous practices that took place in the Balkans during World War II were imports from Western Europe, and if Western Europe could erase these habits during the postwar era, the same should have been possible in the former Yugoslavia: "Therefore, we are making excuses for ourselves when we dismiss the Balkans as a sub-rational zone of intractable fanaticism. And we are ending the search for explanation just when it should begin if we assert that local ethnic hatreds were so rooted in history that they were bound to explode into nationalist violence. On the contrary, these people had to be transformed from neighbors to enemies" (Ignatieff 1993, 15–16.).

My interpretation of these events is as follows. First, Slovenia decided to secede. This met with some opposition in Belgrade, but since Slovenia had only a very small population of Serbs, little fighting took place before Slovenia was de facto acknowledged as an independent state. When Croatia desired to secede, however, problems emerged, since it had a

fairly large Serbian minority (about 11 percent), principally residing in
the province of Krajina. This Serbian minority became worried about
its fate in the new state, especially since the first elections were won by
a nationalist Croat party led by the outspoken Croat nationalist Franjo
Tudjman. Despite this, the Serb leaders in Croatia initially put forth relatively modest political demands and stated they had no intention of taking the Serb minority out of the new Croat republic (Mann 2005). In a
speech delivered to ten thousand Serbs in June 1990, Jovan Rašković,
then the most important Serb leader in Croatia, said:

> The Serbs respect the Croatian people's right to their sovereign state, but they
> [the Serbs] demand in that state an equal position for the Serbian and other
> peoples. The Serbs do not want a second state in Croatia, but they demand
> autonomy. . . . The Serbian people in Croatia should be allowed to speak their
> language, to write their scripts, to have their schools [cheers], to have their
> education programs, their publishing houses, and their newspapers. (cited in
> Silber and Little 1997, 95)

Rašković's claims were modest and in fact pretty similar to those of
the Danish-speaking minority in Germany and the Swedish-speaking
minority in Finland. Thus the prospect that Serbs would be a permanent
minority in a new Croatian state was not sufficient for these leaders to
consider the new state illegitimate. However, the newly elected nationalist Tudjman regime was unwilling to compromise with these moderate
Serb leaders. Instead, the regime did five things that ignited the conflict
and led to the outburst of violence in Krajina, and later in other parts of
the former Yugoslavia.

First, the constitution of the new state ensured that Serbs would be
treated as second-class citizens in Croatia. The moderate Serbian leaders' demand that Serbs be defined as a constituent nation on an equal
footing with the Croats was denied (Gow 2003, 44). Instead, the new
constitution held that Croatia was to be a state for Croatians and that all
other nations were to be considered national minorities. Since the constitution of the Yugoslavian Federation regarded the Serbs in Croatia as
a constituent nation of the Republic of Croatia, this important change
"was a hammer-blow to Rašković. It strengthened the hand of Serb na-
tionalists much more radical than he: those who wanted territorial autonomy, and finally, secession from Croatia" (Silber and Little 1997, 97).

Second, the Tudjman regime began to fire employees from government jobs merely because they were Serbs (Gow 2003; Oberschall 2000). These layoffs occurred in the country as a whole, but also in Krajina, where ethnic Serbs were a majority (Silber and Little 1997; Woodward 1995, 107). "Massive layoffs of Serbs took place almost immediately after Tudjman's election, striking Serbs in the police, army, the judiciary and the educational institutions" (Udovički and Torov 1997, 94). Third, non-Croats were differentiated from Croats in yet another way:

> An official document called a Domovnica (a form providing proof of Croatian origin) was instituted and became an instrument of differentiation between Croats and non-Croats when it came to jobs and privileges. Opening a private business, obtaining medical coverage and the right to retirement pay, getting a passport or a driver's license, even in some cases being qualified to make withdrawals from one's own savings accounts—all these things hinged on the possession of a Domovnica. (Udovički and Torov 1997, 95)

Fourth, from very early on (summer of 1989), the police forces of the new regime failed to protect Serb minorities "from vicious outbursts of anti-Serb terror in some mixed communities" (Woodward 1995, 107). It is noteworthy that these events took place even before moderate Serb leaders had made their demands. Thus, for the Serb minority, the new Croatian state showed itself to be a "weak state" unable to provide even basic protection (Fearon and Laitin 2003, 76). Last, the Tudjman regime deliberately leaked information given to it by the moderate Serb leaders expressing their willingness to compromise and their doubts about more radical Serbian elements of the Serbian community. This delegitimized the moderate Serb leaders in the eyes of their own community and also strengthened more militant Serb leaders in Krajina, whose aim "was not to secure for the Serbs autonomy inside Croatia, but to take the Serbs, and the land on which they lived, out of Croatia altogether" (Silber and Little 1997, 97).

In conjunction with the delegitimizing of the moderate Serb leadership, these policy changes carried out by the Tudjman regime sent a clear signal to the Serb minority that the new constitution was not merely symbolic but would likely have very negative consequences for their life chances. The police could not be trusted to protect Serbs from attacks, no Serbs should apply for government jobs, and they would encounter difficulty in dealing with the new state's Croatian bureaucracy because of a lack of necessary documents.

The resulting violent conflict over the control of the police forces in Krajina empowered Serbian secessionist political entrepreneurs. The secessionists mobilized support for their cause in Belgrade, outmaneuvered the more moderate Serbian leaders, and received military support from the Serb-dominated National Yugoslav Army (Bennett 1995; Oberschall 2000; Silber and Little 1997; Udovički and Torov 1997).[9] Notably, the Milošević regime in Belgrade did not publicly recognize or support the self-declared "Serb Autonomous Province of Krajina" until after the first (two) casualties in a clash between Croatian police forces and the Krajina-Serb militia over the control of a local post office (Silber and Little 1997, 137). Serbian leaders in Belgrade did not protest against Croatia merely because the Serbs were downgraded to a national minority. They took action only after the Tudjman regime made it clear that the Serbian minority in Croatia would be the victims of discrimination.[10]

Interpreting the Causal Logic of Legitimacy

The main lesson from this interpretation of events following the establishment of the Croatian state is that political legitimacy depends more on the output side of the political system than on the input side. As such, it is connected to citizens' perceptions about procedural fairness in the implementation of public policies (cf. Grimes 2006). In fact, the input (will of the people) side of the political system seems rather unimportant: after all, the Serb leaders in the new Croatian state were prepared to accept their new status as belonging to a permanent electoral minority in the new ethnically divided party system. As is the case for many other minorities, the Serbs in Croatia were prepared to accept Croatian rule if they were given cultural autonomy in Krajina and a guarantee of civil and political rights. Not until this option was rejected by the Tudjman government did the Serbs change strategy from compromise and

9. This interpretation of the history of the outbreak of the war should not be taken as an excuse for the many horrible war crimes that the Serbian military and paramilitary forces committed during that war. However, what the Tudjman regime initially did was to give the nationalist hatemongers among the Serbs all the arguments they needed.

10. Needless to say, I do not claim to have intimate or expert knowledge about the outburst of this tragic conflict (and, as can be seen, I have to rely on secondary sources, since I cannot read Serbo-Croatian). Furthermore, it is not unlikely that I have missed something important.

negotiation to violent confrontation.[11] This interpretation of the evolutionary game that took place in Croatia explains why the secessionist Serb leaders could persuade the members of their community that their Croatian neighbors, friends—and in some cases even spouses—were out to harm them. Hence they had better start fighting back.

My argument is not that weak state capacity causes civil war (cf. Migdal 1988). Instead, I suggest that a state that systematically departs from the ideal of impartiality in implementing policy will be seen as illegitimate. Logically, it is more plausible that a strong state can implement systematic discrimination against ethnic or racial minorities. The idea that legitimacy has more to do with the exercise of government power than with access to this power by participating in elections makes a lot of sense. Your ability to vote is unlikely to have a clear and significant impact on your life chances: the likelihood that your vote will be decisive is, of course, minuscule. Many citizens voluntarily abstain from voting and from participating in other forms of political activity on the input side of the political system. However, if the police do not protect you because you are an X-type citizen; if the fire brigade does not come to your house because you are a Z-type citizen; if your children are systematically discriminated against in the schools because they are Y-type children; and if the doctors at the hospital ignore you because you are a P-type person, then you are in real trouble. To be blunt, while what happens on the input side usually has little consequence for the immediate welfare of the individual citizen, what the state does or does not do on the output side may be life threatening. Since Croatia had formerly been a semicommunist society, most social services and insurance, health care, and education were run by government officials (as in most European welfare states). This magnifies the importance of the treatment of citizens on the output side. In sum, ethnic and linguistic minorities that are reasonably well protected against discrimination by government authorities and are granted cultural autonomy are likely to regard their political system as

11. It is not at all certain that the initial moderate strategy of the Serb leaders would have had a chance to become successful. Even if the Tudjman regime had played along, using their propaganda machine, the Milošević regime in Belgrade may have been able to persuade the Serb minority in Croatia to abandon the moderate strategy, not least because the Croatians did not have a very good "history of play" from World War II. However, we can never know this since the confrontational actions by the Tudjman regime against the moderate Serbs effectively prevented a peaceful resolution to the crisis and made the following confrontational propaganda from Belgrade look credible in the eyes of many Serbs.

legitimate. However, attaining legitimacy in a situation like that of Krajina is much more difficult. What the state does with respect to the output side affects people in a direct way (cf. Kumlin 2004). If this analysis
is correct, then it is on the output side of the political system that the battle of broad-based political legitimacy is won or lost.

This interpretation of the outbreak of civil war in the former Yugoslavia is just one illustrative case. Another case that can support this
line of reasoning is the outbreak of civil war in Spain. Recent historical research shows that one can give the same type of explanation for the
outbreak of this civil war in 1936 as for the one in the former Yugoslavia. In brief, the newly elected leftist populist government used the state
to make lots of arbitrary political arrests of members of rightist parties,
gave impunity for criminal action to members of the Popular Front parties, politicized the legal system in order to facilitate political arrests, accepted violation of property rights "en masse," and looked away when
their followers committed horrendous political crimes. As Payne argues,
"By refusing to enforce the law equally and by intensifying its policy of
harassment of the right, the time would come when many moderate con-
servatives would be willing to ally themselves with the radical right"
(Payne 2006, 363; cf. Beevor 2006, 36). What drove many middle-class
citizens into the arms of the Falangist fascists was to a large extent the
unwillingness of the Popular Front government to respect the ideal of
impartiality in the implementation of the law and its policies (Lapuente
and Rothstein 2010). As Beevor argues, the Spanish middle classes did
not need to be reminded of "the horrors which followed the Russian
revolution and Lenin's determination to annihilate the bourgeoisie"
(2006, 36).

Apart from these cases, there is also quantitative empirical work that
supports this conclusion. In a comparative statistical analysis, Öberg
and Melander (2010) show that the occurrence of civil wars is positively related not to democracy, but to bureaucratic quality. They argue
that the relation between democracy and civil war is U-shaped, meaning that such conflicts are most common in what they label as quasi-
democracies.[12] Using data about bureaucratic quality from 141 countries

---

12. An exception is a study by James Fearon and David Laitin (2003), but according
to Öberg and Melander (2010) this is because they include wars of colonial independence,
which implies that a number of Western European countries are coded as having civil wars
during the 1950s and 1960s.

during the years 1984 to 2004,[13] and controlling for a number of other variables (poverty, lack of economic development, time since previous conflicts, ethnic dominance, and political instability), they find that bureaucratic quality is extremely significant for explaining the outbreak of civil wars (Öberg and Melander 2010).

Margaret Levi's (1998b) analysis of compliance with the demand for military service in Canada during World War I offers further evidence that legitimacy is linked to state output. Levi shows that large numbers of French Canadians refused to volunteer for the war and that the Quebecois strongly opposed conscription. This is difficult to explain from a "will of the people" theory of legitimacy, because the francophone Canadian soldiers would have been going to war to defend France on French soil and thus would be saving the homeland. Levi's analysis suggests that most French Canadians believed the Anglo-dominated government and army would not treat them impartially. Although there was no official discrimination against French Canadians in the military, "Francophone servicemen felt and were often made to feel uncomfortable" (Levi 1998b, 149). One possible interpretation is that many French Canadian young men may have thought that if they were to serve in army units led by Anglophones, they would be discriminated against or simply used as cannon fodder.

There is also a wealth of survey-based studies about the determinants of citizens' satisfaction with democracy indicating that performance is more important than support for the "will of the people" ideal (Diamond 1999, 192). In one comparative study based on data from seventy-two countries, Gilley (2006, 57) finds that "general governance (a composite of the rule of law, control of corruption and government effectiveness) has a large, even overarching importance in global citizen evaluations of states." Another example comes from a recent study based on survey data from Latin America that concludes that for most Latin Americans, "democracy was embraced not just as a result of belief in its intrinsic legitimacy or because of any ideological value but mainly because of an ability to deliver expected results" (Sarsfield and Echegaray 2006, 169). Yet another study that points in this direction is Seligson's survey-based analysis of the relation between citizens' experience of corrupt government officials in law enforcement and political legitimacy carried out

13. Their data on bureaucratic quality are from the International Country Risk Guide, see: www.prsgroup.com/ICRG.aspx.

in four Latin American countries. Corruption of law enforcement officials is clearly a departure from the ideal of impartiality on the output
side of the political system, and the study shows that this type of corruption has a negative effect on political legitimacy even after controlling
for whether the correspondents had voted for the incumbent party in the
last election (Seligson 2002). Thus, experiencing low-quality government
is more important for the decline of political legitimacy than being part
of the constituency behind the ruling electoral majority.

Conclusions and Reflections

If the representational system is democratic and public policies are decided according to the rules of this system, citizens will regard political decisions as legitimate—so goes the precept in mainstream democratic theory. They will do this either because they feel they belong to
the political majority or because they accept that the majority rules until the next election. As this presentation has shown, however, this analysis of political legitimacy does not suffice. Instead, the main sources of
political legitimacy are situated on the output side of the political system
and have to do with the quality of government. It is the absence of corruption, discrimination, and similar violations of the principle of impartiality when exercising political power that creates political legitimacy.
The way public administrations are organized is not just a question of
economic rationality and administrative efficiency. In addition, citizens
seem to have strong norms about what to expect when they encounter
government officials who implement public policies. This argument is
built on the fact that citizens generally come into contact with the output side of the political system—with the administration—far more fre-
quently and intensively than with its input side. Moreover, what happens
to them on the output side is often crucial for their well-being. One could
say that the public administration is the political system—as citizens con-
cretely encounter and experience it. The character of the administration
is therefore decisive for the way the political system is viewed. However,
my argument is not that if a country is going to democratize, legitimacy
through impartiality in the exercise of public policies should come before the introduction of representative democracy by free and fair elections (Berman 2007; Carothers 2007). Instead, impartiality as the basic
norm for generating legitimacy on the output side of the political system

should be seen as the equivalent of political equality as the basic norm on the input side. Respect for both norms must be considered central in creating political legitimacy. As Bratton and Chang argue, an increasing number of leading scholars of democratization are now including the importance of impartial state institutions and the rule of law in their definitions of democracy (2006, 1078). If this line of reasoning is correct, it should have important implications for the industrialized world's efforts to promote democracy in developing countries. As the Iraqi case clearly shows, merely bringing electoral democracy to a country is not likely to create political legitimacy. Instead, as Bratton and Chang (2006) propose, representative democracy and state building should be developed simultaneously.

This chapter has argued that political legitimacy ought to be the ultimate goal for any system of governance, and that there is surprisingly little evidence that electoral democracy is the principal political instrument for creating such legitimacy. Given the widespread belief in the superiority of electoral democracy, what accounts for its relatively minor role in creating political legitimacy? Let me very tentatively present four ideas. The first is that the introduction of electoral democracy can create a political opposition.[14] Simply put, it is hard to think of free and fair elections if there is no alternative to vote for. This has other implications. One of the most interesting things about communist dictatorships (and many others) is their inability to solve the problem of succession. Dictatorships and other authoritarian systems have a strong tendency to become gerontocracies. The third argument also concerns the political elite. Any ruling group, whether democratically elected or not, sooner or later loses touch with reality.[15] The reason probably is that, after a while, most systems of power tend to shield leaders from information (or to be more precise, the carriers of information) they do not appreciate receiving. For example, the Romanian communist leader Ceauşescu seems to have been convinced that his people strongly supported him at the very eve of his dismissal from power in 1989. When in 1989 the Polish Communist Party for the first time decided to allow competitive elections for the new senate, they appear to have been convinced up until the eve of the elections that they would get a majority of the seats. In fact, they got none. The same appears to have been the case for Pinochet in Chile and

14. I thank Jan Teorell for this important insight.
15. Thanks to AnnChristin Rothstein for coming up with this idea.

for the Sandinistas in Nicaragua in 1990.[16] My point is that democratic elections force political leaders to pay close attention to reality—or to be more precise, the perceived reality among a majority of the population.[17] Finally, elections may be good for the general political discussion and for educating citizens about public matters, which, ceteris paribus, ought to increase political legitimacy. Politicians have to present alternatives, they have to argue for why their policies are better than their opponents', and in some cases the mass media are said to enlighten citizens about the feasibility and moral logic of these alternatives. However, even in stable democracies like Norway and Sweden, the empirical evidence that elections foster legitimacy is, to put it mildly, not overwhelming (Petersson 2006).

16. Thanks to Adam Przeworski for providing me with this information from his unpublished manuscript, "Studying Democracy—Twenty Years Later," New York University, June 12, 1996.

17. In pure electoral terms, one of the world's most successful political leaders is the Swedish Socialist Tage Erlander, who was prime minister for an uninterrupted period of twenty-three years (1946–69). When he resigned as party leader in 1969, the advice he gave to his successor—Olof Palme—in his speech to the party was: "Listen to the Movement" ("movement" in this case being the Swedish labor movement). He did not say, "Do what the people want you to do," or "Be guided by the will of the people." A reasonable interpretation of "Listen to the movement" is Keep track of reality.

CHAPTER FIVE

Curbing Corruption: The Indirect "Big Bang" Approach

What Is Missing from Political Economy?

In *The Oxford Handbook of Political Economy*, Douglass North, one of the leading scholars in the new institutional economics approach, has a chapter titled "What Is Missing from Political Economy." Having been invited by the editors of this very prestigious handbook of fifty-nine chapters to comment on what has been accomplished in this research area, North criticizes the political economy approach for missing out on "a series of bigger questions." The most important questions that he believes have not been dealt with are: "Why aren't all countries in the world advanced industrial nations? Why do legislatures produce secure property rights and the rule of law in the developed world but not in the developing world?" (North 2006, 1003). He also states that "we have yet to figure out what makes the non-developing countries so stable." In other words, Why is the combination of severe poverty and dysfunctional institutions so difficult to change?

North's explanation for this "black hole" in the political economy approach is twofold: first, current approaches "do not adequately address the problem of non-incremental change" (2006, 1004); second, almost all analyses in political economy focus on the effects of formal institutions while excluding the informal ones, which North considers just as important (if not more so). Since, for example, various forms of corruption are very apt to be seen as informal institutions, and since corruption is likely to be driven by agents' beliefs about other agents' beliefs, it is telling that there is no chapter on corruption or similar QoG issues. In fact, looking at the subject index of this 1,112-page handbook, it is noteworthy that the QoG issue seems to play only a very minor role in the field of political economy. As Michael Johnston recently argued, it is puzzling that "American political science as an institutionalized discipline has remained steadfastly uninterested in corruption for generations" (Johnston 2006, 809). An examination of a number of other recently published "handbooks" in political science and public administration shows that corruption is hardly ever mentioned (Dryzek, Phillips, and Honig 2006; Moran, Rein, and Goodin 2006; Peters and Pierre 2002; Rhodes, Binder, and Rockman 2006).

This chapter will address corruption and anticorruption policies based on the two ideas launched by North: "nonincremental change" and the importance of formal as well as informal institutions. Although corruption, as I argued above, is not the only issue that is detrimental to high QoG, I will focus on this problem in order to follow the main thread in this literature.

Corruption: The Collective Action Approach

The most established idea of how to understand corruption is the "principal-agent" model (Aidt 2003; cf. Teorell 2007). In this approach, corruption is seen as criminal behavior by some agents entrusted to act on behalf of a (honest/benevolent) principal. For example, the benevolent principal can be a cabinet minister, and the criminal/corrupt agents may be the civil servants. One problem with this approach is that in a thoroughly corrupt system, it is difficult to identify who such a benevolent principal might be. For example, the political elites are often the ones who stand to gain the most from rents, and they therefore have no incentive to change the corrupt system (Johnston 2005; Teorell 2007). Another idea in this approach is that "the people" constitute the (honest and benevolent) principal and the political leaders are the (corrupt) agents. The problem here is that, in a thoroughly corrupt system, the evidence that democratic elections work against corruption is simply not at hand (Teorell 2007). On the contrary, corrupt politicians often stand a good chance of getting reelected (Golden 2003). In general, agents at the bottom of a corrupt system, such as the "street level" tax bureaucrats or policemen, have no incentive to refrain from corrupt practices because even if they as individuals start behaving honestly, nothing will change.

As is well known, it makes no sense to be the only honest player in a "rotten game," because benevolent behavior by one or a few agents will not lead to change. This implies that in a political system plagued by systemic corruption, we are not likely to find benevolent "principals" at the bottom or at the top.

Moreover, if corruption did work according to the "principal-agent" model, it would be easy to erase just by changing the incentives. Anticorruption would be simple: principals need to incrementally increase the negative payoff for cheating and corruption (including the risk of being caught) to a point where the fear of being caught is higher than the greed that leads agents to engage in corruption. In a society constructed so that fear was larger than greed, things would go well. The disadvantage with the incentive-based principal-agent approach is that it just forces the problem to become what has been called a *second-order* collective action problem (Ostrom 1998; cf. Rothstein 2000; Teorell 2007). All the agents may well understand that they would gain from erasing corruption, but because they cannot trust that most other agents will refrain from corrupt practices, they have no reason to refrain from paying or demanding bribes. The only reason they would do so is if institutions could be established that would make them trust that most other agents would refrain from corrupt behavior (Rawls 1971, 240). However, establishing such credible institutions is in itself a problem of collective action (Lichbach 1997). From this institutional perspective, the problem is that corruption is self-reinforcing (Aidt 2003; Karklins 2005; Uslaner 2008). In plain language, most empirical research shows that "once the system gets there, it stays there." To use Bardhan's formulation, "Corruption represents an example of what are called frequency-dependent equilibria, and our expected gain from corruption depends crucially on the number of other people we expect to be corrupt" (Bardhan 1997, 1331).

One more important factor needs to be mentioned. While the practice of corruption clearly has cultural traits, it should not be seen as culturally determined. Based on a large survey, Sten Widmalm shows that even in extremely corrupt villages in Madhya Pradesh and Kerala in India, most of the villagers have strong norms against corruption. In this setting, where bribery and absenteeism are rampant, more than 75 percent of respondents agreed with the statement that "civil servants should never take bribes" (Widmalm 2008, 148). Moreover, just as many agreed with statements such as that civil servants/public sector workers "should treat everyone equally regardless of income, status, class, caste, gender, or religion." As Widmalm concludes, the claim that "corruption is more prevalent where it is culturally accepted" finds no support in his data (2008, 166). The same results can be obtained from the Afrobarometer survey (2006), which shows a widespread moral disapproval of corruption in most African countries, even where corruption is rife. When asked whether they consider it "not wrong at all," "wrong but understandable," or "wrong and punishable" if a public official decides to locate a development project in an area where his friends and supporters live; gives a job to someone from his family who does not have adequate qualifications; or demands a favor or an additional payment for some service that is part of his job, a clear majority of Africans deemed all three acts both wrong and punishable. Thus, the idea put forward by, for instance, Heidenheimer (2002) that the public acceptance of what is commonly understood as corruption varies significantly across cultures does not find much support in survey-based research.[1] This result is confirmed by Rasma Karklins (2005), who shows that ordinary people in the often severely corrupt systems in former communist countries usually do not internalize corrupt practices as morally legitimate. Instead, they usually condemn corruption as morally wrong and put the blame on "the system" for forcing them to take part, thus understanding that they are in a "social trap." If they were confident that most other agents would not participate in corrupt practices, their preference would be not to take or give bribes (Smith 2007, 191). However, given the opposite, the interest they de facto act on results in corrupt behavior.

This is important because it makes it clear that while standard ideas of microlevel rationality are important for understanding the "inner" self-perpetuating logic of a corrupt (and noncorrupt) equilibrium, they are of little help if we want to explain why different societies end up in such different equilibriums (given that utility-based rationality is a concept with universal range). Moreover, the neoclassical conception of utility-based rationality cannot be used to explain the huge variation in systemic corruption that exists without adding ad hoc variables. In a critique of the "good governance agenda," Bukovansky argues that if the anticorruption debate remains "dominated by a liberal, individualist rationalism, it

---

1. As Jordan (2009) shows in his study of anticorruption campaigns in thirteenth-century France, medieval understandings of corruption and "good governance" seem remarkably similar to ours. See also Davis 2000, chap. 6, for an analysis from sixteenth-century France.

fails to adequately articulate and fully explore the necessity of moral and political agency in the pursuit of collective good" (Bukovansky 2006, 201). This certainly creates a problem: if variation in levels of corruption can be explained neither by standard utility-based notions of economic rationality nor by reference to culture, then which type of ideas about what guides agency should we use?

One way out of this dilemma comes from the work on *reciprocity* carried out by scholars such as Herbert Gintis, Samuel Bowles, Elinor Ostrom, Robert Boyd, and Ernst Fehr, who combine behavioral economics with experiments (cf. Gintis et al. 2005). One of their strongest results is that behavior based on self-regarding motives ("economic man") is much less frequent than is assumed in neoclassical economics. Opportunistic and treacherous behavior is also much less frequent in so-called public goods experiments than would be expected from the standard axioms in neoclassical economics (Gintis et al. 2005, 15). This research, which is confirmed by, for example, Elinor Ostrom's (1990) field studies of how local groups handle common natural resources in a sustainable manner, shows that humans in general are neither (for the most part) altruists nor strictly self-interested. Instead, in most economic settings and for most agents, the rule is *reciprocity*. Such a person "responds kindly toward actions that are perceived to be kind and hostilely toward actions that are perceived to be hostile" (Fehr and Fischbacher 2005, 153). They add that "whether an action is perceived to be kind or hostile depends on the fairness or unfairness of the intention underlying the action." This idea about reciprocity may help to explain the huge variation in corruption around the world without falling back on intrinsic historical-cultural (or, even worse, biological) explanations. Their major idea is that when analyzing situations of economic interaction, one should take into account not only that all agents may be strategic, but that when deciding how to act, all agents must reason about what strategy is the most likely for all the other agents. This has the following implication: The strategic situation (the "game") does not in itself give the agents the solution to what strategy they should opt for. Instead, when deciding how to act, it is what they believe about the other agents' strategy that is important. As I will show in the next chapter, this information about the honesty and trustworthiness of (most) other agents is most commonly derived from the institutional setting that surrounds the agents' strategic situation. As Fehr and Fischbacher (2005, 167) state: "If people believe that cheating on taxes, corruption and abuses of the welfare state are widespread, they themselves are more likely to cheat on taxes, take bribes, or abuse welfare state institutions." Thus, behavior depends on how the existing institutions inform the agents' mutual expectations—for example, the expectation about whether the other agents will take part in corrupt exchanges. This very problem is in fact described by John Rawls in his "modern classic" *A Theory of Justice*:

> For although men know that they share a common sense of justice and that each wants to adhere to existing arrangements, they may nevertheless lack full confidence in one another. They may suspect that some are not doing their part, and so they may be tempted not to do theirs. The general awareness of these temptations may eventually cause the scheme to break down. The suspicion that others are not honoring their duties and obligations is increased by the fact that, in the absence of the authoritative interpretation and enforcement of the rules, it is particularly easy to find excuses for breaking them. (Rawls 1971, 240)

According to Rawls, what can solve this problem is the establishment of impartial institutions that ensure the agents that most of "the others" will be "honoring their duties." Or as Fehr and Fischbacher (2005, 167) put it, "It is therefore important that public policy prevents the initial unravelling of civic duties, because once people start to believe that most others engage in unlawful behavior, their belief-dependency of individuals' behavior may render it very difficult to re-establish lawful behavior."

The specific question is how we can perceive the way real-life agents in a society marked by systemic corruption make up their minds about whether to participate in corrupt exchanges. We have to think of an agent who has lived his or her whole life in a society where corruption is "systemic." This is a system where the need to offer and demand bribes in order to maintain what are deemed the necessary services or economic standard is ingrained in most agents' "mental maps"—so much so that this has become an informal institution. When you go to the doctor, when you see your children's schoolteacher, when you put in a bid for a public contract, when you need a license for your restaurant, when you want to take an exam at the university, when you apply for a job in the public sector, when you are stopped by the police, then paying bribes or carrying out similar illegal actions is simply "standard operating procedure" (Jordan Smith 2007; Wrong 2009). You have done so all your life,

as has everyone you know, and this way of doing things has since long
been established as "common knowledge." To give one example: In 2002
the United Nations Development Program, the organization responsible for the UN's yearly "Human Development Reports," launched a "regional study" of Bosnia and Herzegovina. The report has a section about
corruption that presents results from a survey showing that about 70 percent of the population in Bosnia and Herzegovina believe their local authorities are "severely corrupt." This was maybe not so surprising, but an
equal percentage believed that the international aid organizations working in the region, including the UN organizations, were just as corrupt.
The interpretation of the situation in the report reads as follows: "For
the average citizen, therefore, it seems that corruption has broken down
all barriers and dictates the rules of life. That is not very different from
saying that *they interpret life in terms of corruption*" (UNDP 2002, 72).

If people "interpret life in terms of corruption," this amounts to what
reasonably can be called a *deeply held system of beliefs about what can
be expected of other agents*. This, I argue, is generated by the historically established institutions the agents live under. The ideas presented
here, that corruption is reinforced by such beliefs and that we should understand rationality as "interactive," have a number of implications for
what can count as an anticorruption strategy with a reasonable chance
of success.

The State of Anticorruption Research and Policy: A Critique

A society faced with the task of addressing systemic corruption and establishing "good governance" needs to ask itself two principal questions.
First, what types of structural reforms are necessary to reduce corruption? Common suggestions are creating new legal institutions or changing existing ones in order to alter incentive structures for taking or offering bribes. Second, which types of *processes* are likely to be successful
for enacting such reforms? Most research on corruption has focused
mainly on the first, structural question, while the second one about the
change of processes, strategies, and agents' cognition has to a large extent been ignored.

One case in point is Rod Alence's article "Political Institutions and
Developmental Governance in Sub-Saharan Africa," which examines
how different types of political institutions affect the degree of corrup-

tion in thirty-eight African countries. The conclusion is that a combina-tion of electoral competition and institutional checks and balances on executive power has a negative effect on the frequency of corruption. In other words, this strategy suggests that the idea and the practice of lib-eral democracy work counter to corruption (Alence 2004, 163). Another example is the article "Seeds of Corruption: Do Market Institutions Matter?" in which Harry Broadman and Francisca Recanatini identify a number of market economic institutions that are key to change—among others, "clear and transparent rules . . . and a robust competitive envi-ronment" (2001, 359).

What these examples of the anticorruption literature tell us is that, in line with the principal agent theory, "fixing the incentives" would solve the problem of corruption. There is just one difficulty left: construct-ing such institutions is in itself a problem of collective action that is not likely to be solved within a society dominated by corrupt agents (Fala-schetti and Miller 2001). Or to use Elinor Ostrom's (1998) words, there exists a collective action problem *of the second order*. Why would agents who either stand to gain from corrupt practices or can only lose by re-fraining from corruption at all be interested in creating such "efficient" institutions?

In fact, the list of authors who are content with establishing that the institutions characteristic of stable democracies with a well-functioning market economy show a relation to low levels of corruption is very long. But as Blomkvist (2001), Grindle (2004), and also Bukovansky (2006) have asserted, much of the advice on how to curb corruption emanating from works like the ones mentioned above and from organizations like the United Nations Development Program, the International Monetary Fund, and the World Bank presumes access to the kind of administra-tive praxis and institutions that notoriously corrupt countries lack.

Instead of explaining the causes of corruption, authors in this ap-proach have simply described how the institutional systems in corrupt and noncorrupt countries differ. To offer transparency, democracy, in-dependent judicial anticorruption agencies, or "good governance" as ex-planations of and solutions to the problem of corruption leaves many im-portant questions unanswered, even in the best-case scenario. A more fundamental critique is that in many cases this produces tautologies. In the language of causality, it could be formulated as if the dependent and independent variables become identical. In states blessed with an inde-pendent and honest judiciary, effective institutions for anticorruption

measures, effective audit systems, and effective laws guaranteeing freedom of information and a free media, where liberal and human rights
are effectively protected, it is obviously quite right that these institutions promote political accountability and counteract corruption. However, in states that suffer from systemically corrupt structures, it is likely
that the causal mechanism works in the opposite direction, meaning it
is the corruption of precisely these types of institutions that is holding
back development toward democratic governance (Diamond 2008). In
the search for universal theories on causes and solutions concerning corruption, many researchers do not recognize the built-in institutional inertia (or path dependency) of corrupt systems. In the words of Harris
Robert, "Just as a predominantly non-corrupt system will self-correct to
deal with corrupt individuals and the legislative or political flaws that fa-
cilitated their corruption, so will a predominantly corrupt system self-
correct to maintain its corruption following a purge" (Robert 2003, 63).

Or to quote Nuhu Ribadu, a former high-level police officer in charge
of an anticorruption task force in the government of Nigeria, who had to
flee his country after revealing high-level corruption, "If you fight corruption, it fights you back."[2] Another example is the recent development
in Italian politics, where despite strong efforts in the early 1990s to erad-
icate political corruption, the current situation is described in some areas as worse than before the "clean hands" operation (Della Porta and
Vannucci 2007; cf. Wrong 2009). A recent media report points to the failure, impotence, and closing down of anticorruption agencies in countries
like Nigeria, Kenya, and South Africa.[3] As Claus Offe has argued, questions remain about what brings countries into a vicious circle with corrupt institutions and also, in a corrupt context, "which motives, values,
and political forces would actually push forward the reform project. . . .
what are the incentives to introduce incentives designed to control corruption or to redesign opportunity structures?" (Offe 2004, 91).

In addition, if new institutions have to be created, the questions about
agency become central. The central problem with establishing impartial
and universal political institutions is that by their very nature they are to
serve "the common good," and interest-based actors have no reason to

2. As reported by Cecila W. Dugger, "Battle to Halt Graft Scourge in Africa Ebbs,"
New York Times, June 10, 2009.

3. Ibid.

support their creation (Bukovansky 2006; Falaschetti and Miller 2001). It seems as if the search for structures that covary with low levels of corruption has taken place at the expense of the attention to what agents could possibly overcome the collective action problem in establishing "good governance." If we are to establish a thorough picture of what can become a successful reform process, research should start to identify different agents' roles and interests. Essential questions are, for example, What groups can be expected to oppose reforms, and how should this resistance be dealt with? Who are likely to support change, what strategies can they use, and how can they best be involved in the struggle against corruption?

Many social scientists nowadays are inclined to understand social changes in a path dependent and incremental way. The current situation can be explained by going back to some kind of "critical juncture" or "formative moment" when an often minor institutional change set in motion a "feedback mechanism" that has led to a virtuous (or vicious) causal circulation between two or more variables so that they reinforce one another over time and keep the society spinning along a "chosen path." As Paul Pierson puts it, "As feedback loops become central to the process that follows a critical juncture, it becomes impossible to delineate clear causes and effects; instead, a set of factors mutually reinforce one another" (Pierson 2004, 95).

In this line of thinking, analyses about curbing corruption and establishing QoG are geared toward finding those "initial steps" serving as a "magic key" in the form of a small device that will make a country start spinning on a new path out of systemic corruption. This idea can, for example, be found in the World Bank's report about policy measures to combat corruption. To successfully implement anticorruption policies, the report states, the challenge is to find "an appropriate *entry point* for anticorruption work." Furthermore, "it is critical to begin at a point where the goals are feasible and tangible results can be realized within a time frame that builds support for further reforms. Small gains can provide essential levers to sway public and official opinion" (World Bank 2000, 75). Similarly, the UN's *Global Programme Against Corruption* describes the best strategy as "a long-term process whereby corrupt values and practices are gradually identified and eliminated" (United Nations 2004, 17). Thus, if we could only find the *magic key* (the "entry point") and change this institutional device, we would be able to advise policy makers on this important topic. If large differences start with small changes, we need to find these small things, because huge (societywide) things like systemic corruption are otherwise hard to change.

With reference to Romania, the opposite line of thinking has been launched by Alina Mungiu-Pippidi. She has stated that although international donor organizations put great effort into anticorruption policies, there seems to be little evidence that this has accomplished much, and there are few success stories. She warns that the many campaigns and efforts that turn out to be ineffective "render voters extremely cynical and threaten to subvert public trust in emerging democracies" (Mungiu-Pippidi 2006, 82). The problem is that these campaigns fail to take into consideration that corruption in a country like Romania is rooted in a *particularistic* political culture in which almost all public goods are distributed on a "nonuniversalist basis that mirrors the vicious distribution of power." The risk is therefore that the anticorruption measures put in place with support from international organizations, such as a special anticorruption agency, will be taken over by corrupt or semi-corrupt networks. Mungiu-Pippidi argues that the root of systemic corruption is a particularistic political culture, which is defined as a system in which the government's treatment of citizens "depends on their status or position in society, and people do not even expect to be treated fairly by the state; what they expect is similar treatment to everybody with the same status" (2006, 82).

In such a particularistic political culture, what you get from the public sector depends on your connections, your ability to bribe, or your participation in various corrupt networks. In this state of affairs, the establishment of a few new "Western-style" benevolent "principals" will not help against corruption, because they will become impregnated with the dominating particularistic political culture (cf. Doig, Watt, and Williams 2007). According to Mungiu-Pippidi, even the most famous of Swedish anticorruption institutions, "the Ombudsman," which has been reproduced in many emerging democracies, "has been largely unsuccessful, as the historical process that promoted universalism at the expense of particularism in the Scandinavian countries has not been replicated as well" (2006, 96).

This conceptual division between universal and particularistic political cultures is in line with North, Wallis, and Weingast's idea of distinguishing between "limited access social orders" and "open access social orders." In this typology, the former are characterized by privileged access to valuable rights and activities that are built on *personal* relationships (North, Wallis, and Weingast 2009). Examples are aristocratic-feudal states, third world "crony-capitalist" autocracies, or the former Soviet-style states. In contrast, the "open access social order" (mainly the advanced OECD countries) is characterized by free access to political and economic arenas of competition based on *impersonal* contractual forms (ibid., 40). They make a convincing case that, seen from a historical and comparative perspective, what they call "limited access orders" and what here are called "corruption and similar practices" constitute the natural state of affairs and are to be expected. It is thus not the existence of corruption that needs to be explained, but the relatively few cases in modern history that have been able to take the step from high corruption ("limited access order") to low corruption ("open access order").

Both North, Wallis, and Weingast and Mungiu-Pippidi argue convincingly that corruption and similar practices are rooted in deeply held beliefs about the proper order of exchange in a society: personal-particularistic versus impersonal-universalistic. The implication is that to effectively curb corruption and establish QoG, the whole political culture has to move from the "limited access" or "particularistic" equilibrium to the very different equilibrium characterized by "impersonal" or "universal" forms of exchange. Accepting their approaches implies that corrupt and noncorrupt societies are seen as different "states" or "equilibriums." This can certainly be questioned, since according to several empirical studies, many contemporary societies are in between systemic corruption and being (almost) noncorrupt. However, the arguments these authors present for understanding the problem as different "states" are both empirically convincing and theoretically illuminating.

The implication from this perspective is that taking small steps by installing a few specific institutions, such as the Swedish "ombudsman" or an "anticorruption commission," to induce change from one political culture/social order to the other is in all likelihood in vain. As North and his colleagues argue, history "does not seem to present us with a wide spectrum of societies gradually making a transition from old to new political and economic institutions" (North, Wallis, and Weingast 2009, 33). Unfortunately, we know very little about how such a transition can be made. The establishment of *universal, impersonal,* and *impartial* political institutions that make "credible commitments" between competing actors possible remains something of a mystery, at least from a rational-choice perspective (Falaschetti and Miller 2001; Hechter 1992; Lichbach 1997). Or, as it is stated in a handbook on institutional economics, the puzzle is that such "efficient" institutions "operate in a few advanced contemporary countries and only in recent times. We know surprisingly little, however, about the institutional developments that led to these modern successes" (Greif 2005, 773).

The problem is not confined to changes in formal institutions but includes the role of informal institutions as well. The operation of such institutions is of course difficult to detect, but one clue may be found in the strong correlation between high levels of social trust and high levels of trust in the legal system and low levels of corruption. There is a vast discussion on how the standard general trust question can be interpreted, and I agree with Delhey and Newton that when people answer the survey question on whether they believe "most other people can be trusted," this can be interpreted as their evaluation of the moral standard of the society they live in, that is, the quality of the informal institutions in their society (Delhey and Newton 2004). Following the logic of reciprocity described above, if most people think that most people in their society will behave in an honest way, the individual agents who enter into a transaction with someone unknown to them have less reason to fear becoming a victim of treacherous or exploitative behavior. Therefore cooperation between people who do not have personal knowledge about one another will be more common in a society with a high level of social trust. If we follow the idea of reciprocity as stated above, the outcome of social and economic interactions depends on how the "real-life context" somehow has constructed the "mutual expectations," for example, about whether the other players can be trusted.

So far, the implication of this analysis is quite negative. First, corruption is driven by the workings of a large set of historically rooted formal and informal institutions in a society. Second, neither the formal nor the informal institutions are easily changed, since they constitute "self-reinforcing" equilibriums. If an agent tries to reform a single institution or a small set of institutions in a corrupt-particularistic-limited access political culture, the attempt will in all likelihood backfire, since the new institutions will be overtaken by the corrupt/clientelist networks and dominated by practices that, in turn, will increase cynicism among the population and delegitimize future efforts to improve the quality of government (cf. Doig, Watt, and Williams 2007).

The Transition Away from Corruption in
Nineteenth-Century Sweden

Sweden and the other Nordic countries present a puzzle in this discussion. On the one hand, they are characterized by most of the features that according to standard economic theory should make them corrupt beyond repair (Alesina and Angeletos 2005). For example, they have very large public sectors, interventionist governments, and large bureaucracies with lots of discretionary power over many types of regulations. Yet the most commonly used comparative measures of national levels of corruption show precisely the opposite—that the Scandinavian countries have the lowest levels of corruption in the world (Hopkin and Rodrîguez-Pose 2007; Uslaner 2008). However, contrary to what is often believed, during the eighteenth and early nineteenth centuries the Scandinavian states were by today's standards thoroughly corrupt (Frisk Jensen 2008; Rothstein 1998b). This changed dramatically during the latter part of the nineteenth century. Understanding corruption as a universal (and not culturally specific) problem, examining how nineteenth-century Sweden managed to overcome corruption could provide some important insights.

To give some examples: In the early nineteenth-century Swedish civil service, it was common for the same civil servant to hold five or six full-time positions. Personal contact with the king's court was more important than impersonal laws. The nobility had precedence for positions in the courts and the civil service. Obedience to laws was seen as more or less voluntary compared with personal instructions from the king's court. The *accord system* allowed civil servants and military officers to buy and sell paid positions within their corps (Frohnert 1993, 287). No age limit was established for when a civil servant or military officer could be forced to leave his position, reflecting a premodern view of public positions as feudal property. Neither severe illness nor other gross inability to carry out one's duties was valid grounds for removing someone from public office. During the eighteenth and nineteenth centuries a number of royal prohibitions were issued that addressed this position purchasing. That these hardly made an impact provides insight into the legislative system of a particularistic limited-access society (Myrberg 1922).

The requirements for education and skills are another example. In a Weberian bureaucracy, civil servants have to have a certain degree of specific knowledge about the legal and administrative systems of the state, and recruitment has to be meritocratic. In early nineteenth-century Sweden, the opposite was true. The education in law at the universities during this period has been characterized as an intellectual as well as organizational morass that lasted into the first decades of the nineteenth century (Lindroth 1976; Gierow 1971, 224). For example, in 1797 there were complaints from the chancellery college to the governing board of Lund University:[4] "At times we must understand that the young men who seek entrance to the chancellery offices have not possessed the knowledge in science and language necessary for a chancery subject, notwithstanding they were furnished with academic qualifications" (Gierow 1971, 225).

This slump pertained, not least of all, to the so-called *ämbetsexamina* (the degree qualifying candidates for higher civil service posts), which served as the foremost recruitment instrument for employment in the central administration. In 1859 law professor Knut Olivecrona writes in his historical account of the education at Uppsala University School of Law in 1785–1823: "During the long period when Hernberg, Lundström and Drissel occupied the prominent juris patrii profession, the purely legal studies sank to their lowest point of ruin. The so-called *Hofrättsexamen* became insignificant, the Bachelor of Law degree was implemented with the highest degree of ease, and in the study of Roman jurisprudence, even the most cursory knowledge was not required" (Olivecrona 1859, 14).

Legal exams during this period have been described as pure travesty (Lindroth 1976, 165).

In 1797, in response to the criticism against the low quality of education of its graduates, the university's chancellor explained that the one factor primarily responsible for the unfavorable conditions was that "small children" were being enrolled as students in the universities. He was referring to adolescents in their early teens, who for understandable reasons could not benefit from the education offered. This in turn happened because "parents and relatives, whose main goal is only to hasten the early entrance of their children to a civil service career, either

4. Sweden at this time had had only two universities, one in Lund, the other in Uppsala.

out of conceit or ignorance, . . . build their hopes of future advancement more on wealth and privileged connections than on duly founded ability through hard-earned requisite learning" (Gierow 1971, 238).

Since seniority was the most important principle for competitive advancement, it was a matter of gaining entrance for one's offspring to a department where he could already be employed as a two-year-old (naturally without being required to work or receive compensation).

Eventually rules were introduced that established guidelines for the minimum time of study, as well as age limits for employment in the civil service departments. Nevertheless, in response to a letter regarding the education of future civil servants, law professor Holmbergsson at Lund University stated in 1831 that education was not going to be improved by establishing minimum time of study regulations and age limit requirements. Holmbergsson proposed that what needed to be done instead was to change the promotion system of government departments so that actual merit and years of service, rather than personal relationships, decided career advancement (Gierow 1971, 244).

In addition, the system of pay was far from universal and impersonal during the first half of the nineteenth century. Even though payment in kind was the most common compensation, monetary remuneration did exist. Perquisites and fees for job-related services, or bribes by today's standards, were abundant (Westerhult 1965). It was also common for the civil servants to receive income from land and residences that belonged to the position. Civil servants were often appointed, especially within the higher administration and the universities, without sufficient funds to pay them and with no expectation that they were going to perform any work (Gierow 1971, 25–27). In the local government administration, for example, income for the very same job was "so varying that many of the best-paid civil servants had twice the pay of their less fortunate colleagues" (Westerhult 1965, 167). A study of local bailiffs during the eighteenth century shows that "a large portion of wage income was . . . tied to individual peasants who were obliged to deliver grain, money or other goods" (Frohnert 1993, 367). In a letter to His Majesty the King in 1811, the directors of the Exchequer Board pointed out that since the pay had fallen to such a low level, a large number of civil servants had taken work in other national boards or agencies, or with county governments (all the while retaining their old positions, of course), and that this had considerably complicated and delayed work within the central part of

the national civil service (Edén, Berglöf, and Schalling 1941, 278). Holding several positions in this way was very common, and the practice was
not prohibited until 1879. In a report from 1822, the government depart-
mental committee appointed in 1819 declared that, owing to the poor
pay, those civil servants who did not have private fortunes were forced
to either look for other posts and public offices or gain their livelihood
through private business affairs (Rothstein 1998b). In sum, as (under)
stated by one of Sweden's foremost political scientists, Gunnar Heckscher, in his landmark book about the Swedish Civil Service from 1952,
in the beginning of the nineteenth century the public administration in
Sweden was "pretty bad" (Heckscher 1952).

The change toward a Weberian civil service came between 1860 and
1875 and was both "nonincremental" and dramatic. Most important, the
whole idea of what it meant to be a civil servant changed. The idea of
seeing a public position as equivalent to a feudal enfeoffment that the
"owner" could use for extracting rents pretty much according to his own
will was abandoned. It was replaced with the view that a full-time position with a fixed wage could be offered only in an open, meritocratic
competition carried out according to stipulated universal rules and laws.
In his book about the Swedish public administration published in 1896,
Emil Hildebrand, the historian and head of the Swedish National Archives, reported that "the old view of an administrative office as property was beginning to disappear" (Hildebrand 1896, 653). Corruption
and similar practices did of course still occur to some extent, but they
were no longer seen as "standard operating procedure." Maybe the most
telling evidence for this is the novel *The Red Room*, published in 1879
by Sweden's still most famous author—August Strindberg. In this novel,
Strindberg (who was a leftist radical) gave a very vivid and negative description of a prototypical civil service administration (the fictitious National Board for the Payment of Wages for the Civil Service). The bureaucrats were described as utterly conservative, lazy, and ineffective
(this still makes a good read). However, he did not portray them as corrupt. A fair guess is that if civil servants had been generally considered
corrupt at this time, Strindberg the radical would have added this to his
long list of faults. But he did not do so, and a fair guess is that it would
not have had broad resonance in the public opinion at this time. In any
case, what is remarkable for this period is the many and dramatic institutional changes toward establishing QoG that took place in a fairly short
time. Below is just a partial list:

Reforms That Changed Sweden from Corruption/Particularism to Impartiality/Universalism

· 1840 to 1862: Several new public boards/agencies are established for carrying out large investments in communications infrastructure (National Railway Board 1862, National Board for Telegraphic Communication 1856, National Board for Roads and Canals 1841). This brought in a whole new cadre of more professionally trained civil servants. Technical skills and merits became important.

· 1842 to 1862: Major reforms are made to the public school system—mandatory and free basic education for everyone is established and implemented during the 1860s, together with the National Board of School Inspectors.

· 1845: The government's right to confiscate newspapers is abolished (leading to the de facto establishment of a newspaper-driven debate about public affairs from the 1850s).

· 1845: The last formal aristocratic prerogative for higher positions in the state is abolished. In practice, the nobility's privileged rights to top positions are de facto implemented during the mid-1860s.

· 1845: A law establishes equal rights to inheritance between men and women.

· 1846: The guild system is abolished.

· 1848: The joint-stock company law is introduced.

· 1855 to 1860: Major revision is made to the wage system in the civil service to create a Weberian system of pay.

· 1858: Freedom of religion is established.

· 1860: The right to leave the state church for other congregations is granted.

· 1862: New local government law and new law about regional authorities establish new regional and local self-government bodies.

· 1862: A new general criminal code includes a law on misconduct in public office.

· 1862: New laws for cities, county councils, and local municipalities greatly increase political decentralization.

· 1863: New rules for university education establish higher standards for degrees.

· 1864: Freedom of trade is established.

· 1866: Major reform is made to the Parliament—the four-estate system is abolished, and a "modern" bicameral parliament is established.

· 1868: Parliament decides to start abolishing direct payments for services to individual civil servants. The fees citizens pay for various services should no longer belong to the individual civil servant but should be state property.

- 1869: Parliament decides that taxes must be paid in money instead of in goods.[5]
- 1870: Jews can now be civil servants and representatives in the Swedish parliament.
- 1876: There is major reorganization of the national bureaucracies from collegial decision making (the court model) to the modern bureau system with hierarchical structure.
- 1878: The "accord system" is getting dismantled and a working pension system for civil servants is introduced. The "accord system" seems to have finally been abolished about 1886.

A look at this long list of institutional changes reveals four things. First, although some of the reforms started in the 1840s, their lagged effect (especially school reform and the establishment of a free popular press) shows that there is a stark concentration in time, with the 1860s as the main decade. Second, the time frame of the Swedish case is consistent with the analysis North, Wallis, and Weingast (2009, 27) carried out on the periods of transition from "limited" to "open access" orders in Britain, France, and the United States. If anything, the time frame of the transition in Sweden is a bit shorter than the "about fifty years" they portray for their three cases. The third thing to notice is that few of these changes directly targeted corruption. Instead, this case reveals a more *indirect approach* that was directed not at corrupt practices in particular but at the general framework of what seems to be the full set of political institutions in the country. Instead of just attacking corruption and clientelism head-on, this indirect approach changed the political culture from a particularistic understanding of *what politics is* to a universalistic one.

Note that this has a clear parallel to the strategy launched by what most experts hold to be the most prominent military strategist of the twentieth century, Basil Liddell Hart. His famous "indirect approach" in military strategy holds that an enemy that is attacked directly will easily reinforce his strength at the position attacked and so be very difficult to defeat. Against this, Liddell Hart's famous "second principle" reads: "*To defeat the enemy one must first upset his equilibrium, which is not accomplished by the main attack, but must be done before the main attack can succeed*" (Liddell Hart 1967, 167 [italics added]; cf. Danchev 1999). The "indirect strategy" implies that it is most important to achieve the

5. Thanks to Dr. Maria Cavallin Ajmer for providing most of this information.

enemy's psychological dislocation, which in the terminology applied here would be the same as changing his "logic of reciprocity," that is, what he can expect from "the others" in the corrupt networks.

Fourth, one can clearly characterize this period as a nonincremental, indirect "big bang" change. Not just a few, but almost all major political, social, and economic formal institutions were transformed during a relatively short period, with the 1860s as the central decade. Sten Carlsson, the well-known Swedish historian of this period, speaks of the years between 1856 and 1886 as "Liberalism's high tide" (cited in Nilsson 2001, 258). Politically, the old corporative feudal order was replaced by a new dominant principle that put the individual at center stage (ibid.).

Space permitting, I could provide a detailed explanation for each of these reforms. But explaining why so many reforms, pointing in the same direction, took place within this relatively short period is more difficult. Nevertheless, as with neighboring Denmark, these reforms started after the countries had experienced crushing military defeats (and ruined state finances as a consequence), threatening their very existence. Faced with such a severe threat, it seems that the elites in both countries realized the importance of genuine institutional change (cf. Frisk Jensen 2008). As is known from research on group behavior, a severe external threat usually increases internal cooperation (Hardin 1995).

As stated above, not only formal but also informal institutions (such as generalized trust) should be important drivers behind this development. Changes to informal institutions earlier in time are by their very nature more difficult to research, but in one important area there are some indicators that this period also saw changes in this respect. The mid-nineteenth century in Sweden was also a time of dramatic increase in the number and activity of voluntary associations. What is important is that they were not closed, "guildlike" organizations but usually stressed that they were open to people from all social classes. Second, there was a strong emphasis on "the common good," "communality," and "serving the nation" in their discourse as well as in the written goals, rules, and regulations that many of them established (Jansson 1985, 241). According to the most detailed historical study of this process, the phenomenon was so strong that one could speak of it as a "meta-ideology" (ibid., 242) and as their way to achieve respectability (Pettersson 1995). Strong support for the "free associations" also came from important members of the new capitalist class, not least from the founder of the famous Swedish Wallenberg dynasty (Nilsson 2001, 123).

This is not the place for a full comparative study of political changes aimed at erasing systemic corruption in other Western countries, but there are clear indications from other nations of similar major changes during this period. Denmark shows a similar massive institutional change between 1840 and 1860, "when corruption is almost eradicated" (Frisk Jensen 2008, 291). The United States saw a similar overhaul of a corrupt and patronage-ridden political culture during the "Progressive movement" that started in the late nineteenth century. According to Arnold, the movement cannot be understood as driven simply by the effort to increase government efficiency. Instead, its goal was nothing less than "the moral purification of government" (Arnold 2003, 205; Root 2006). Especially the Civil Service Reform League managed to change the very nature of "the public understanding of what ought to be the character of American politics and the federal government." According to Arnold the movement was "completely" successful in combating patronage and corruption in the federal government not by concentrating its efforts on corruption but by including this "war on corruption" in a broader framework to change the overall political culture (2003, 205–6). A third example is the famous Northcote-Trevelyan report launched in Britain in 1853 that argued for the establishment of a meritocratic recruitment system. However, the report not only was directed toward eradicating corruption but also took a broader universalist perspective on the civil service as a part of the British political culture (Chapman and Greenaway 1980; Harling 1996). A fourth example of such a "big bang" change of the overall political culture is the "revolution from above" that took place in Bavaria in the earlier part of the nineteenth century when the prime minister, Maximilian von Montgelas, not only introduced a meritocratic and rule-bound civil service but also modernized and secularized all of Bavarian society very much along the same lines as in the Swedish case (Weis 2005).

Conclusion: The Indirect "Big Bang" Approach

In a thoroughly corrupt setting, even people who think corruption is morally wrong are likely to go along because they see no point in doing otherwise, since "all" other agents take part in the corrupt game (Della Porta and Vannucci 1999). In encouraging change, recognizing this fact has important implications. Changing norms about what is good or bad are of little relevance, since most people already know about them. The important thing will be to change agents' beliefs about what "all" the other agents are likely to do when it comes to corrupt practices. This is an answer to North's demand, mentioned in the introduction to this chapter, for handling "nonincremental change" and putting more focus on informal institutions.

From a policy perspective, this has some important implications. First, this approach does not point out any single set of institutions as most important for change. The courts are not more or less important than the civil service, the integrity of the politically elected leaders, civil society, or the mass media. Second, targeting corruption directly is probably not going to lead to change unless it is accompanied by a Liddell Hart–type "indirect" strategy in which many, if not most, other public institutions are converted from particularistic practices to universalism and impartiality. One can think of this as the need to reach a "tipping point" in order to reach a new equilibrium (Schelling 1998). If the anticorruption policies are limited to small measures ("entry points"), they will not convince enough agents that continuing their corrupt practices is no longer a viable option, and the likely result is that the system will not reach the crucial "tipping point" but will slide back into its old practices of systemic corruption. As I pointed out earlier, Larry Diamond, one of the most renowned scholars in democratization, has recently argued, "Endemic corruption is not some flaw that can be corrected with a technical fix or a political push. It is the way that the system works, and it is deeply embedded in the norms and expectations of political and social life. Reducing it to less destructive levels—and keeping it there—*requires revolutionary change in institutions*" (Diamond 2007, 119; emphasis added).

Quality of Government and the Welfare State

Why Are Modern Welfare States So Different?

It is common to see problems related to quality of government as mostly pertaining to developing or "transition" countries. For the most part this is probably true. However, in this chapter I argue that to quite some extent the QoG variable can also explain why Western industrialized capitalist countries have developed such very different systems for social protection and social insurance. It is of course easy to put forward arguments for why the QoG factor would have a huge effect on, for example, public spending on health care if one compared two oil-rich countries such as Norway and Angola. If one could show that the QoG factor also can explain variations in spending on social insurance and social services in countries that are at about the same economic level, this would increase our belief in the importance of this variable.

How to explain the substantial variation in social spending among the rich OECD countries has generated a huge amount of research over the past three decades, in part because these societies share basic structural, social, political, and institutional features. This, one could argue, should have produced similarity and convergence in their levels of social protection and equality-enhancing policies, not the huge persisting, and in some cases increasing, differences that exist (Alber 2006; Huber and Stephens 2001; Iversen 2005; Kenworthy and Pontusson 2005; Korpi and Palme 1998; Pontusson 2005; Scruggs and Allan 2006). For example, given that all are culturally seen as Western liberal market-oriented democracies, the variation in their systems of social protection can hardly be explained by historically inherited cultural traits resulting in generally held beliefs about what is just and fair, or what sort of risks should be individual responsibilities rather than handled by collective/public systems. As Larsen and others have shown, there is in fact very little evidence that the variation between, for example, the encompassing and universal character of the Scandinavian welfare states and the residual and targeted system for social protection that exists in the United States can be explained by variation in popular beliefs about social justice or wage inequalities (Larsen 2006).

A different approach to the values/beliefs explanation would be to refer to the level and spread of religious beliefs in the population. But if the extent and coverage of the welfare state are connected to Christian values, whereby humans are obliged to support the poor and the needy, then why are the most secular countries also the ones with the most extensive programs for economic support, and why do they have the lowest percentage of children living in poverty (Norris and Inglehart 2004; Smeeding 2004)? The United States, one of the world's richest and, among developed nations, most religious societies, also has the highest percentage among Western countries of children living in poverty and the highest percentage of newborns who do not reach their first birthday. Simply put, why are the least religious countries in the developed world the most generous to the least fortunate and most vulnerable of their members?

A more utility-based line of thought could start from neoclassical economic theory, which should predict that, given that these are all societies where the logic of the market dominates the economy, economic agents (workers, employers, unions, firms, associations, bureaucracies, etc.) should have acted based on similar utility functions and perceptions about risks, and their demand for protection from these risks and the following interactions should then have resulted in similar systems for social protection. Alternatively, by the logic of increased global economic competition, the less efficient social insurance systems should have been weeded out by the more efficient ones. However, what we see is that the differences, in terms of both institutional configurations and coverage, are huge and stable (Alber 2006; Pontusson 2005; Swank 2002).

One of the most successful approaches for explaining variation in the size and coverage of welfare states is the so-called power resource theory (henceforth PRT), according to which this is largely a function of working-class political mobilization (Huber and Stephens 2001; Korpi

1988). However, when PRT scholars reflect on the importance of institutions for explaining variations in welfare states, they do not touch on issues such as legitimacy or quality of government. Instead, institutions are just seen as arenas for political conflicts generated by forces of social class or as useful political tools for the parties involved in this struggle. In other words, in the PRT, institutional factors do not have an independent explanatory power (Korpi 2001).

My argument is precisely the opposite. In each country the historically inherited government institutions are an important influence on the choices of individual wage earners and their representatives about whether to give the state the responsibility for extracting resources and implementing policies for social insurance and welfare state redistribution. More precisely, this causal effect springs from the generally established perceptions and the following ideological and political discourses of the quality of the government institutions (Schmidt 2009). Let me underline, however, that the argument I present here is not a rebuttal of the power resource theory but a complement to it. Working-class mobilization is a key to understanding welfare state expansion, and my ambition is to clarify the hitherto largely neglected underlying conditions for when this process is likely to take place—an environment of high QoG.

The Power Resource Theory: Appraisal and Critique

The power resource theory grew out of the efforts of a group of scholars who during the late 1970s tried to find a "middle way" between the then popular Marxist-Leninist view that the welfare state should be understood as merely a functional requisite for the reproduction of capitalist exploitation and, on the other hand, the idea that welfare states follow from a similar functionalist logic of modernization and industrialization. As a reaction against these functionalist explanations, the PRT puts forward two important considerations. First, the PRT scholars were the first to point out that the variation in things like coverage, extension, and generosity among existing welfare states needed to be explained. Second, to explain this variation they introduced the importance of political mobilization based on social class (Korpi 1974, 1983). According to this theory, variation in welfare states reflects "class-related distributive conflicts and partisan politics" (Korpi 2006, 168). The more political resources the working class is able to muster, such as a strong and united

union movement that gives electoral support to labor or social democratic parties, the more extensive, comprehensive, universal, and generous the welfare state would become (Esping-Andersen 1990). The reason for this, according to the theory, is that the splits in the employment
situation reflect the class divisions that "generate interactions between
class, life-course risks and resources, so that categories with higher life-
course risks tend to have lower individual resources to cope with risks."
The argument is that such diversity of social risks would generate "a potential for class related collective action" (ibid.). Although the theory has
been challenged, the power resource approach has been more successful
than its competitors in explaining the size as well as the structure of welfare states (Allan and Scruggs 2004; Huber and Stephens 2001; Korpi
and Palme 2003).[1]

The analytical problem in the power resource approach is that while I
agree that social class positions give rise to different social risks and that
reasonably rational wage workers (and their representatives) would opt
for some kind of protection from these risks, we still need to explain why
they would turn to the state for such protection. There are many other
possibilities, not only in theory. First, unions or national union movements could have taken care of many of these risks and created large
insurance organizations that also could have worked as "selective incentives" when recruiting and keeping members (cf. Rothstein 1992a).
Second, strong unions could have forced employers (or employers' organizations) to take on either all or part of the costs. A third possibility was
that various "friendly societies" or similar voluntary nonprofit organizations connected to the working-class movement would have handled the
demand for social protection. Another possibility would of course have
been to rely on extended family networks (de Sousa 2008). The point I
want to make is that in order for wage earners and their representatives
to turn to the state for protection against social risks, they have to have
a high degree of confidence in "their" state. This can readily be seen
from a Nordic perspective (the countries in which the PRT originally

1. The PRT has been challenged by theories focusing on the importance of employers and cross-class alliances (Mares 2003; Swenson 2002); variation in systems of skill formation (Estevez-Abe, Iversen, and Soskice 2001); the importance of autonomous state bureaucracies (Weir and Skocpol 1985); and the importance of electoral systems (Iversen and
Soskice 2006). In my evaluation of the debate, the first case has been successfully refuted
(Korpi 2006; Paster 2009), and the latter three should be seen as complements and addi-
tions to the PRT (see, e.g., Iversen and Stephens 2008).

developed). In these countries, political corruption or clientelism have hardly ever been on the political agenda. As I showed in chapter 5, even before the emergence of democracy, the Nordic states were historically less corrupt, less clientelist, less prone to use violence against their citizens, and more open to popular influence than most Continental and southern European states.

However, in other countries the state turned out to be much more problematic for the union and labor movement. For example, at the beginning of the twentieth century, the unions in the United States encountered courts that systematically produced decisions they thought of as hostile to their interests, and this in turn turned the unions' political strategy away from relying on the state for social protection (Forbarth 1989; Hattam 1993). In France in 1905, a conservative government wanted to involve the unions in administering an unemployment insurance system, but remembering the bloody defeat of the Paris Commune in 1871, the radical unions refused to collaborate with the French state (Alber 1984). On a more general level, while great distrust of government authorities is rare in the Nordic countries, the opposite is certainly true for much of the rest of the world, not least in developing and transition countries. High levels of corruption, clientelism, and patronage hamper government's ability to collect taxes and to deliver services to its population (Adésínà 2007; Bräutigam, Fjeldstad, and Moore 2008; Kornai, Rothstein, and Rose-Ackerman 2004; de Sousa 2008; Riesco and Draibe 2007; Rothstein and Uslaner 2005; Sorj and Martuccelli 2008). A close observer of the situation in Latin America has described this situation: "I don't think there is any more vital issue in Latin America right now. . . . It's a vicious cycle that is very hard to break. People don't want to pay taxes because their government doesn't deliver services, but government institutions aren't going to perform any better until they have resources, which they obtain when people pay their taxes" (Rother 1999).

Note that in the very early forms of "workers' insurance" established in, for instance, Germany and Sweden, the question of the trustworthiness and legitimacy of the institutions that were to implement the policies was central. In both countries, the solution was to give trade unions representation in, and sometimes direct control over, the various insurance funds that were to implement the system (Rothstein 1992a; Steinmetz 1991). Moreover, in some cases the unions could use this control as a form of "selective incentive" to increase their membership and thereby their organizational strength (Scruggs 2002; Western 2001). There are thus good arguments for why unions could have solved the demand for social protection themselves instead of putting this demand on the state.

The conclusion to be drawn is that the causal logic in the power resource theory is too "monochrome" in its ontological foundations (cf. Hall 2003). The idea of a linear causal logic between how politically mobilized wage earners are and the size of the welfare state omits the existence of what have been called *feedback mechanisms* that focus on the existence of a reverse causal link from the implementation of policies to public opinion (Soss and Schram 2007). The theory is simply not political enough, since it pays too little attention to the ramifying political conditions under which the working class (or, more precisely, its political representatives) is likely to succeed in mobilizing support for social protection or redistribution *by the state*.

What Happens When the State Is Brought Back In?

In *Protecting Soldiers and Mothers*, Theda Skocpol (1992) shows that the welfare sector in the United States was quite large during the late nineteenth century. A central part of this was the pension system for veterans of the Civil War and their dependent family members, a program that during the decades after the war became a huge operation in terms of both finances and the number of people it supported. The problem was that the system for deciding eligibility was complicated and entailed a large portion of administrative discretion. It is easy to imagine that it is difficult to decide what health issues should count as resulting from military service or from other sources. The result, according to Skocpol, was that "the statutes quickly became so bewilderingly complex that there was much room for interpretation of cases" (Skocpol 1992, 121). What happened was that war veteran pension administration became a source for political patronage:

> Because the very successes of Civil War pensions were so closely tied to the workings of patronage democracy, these successes set the stage for negative feedbacks that profoundly affected the future direction of U.S. social provisions. During the Progressive Era, the precedent of Civil War pensions was constantly invoked by many American elites as a reason for opposing or delaying any move toward more general old-age pensions. . . . Moreover, the party-based "corruption" that many U.S. reformers associated with the im-

plementation of Civil War pensions prompted them to argue that the United States could not administer any new social spending programs efficiently or honestly. (Skocpol 1992, 59)

The point Skocpol makes is that the reason the United States of today has a comparatively small, targeted, and not very redistributive welfare state cannot be explained only by the lack of a social democratic type of labor movement or by normative ideals about "rugged individualism." On the contrary, the United States welfare state was comparatively well developed at the beginning of the twentieth century, but it was thereafter politically delegitimized owing to what was generally perceived as its low quality of government. For the United States, the QoG problem for the overall legitimacy of the welfare state seems to have had a lasting impact. A case in point is the efforts made in the 1970s in the United States to launch a federal active labor market policy known as the Comprehensive Employment and Training Act (CETA). Despite strong public support for the notion of a work ethic that this program was based on, this active labor market policy largely came to an end because of accusations of "corruption, waste and mismanagement" (Weir 1992, 126). According to one observer, by the time it was discontinued, CETA had almost become "a four-letter word" in the public debate (Donahue 1989, 181).

Skocpol's argument can thus be generalized in time and space. As shown in the previous chapter, many of the northern European countries that started to develop encompassing welfare states during the first half of the twentieth century had successfully increased their quality of government during the preceding century. For example, during the nineteenth century Bavaria, Prussia, Britain, Denmark, and Sweden carried out large-scale changes in their government institutions that did away with systemic corruption and pervasive patronage and introduced impartial (meritocratic) systems for recruiting civil servants and implementing public policies (Frisk Jensen 2008; Harling 1996; Heckscher 1952; Rubinstein 1987; Weis 2005). These countries, when starting to build their welfare states, could thus start from a comparatively very advantageous position regarding how their citizens perceived the trustworthiness, competence, and reliability of the government authorities that would be given the sensitive and intricate task of implementing the policies (Rothstein and Uslaner 2005). However, although Skocpol's analysis was impressive, it dealt with just one case (albeit an important one). It is noteworthy that in only one of the literally hundreds of comparative statistical analyses the welfare state research industry has produced during the past three decades have I found any attempt to test the hypothesis originally launched by Skocpol.[2] Interestingly enough, the problem of low quality of government is not mentioned even in recent works that argue for the need for welfare state research to move beyond the advanced industrial countries and focus on the developing world (Carnes and Mares 2007).

The Quality of Government Theory of the Welfare State

For most people, making a living in a market economy carries a lot of well-known risks, such as unemployment or having to pay for costly medical treatment. When facing risks, for most individuals a rational response is to try to find ways to get insurance or other support. But welfare states are complicated organizations, and therefore it not easy to theorize about them "in toto." They usually have different systems for improving equality, redressing severe poverty, and handling social risks either for specific groups or for their whole population or very broad segments of it. Thus they are intended for redistribution as well as for insurance against risks (Iversen 2005, 21). However, as shown by, for example, Åberg (1989) and Korpi and Palme (1998), systems that are meant to be mostly redistributive may be less so than those intended mostly to provide social insurance. As Moene and Wallerstein have argued, social insurance systems "generally provide insurance against a common risk on terms that are more favourable for low-income individuals than for high-income individuals" (2003, 487). Moreover, if generally available services such as basic education, day care, elder care, and health care are included, the redistributive effects of welfare state policies increase dramatically (Zuberi 2006). Even if taxation is proportional to income (and not progressive), costs for services are on average nominal, and the net effect of proportional taxation and nominal benefits is massive redistribution (Åberg 1989). Thus, whether the welfare state is understood as providing social protection, social services, or social insurance, the overall tendency is that "more encompassing" generally implies increased redistribution. The same underlying microfoundations thus apply whether

2. The exception is Mares (2005), but she concentrates her theoretical argument on the importance of economic volatility.

preferences for welfare state generosity are based on demand for insurance or for redistribution, although I will mostly argue in terms of the former.

Based on this line of reasoning, citizens (and political representatives) have to handle three problems when deciding if they are going to support a social policy, for example, unemployment insurance or a public health care system. The first concerns the normative side of the question—whether such policies are to be considered a "good thing." Second, and more important for the QoG theory, for most citizens/ wage earners, the enactment of welfare state policies implies that they will have to part with a substantial portion of their money through taxation or other contributions. They are likely to accept this only on condition that they believe taxes are collected in a fair, incorrupt, transparent, nondiscriminatory, impartial, and competent manner (Scholz 1998).

Moreover, it is reasonable to believe that the perceived quality of the institutions responsible for implementing the various programs enters into this calculus. All systems of insurance have to be based on trust, and—as is well known—such trust is a delicate thing. In anonymous large-n systems like these, at least two complicated "trust games" are involved. Citizens have to trust that when they need and are entitled to support, the system will actually deliver what it has promised. In some cases we must think of this as a "leap of faith." Not only is the demand substantial in that it concerns the quality of outcome, but in all likelihood it is also procedural. People not only want the "technical side" of, say, health care delivered to them according to professional standards. They also want to be respected and listened to, and to have the right to appeal when they believe that they have not been treated professionally and fairly (de Sousa 2008). In other words, the perceived level of procedural fairness is probably as important as the level of substantial fairness (Tyler 1998). Using very detailed survey data from Sweden, one of the most encompassing welfare states in the world, Staffan Kumlin has shown that citizens' direct experience from interacting with various social policy programs has a clear influence on their political opinions. Moreover, such experiences are more important than citizens' personal economic circumstances when they form opinions about supporting welfare state policies (Kumlin 2004, 199–200). Based on a large survey from four Latin American countries, Mitchell Seligson concludes that the perceived level of corruption has a strong negative effect on beliefs about the legitimacy of the government, controlling for partisan identification (Seligson 2002). Using World Values Survey data from seventy-two countries, Bruce Gilley states that a set of variables measuring the quality of government (a composite of the rule of law, control of corruption and government effectiveness) "has a large, even overarching, importance in global citizen evaluation of the legitimacy of states" (Gilley 2006, 57).

In addition, many welfare state programs, both those intended to be redistributive and those oriented more toward social insurance, have to establish safeguards against overuse and outright abuse. For example, even people who favor generous unemployment insurance are likely to demand that people work if they are able and if there are suitable jobs. Neither tolerance for "free riding" nor willingness to be the "sucker" is generally very high. This is the third question facing citizens in need of social protection. The issue of whether the welfare state system will undermine personal responsibility is thus important, and such discourses can lead to a loss of legitimacy for the general idea of social protection by the state (Schmidt 2002). In other words, to be legitimate, the welfare state system should be able to distinguish between personal risks for which agents should have to take private responsibility and risks for which they have the right to claim benefits (Paz-Fuchs 2008). Those who favor a generous system for workers' compensation insurance or the right to early retirement for people hit by chronic illness may have legitimate reason to fear that such systems can be abused. I want to make the point that even people who are true believers in social solidarity and have a social democratic vision of society are likely to withdraw their support for an encompassing welfare state if these three requirements are not met. Put differently, their support is "contingent" on how they view the quality of the public institutions that are to implement the programs (Levi 1998a). In sum, we can think of this as citizens facing three interrelated questions when they decide if they should support a policy for social insurance or redistribution: the policy's *substantial justice*, its *procedural justice*, and the amount of *"free riding"* that can be expected. For example, an agent may agree that it is right to have universal health care but still take a political stand against it because she believes the government is incapable of implementing such a program in accordance with her demands for procedural justice. One can think of the success opponents of universal health care insurance in the United States have had in branding this policy "socialized medicine." I should underline that these issues are likely to play a role not only, as is obvious, in programs that are modeled as social insurance systems but also in programs for redistribution. This is evident from the long-standing discussion, especially in the United States, about how to distinguish between the "deserving" and the "undeserving" poor (Skocpol 1987). The welfare state contract, whether "new" or "old," is for the individual citizen a contract both with all other citizens (Will they pay their taxes and refrain from abusing the system?) and with the government authorities (When the day comes to collect the insurance or service, will they deliver? And, if so, will it be done in an acceptable way?). This can be thought of as the "moral economy" of the welfare state (Svallfors 2007).

I will leave the first, normative, question about a policy's substantial justice out of the discussion and concentrate on the second and the third. Both these problems concern how the agents perceive the competence, honesty, and trustworthiness of the government institutions that are to implement the policies in question. As I argued in chapter 1, *quality of government* can be conceptualized as founded on one basic norm: impartiality in the exercise of public power. This discussion is connected to the more recent focus in development studies and institutional economics on the importance of "good governance" (Acemoglu and Robinson 2008).

The central hypothesis, following the argument in the previous chapters (and especially in chapter 1) is that without a reasonably high level of QoG, political mobilization for welfare state policies in the way that PRT has outlined is not likely to have broad appeal. Let me underline again that I think of these approaches not as mutually exclusive, but rather as complementing one another. In other words, both political mobilization according to PRT and a high level of QoG are necessary, but on their own neither is sufficient to create an encompassing, universal, and thereby more redistributive welfare state. This has two implications for the initial question about how to explain the existing variation in systems of social policy. The first has to do with the origins of the welfare state system. If the QoG theory is correct, we should not expect countries with low QoG—that is, countries that have high levels of corruption in their government systems or that are characterized by clientelism and patronage—to develop encompassing welfare states. Second, we should expect high QoG to work as a ramifying condition for the success of PRT. More precisely, the effect of working-class mobilization on welfare state expansion should increase with the level of QoG.

Data and Design

To test my hypothesis on a broader scope of observations than the historical case of the United States, it is necessary to measure two things: the size of the welfare state and its quality of government. Starting with the former, the lion's share of the large-n literature on determinants of the welfare state has relied on social spending data (see, e.g., Huber and Stephens 2001; Swank 2002). Including government spending on both cash benefits and social service provisions, this is arguably a reasonable proxy for welfare state effort. Since the causal mechanism underlying the QoG theory is based in part on the notion that ordinary citizens or their representatives refrain from trusting the state with the huge sums of money that an encompassing welfare state requires, this proxy actually suits this purpose well. As a first measure of welfare state development, I will therefore use total public social expenditure as a percentage of annual GDP of eighteen countries between 1984 and 2000, from the OECD Social Expenditure Database (OECD 2007), taking into account missing data in the independent variables.[3]

True, there are well-known drawbacks to using social spending data. Some of these are more technical and hence more easily handled. For example, without proper controls for business cycles and the size of the target population, figures on social spending might tap into phenomena other than welfare state effort (see, e.g., Korpi and Palme 2003; Scruggs 2007). The more fundamental problem with the spending data, however, concerns their risk of being "epiphenomenal to the theoretical substance of welfare states" (Esping-Andersen 1990, 19). When ordinary citizens ponder the social risks involved in being laid off from work, for example, they are likely to demand some form of unemployment protection, not simply the macromeasure of "increased social spending on the unemployed." Similarly, when political parties and representatives propose new legislation to increase social protection for sick leave, they frame their proposals in those words, and not in terms of the budgetary increases these reforms require. In Esping-Andersen's famous words, whereas social spending definitely taps into increased welfare efforts, "It is difficult to imagine that anyone struggled for spending *per se*" (1990, 21).

3. If not otherwise indicated, all data used in this chapter are taken from the freely available QoG social policy data set (Samanni et al. 2008).

For this reason, the social spending indicator will be complemented with the hitherto broadest-ranging measure of welfare state effort based on actual social policy reforms rather than on their implied costs. This measure is Lyle Scruggs's (2006) "benefit generosity index," which draws on detailed information on replacement rates, eligibility criteria, and the size of the population that is insured against unemployment and sickness and that participates in public pension schemes. The index theoretically varies from 0 to 64, and it covers eighteen countries annually from 1984 to 2000. Since this index captures more directly the kinds of social policy reforms that are more likely to be implemented in systems with high QoG, I believe it is a more realistic proxy for the outcome the QoG theory purports to explain. However, one potential drawback with the benefit generosity measure deserves to be mentioned: it excludes the social service production part of the welfare state.

Second, QoG must be measured. Although cross-national indicators of QoG or "good governance" have proliferated in recent years, only one of them gauges the quality of government institutions over a longer period: the International Country Risk Guide's indicators (www.prsgroup .org). We need over-time (apart from cross-national) variation in QoG, since the implication of the theory is that the cumulative experience of the state, not one-shot encounters, should be what matters (more on this below). Three of the ICRG indicators are of particular interest, since they are based on expert perceptions of risks to international business and financial institutions stemming from corruption (e.g., special payments, bribes, excessive patronage, and nepotism); lack of law and order (e.g., weak and partial legal systems, low popular observance of the law); and low quality of the bureaucracy (lack of autonomous and competent bureaucrats). The ICRG indicators have a distinguished history in the field of cross-national measurement of QoG, going back at least to Knack and Keefer (1995). Thus, as the key independent variable in the subsequent analyses I use the average of these three indicators, restricted to range from 0 (low) to 1 (high quality), and covering the same eighteen countries from 1984 to 2000.[4]

As shown in table 6.3 and at the end of this chapter, where basic descriptive information on all variables is displayed, it comes as no surprise

---

4. The other three indicators have been checked for individually, but with no substantial change in results.

that the countries for which data are available belong to the least corrupt group and hence can be argued to have the highest quality of government in the world. This means that the variation in QoG that pervades these countries applies to the higher end of the scale: the mean value is .94, ranging from Italy with an average of .75 to Canada with an average of .99. Clearly this weighs against the tests of the hypothesis. If it would be possible to find evidence of an effect of QoG on welfare state effort in this restricted set of countries, there is reason for more optimism about finding such a pattern on a more global scale (had the data for this been available).

Ideally, however, one would prefer data on the quality of government that goes further back in history, all the way back to the buildup stage of the modern welfare state. Unfortunately the period the available data cover is from the era of retrenchment around the mid-1980s and onward, when most social security provisions in the Western world had been scaled back. This poses a problem for testing the QoG theory, since it is reasonable to argue that the causal mechanism underlying the hypothesis relates more strongly to the political logic of welfare state *expansion*. My solution is to rely on levels in the dependent variables, rather than changes. These levels may be viewed as a long-run tally of all previous changes (positive or negative) in welfare state effort and should predominantly capture the extent of welfare state expansion rather than retrenchment.[5]

This means that the methodological setup of Huber and Stephens (2001, chap. 3) is closely followed, which hitherto has provided the most encompassing quantitative support for PRT as an explanation for welfare state expansion. This has the additional advantage of highlighting the more exact contribution from the QoG factor. The Huber and Stephens (2001) measurement strategy is also closely followed for the partisan variables, based on their own data (Huber et al. 2004): left and Christian democratic cabinets, respectively, are the cumulative share of left and Christian democratic party governments (or fraction of parlia-

5. The use of levels comes at a cost, however, since it introduces substantial amounts of autocorrelation biasing the variance estimates. This has been corrected using the Prais-Winsten transformation based on the assumption of an AR(1) error structure common to all countries. It should be noted that all independent variables (except year dummies) are lagged one year.

mentary seats for all coalition member parties in coalition governments) since 1946.[6] The rationale for using the cumulative, rather than the annual, shares is again our focus on long-term development. For example, there is no reason to expect a left party cabinet to be able to substantially alter the welfare state effort in its country from one year to the next. But the longer left parties have been in government in a country, the more welfare state expansion we should expect to find. Following the same logic, the cumulative score of the quality of government variable is computed as well (in this case the cumulative mean rather than the cumulative sum). The QoG factor each year thus reflects the entire history of quality of government for that particular country since the first year of measurement (that is, 1984). This is because measurement strategy resonates well with the cognitive mechanisms the QoG theory is based on, since citizens or their representatives are likely to judge the trustworthiness of their state institutions not as a single-shot evaluation at each time point but as a running tally of previous experiences.[7]

Finally, a set of control variables is included. Globalization is measured with two variables: openness to trade (Heston, Summers, and Aten 2002) and an index of the liberalization of the regulation of capital and current transactions (Huber et al. 2004; originally from Quinn 1997). To control for business cycles, measures of unemployment have been included as well as budget deficits as a percentage of GDP (Armingeon et al. 2008; IMF 2008).[8] Since Huber and Stephens (2001) have shown that women's participation in the labor force has a significant effect on the expansion of the welfare state, a measure of the percentage of women in the labor force is included (OECD 2006). In addition, constitutional veto points have be theorized to hinder welfare state expansion. To control for this, an additive index based on federalism, presidentialism, bicameralism, and frequent use of referenda is used (Huber et al. 2004; Huber and Stephens 2001, 55–56). Finally, the percentage of the population over sixty-five years of age, GDP per capita, and inflation are

6. The cumulative cabinet variables are not included in the QoG social policy data set (Samanni et al. 2008), and these data are instead taken directly from Huber et al. (2004).

7. Since the use of levels in the dependent variable and cumulative scores for the independent variables may introduce a spurious correlation of time trends, all results are controlled for year-fixed effects (or year dummies).

8. The IMF data on budget deficits are not included in the QoG social policy data set (Samanni et al. 2008) and have been taken directly from IMF (2008).

controlled for (Heston, Summers, and Aten 2002; OECD 2007; World Bank 2007).

Again, most of these variables can be expected to influence the level of the welfare state effort only in the long run, and they will therefore be measured cumulatively. Again, Huber and Stephens's (2001) research strategy is closely followed and measures the following variables as the cumulative mean from the first year of observation: liberalization of capital and current transactions, female labor force participation, constitutional veto points, population over sixty-five, and inflation. A few of the variables can be argued to influence the extent of the welfare state in the short run. Higher unemployment means more recipients, which should increase social spending without making the system more generous. The same applies to openness to trade, which has been said to increase workers' sense that they risk being displaced (Huber and Stephens 2001, 63; Mares 2005). GDP not only is the resource base for expanding the welfare state in the first place, but also is the denominator in the spending measurement, and this is why short-term changes can be expected to influence the dependent variable. Finally, there is reason to expect that budget deficits tend to force governments to make cuts in the welfare state in the short run, so the budget deficit variable is not measured cumulatively.

Empirical Results

To illustrate the patterns observed, the two graphs presented below give a more visual feel for the data. Figure 6.1 displays the positive relation *at the country level* between QoG and the level of welfare state effort, measured as the benefit generosity index. Both the QoG and the welfare state measures are here computed as the mean value of all observations from 1984 to 2002 for each country. As the theory predicts, the encompassing Scandinavian welfare states can be found at the upper right, that is, among countries with both high levels of QoG and benefit generosity. On the other side of the spectrum are countries with lower QoG and smaller welfare states, such as Italy and Japan, and they are located to the lower left.

Figure 6.2 illustrates how QoG works as a ramifying condition for the effect of cabinet partisanship on welfare state generosity. The graph presents data for all the available *country year* observations from 1984

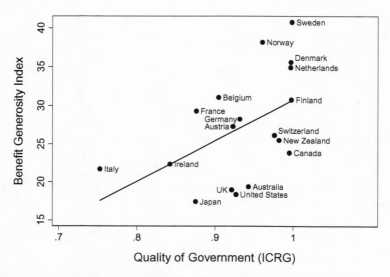

FIGURE 6.1. Benefit generosity and QoG in eighteen OECD countries, 1984–2002. R^2 = .25; b = 53; $p > |t|$ = 2.32. *Sources*: Scruggs (2006); ICRG. *Comments*: Both the QoG measure and the benefit generosity index are here computed as the mean value of all observations for each country from 1984 to 2002.

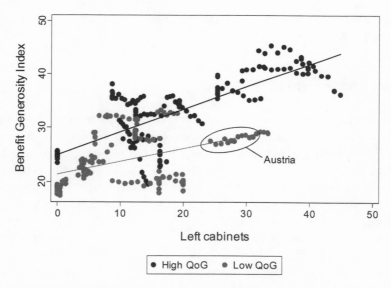

FIGURE 6.2. Interaction in eighteen OECD countries, 1984–2002. *Sources*: Scruggs (2006); Huber et al. (2004). *Comments*: Each dot represents one country and one year (e.g., Sweden 1984). The observations are split into two equal-sized groups based on their level of QoG. The regression lines show that the effect of left cabinets on the benefit generosity index is bigger for the observations with high QoG than for the observations with low QoG.

to 2002 in the eighteen OECD countries for which data are available. In the figure, the observations are divided into two equal groups based on their value of the QoG variable (the cumulative mean): the high-QoG observations are in black, the low-QoG in gray. The two regression lines track the relation between left cabinets and the benefit generosity index, respectively, for these two groups. As can be seen, the dark gray regression line, representing the group with high QoG, is steeper than the light gray regression line. This means that the effect of left cabinets on the benefit generosity index is bigger in the group with high QoG than in the one with low QoG. Thus, the effect of left cabinets on the level of welfare state effort is dependent on the level of QoG.

This latter result, however, depends critically on the inclusion of one country—Austria—whose observations have been circled in the figure. Although one could interpret this as a sign of nonrobustness (more on that below), note that the Austrian case fits the theoretical argument well. Among countries with more extensive experience of leftist governments, Austria is alone in having a relatively less generous welfare state (all other countries being Scandinavian). The QoG theory can explain why this is so: Austria also has lower quality of government, implying that workers' mobilization has not resulted in welfare state expansion to the same extent as in Scandinavia. This finding is well in line with qualitative work on the history of Austria. After 1945, the country's politics became dominated by the "Proporz" system, in which the two main parties divided power. From the early 1960s, this high-level political consensus degenerated into a full-fledged system of patronage and clientelism in which even minor positions in public administration, such as public school principals and chairs in the public universities, were divided along party lines. However, from the 1990s, this degeneration of the Proporz system came under widespread criticism. Identifying Proporz as corruption became a major asset for the new populist party that gained strong electoral support in the late 1990s (Fallend 1997; Heinisch 2002). To my knowledge, Austria is the only Western European country that has institutionalized systematic clientelism in its civil service.

Let us now turn to the more systematic evidence underpinning these descriptive relationships. In table 6.1, four empirical models are displayed that together show how QoG is part of the explanation of the generosity of the welfare state. The models again include all eighteen OECD countries from 1984 to 2000. In model 1 and model 2, social spending is used as the dependent variable. Model 1, where QoG is *not* included,

TABLE 6.1. **Regression estimates for QoG in eighteen OECD countries, 1984–2000**

	(1) Social spending (% of GDP)	(2) Social spending (% of GDP)	(3) Benefit generosity index	(4) Benefit generosity index
Quality of government		21.3*** (4.24)		35.6*** (5.19)
Left cabinet	0.23*** (5.93)	0.13** (3.08)	0.38*** (6.58)	0.26*** (4.57)
Christian democratic cabinet	0.12*** (3.57)	0.15*** (4.12)	0.12* (2.41)	0.20*** (4.81)
Openness to trade	−0.011 (−1.04)	−0.022* (−2.11)	0.069*** (4.31)	0.054*** (3.71)
Liberalization of capital and current transactions	1.16*** (5.55)	0.93*** (4.14)	1.04*** (3.61)	0.77** (2.87)
Constitutional veto points	−1.11*** (−5.77)	−0.92*** (−4.74)	−1.46*** (−4.38)	−1.54*** (−5.17)
Budget deficit/ surplus	−0.088* (−2.30)	−0.12** (−2.86)	−0.013 (−0.29)	−0.054 (−0.97)
GDP per capita	−0.24* (−2.42)	−0.35*** (−3.35)	0.46** (3.22)	0.50*** (3.74)
Female labor force participation	0.13* (2.35)	0.11 (1.70)	0.16** (2.67)	0.13** (2.65)
Inflation	0.10 (0.57)	0.70*** (3.92)	0.16 (0.58)	0.76** (2.89)
Population over 65	0.30 (1.41)	0.72** (2.96)	−0.31 (−1.04)	0.040 (0.14)
Unemployment	0.082 (1.28)	−0.011 (−0.14)	0.00095 (0.01)	−0.046 (−0.54)
N	339	279	353	285
R^2	0.85	0.89	0.83	0.89

Note: t statistics in parentheses; * $p < .05$, ** $p < .01$, *** $p < .001$
Comments: Prais-Winsten's regression with heteroskedastic panel corrected standard errors and AR1 autocorrelation structure. Year dummies are included in the model. Most independent variables are measured cumulatively (see text). All independent variables are lagged one year (except year dummies).

confirms that the data are in line with PRT. That is, as predicted, both the left cabinet and the Christian democratic cabinet variables are positively related to social spending.

Turning to model 2, the main hypothesis is confirmed. QoG has a positive and significant effect on the level of welfare state effort measured as spending. Since the QoG variable in this sample varies from .75 and 1, it is easy to interpret the coefficient: the model predicts that a country with the best possible level of QoG will spend about five (i.e., 21 × .25) percentage units more of its GDP on the welfare state compared with a country with the lowest level of QoG. This can be compared with the between-country standard deviation in social spending, which, incidentally, is 5 percent of GDP.

In addition, model 2 shows that both left and Christian democratic cabinets still have a positive effect on the level of social spending when QoG has been included in the model. The effect of left cabinets, however, is almost halved, while the effect of the Christian democratic cabinet becomes somewhat bigger. The implication of this is that previous tests of PRT, where QoG has not been controlled for, have overestimated the effect that left cabinets exert on welfare state expansion and underestimated the effect of Christian democratic cabinets. The probable reason is that left parties have held power for longer spells in high-QoG countries like, for example, the Scandinavian countries, than their lower-QoG counterparts in southern Europe.

Turning to model 3 and model 4 of table 6.1, in which the benefit generosity index from Scruggs (2006) is used as the dependent variable, the results from models 1 and 2 are repeated. Without QoG in the model, left and Christian democratic governments have a significant and positive effect on the generosity of the welfare state (model 3). However, the effect of left cabinets is reduced by one-third when QoG is introduced in the model, and the effect of Christian democratic cabinets increases by two-thirds (model 4). In model 4 the main hypothesis that QoG is positively related to the dependent variable is again confirmed. The coefficient of 35.6 implies that an increase in QoG from the level of Italy (at .75) to the level of Canada (at about 1) would lead to an increase in benefit generosity of about 8.7 (35.6 × .25). In substantial terms, this effect is even slightly bigger than the between-country standard deviation in benefit generosity (which is about 7).

In sum, models 1–4 confirm the hypothesis. Quality of government has a significant and positive effect on the level of welfare state effort, regardless of whether it is measured as spending on the welfare state or through the benefit generosity index. However, the effect of the cabinet partisanship still holds when QoG is included in the model. As predicted, the power resource theory is therefore complemented rather than refuted by the QoG theory of the welfare state.

The more systematic test of the second and supplementary hypothesis, that the size of the effect of cabinet partisanship is conditional on the level of QoG, shows the following result. In table 6.2, the results with regression estimates are presented, still limited to the eighteen OECD countries from 1984 to 2000 and using the same control variables as in table 6.1. The two interaction variables are simply the QoG variable multiplied with the left and Christian democratic cabinet variables, respectively. The coefficients for these interaction terms should be interpreted as the effect QoG exerts on the effect of either type of cabinet. In other words, if this second hypothesis proves correct, then we should expect a positive and significant interaction term.

This hypothesis is in part confirmed. There is a positive and significant interaction effect when the welfare state level is measured with the benefit generosity index (model 6), but not when it is measured as spending on the welfare state (model 5). In other words, the positive relation between left and Christian democratic cabinets and spending on the welfare state does not vary with the level of QoG. However, the effect of left cabinets on benefit generosity increases with higher QoG. This means that the QoG hypothesis is at least confirmed in the model with the most realistic proxy for welfare state effort.[9]

There are more indications that the first hypothesis, on the general effect of QoG on welfare state expansion, is the more robust of the two (these robustness tests are available from the author on request). To begin with, it holds even when all cross-country variation has been parceled out through the use of country-fixed effects (a rather hard test, considering that the variables are pretty stable over time). In this case the QoG variable holds up as an explanation of the level of welfare state effort, regardless of what measure is used for the dependent variable. As a matter of fact, it holds even when, apart from year- and country-fixed effects, the lagged dependent variable is controlled for, in effect turning the estimates into a model of change. But the hypothesis about the interaction effect does not stand these tests of robustness. The main reason, as should be expected from the discussion about figure 6.2 above, is

9. One might suspect that this is because the contingent effect of left cabinets holds only for social insurance, not for social service provision (since the benefit generosity index does not capture the latter). A finer-grained analysis, however, reveals that this is not the case. The second hypothesis is confirmed neither when spending on service is used as a dependent variable nor when cash transfers are used.

TABLE 6.2. **Regression estimates for interaction effect of cabinet partisanship and QoG in eighteen OECD countries, 1984–2000**

	(5) Social spending (% of GDP)	(6) Benefit generosity index
QoG–left Interaction	−0.56 (−0.95)	1.92* (2.48)
QoG–Christian democratic interaction	0.13 (0.47)	−0.014 (−0.04)
Quality of government	24.5** (2.87)	18.9 (1.67)
Left cabinet	0.67 (1.21)	−1.57* (−2.16)
Christian democratic cabinet	0.046 (0.19)	0.18 (0.58)
Openness to trade	−0.024* (−2.12)	0.052*** (3.39)
Liberalization of transactions	0.91*** (3.80)	0.85** (3.17)
Constitutional veto points	−0.94*** (−4.62)	−1.53*** (−5.20)
Budget deficit/ surplus	−0.12** (−2.84)	−0.050 (−0.90)
GDP per capita	−0.32** (−2.80)	0.44** (3.10)
Female labor force participation	0.13 (1.75)	0.075 (1.39)
Inflation	0.82*** (3.76)	0.44 (1.43)
Population over 65	0.69** (2.76)	0.090 (0.30)
Unemployment	−0.0064 (−0.08)	−0.054 (−0.62)
N	279	285
R^2	0.89	0.89

Note: t statistics in parentheses; * $p < .05$, ** $p < .01$, *** $p < .001$.

Comments: Prais-Winsten's regression with heteroskedastic panel corrected standard errors and AR1 autocorrelation structure. Year dummies are included in the model (coefficients not reported). Most independent variables are measured cumulatively (see text).

the critical case of Austria. When Austria is excluded (or when all cross-country variation is canceled out) the interaction effect does not hold.[10] But the main effect of QoG on welfare state expansion is not sensitive to the exclusion of any particular country. It is thus clearly the more robust finding of the two.

Conclusions

The argument presented in this chapter started out from a discussion of how to explain variation in the extension of social insurance and social protection systems among the developed liberal democracies. I argued that so far the theory most successful in explaining this variation has been the power resource theory (PRT). My criticism of this theory is that it has taken it for granted that the state as an organization can always be seen as a suitable and unproblematic tool for implementing welfare state policies. Building on Skocpol's and others' historical case studies, the quality of government theory (QoG) implies that the political legitimacy of the state is central for getting political support for public programs for social insurance and systems of redistribution.

This theory was tested with data from eighteen OECD countries, and the results show that QoG has a significant and positive effect on a country's efforts for social protection and social insurance, both when this is measured as the level of spending and when it is measured by how generous the specific benefits are. However, since the effect of cabinet partisanship still holds when QoG is included in the model, the power resource theory is, as was expected, complemented rather than refuted. For the second hypothesis, that the size of the effect of cabinet partisanship is conditional on the level of QoG, this interaction effect was confirmed when using benefit generosity as the dependent variable but not when overall spending was used. I would argue that this means the QoG theory is confirmed when the data with the highest validity for measuring welfare state effort are used. I should add that a country for which the empirical analysis is very telling is Austria, which has had a

10. Austria is most likely also the reason the interaction effect works for the benefit generosity index but not for social spending: compared with its counterparts (Scandinavia) in terms of having a strong tradition of leftist government, Austria does have a less generous welfare state but not on average much less social spending.

TABLE 6.3. **Descriptives**

Variable	Mean	Min. value	Max. value	Standard deviation Overall std. dev.	Standard deviation Between std. dev	Standard deviation Within std. dev
Social spending (% of GDP)	21	11	36	5.4	5.1	1.7
Benefit generosity index	28	17	45	7.2	7.0	1.7
Quality of government	0.94	0.75	1	0.067	0.067	0.010
Left cabinet	15	0	45	11	11	2.0
Christian democratic cabinet	8.5	0	40	12	13	1.0
Openness to trade	63	14	186	32	30	12
Liberalization of capital and current transactions	11	6.6	14	1.8	1.9	0.36
Constitutional veto points	1.5	0	6	1.8	1.8	0.034
Budget deficit/surplus	−2.4	−12	11	3.8	2.4	3.0
GDP per capita	21	11	33	3.4	2.7	2.1
Female labor force participation	53	35	70	9.1	9.0	1.8
Inflation	5.8	2.4	13	1.7	1.7	0.61
Population over 65	12	7.7	16	2.1	2.1	0.3
Unemployment	7.5	0.46	17	3.6	3.0	2.1

Note: The "Between std. dev." is the standard deviation between countries, that is, when the year variable is held constant. The "Within std. dev." is the standard deviation over time, that is, when the country variable is held constant.

high level of social democratic cabinet members but a comparatively low level of welfare state effort. This fits well with the QoG theory, since the Austrian state is the only one in the sample that has had an openly institutionalized system of political clientelism, which has been successfully used by populist parties to delegitimize the established political order.

One way to evaluate the strength of a social science theory is to ask how well it "travels." The more cases it can explain, the stronger it stands. In this case, the power resource theory has been shown to be fairly good at explaining the extent and institutionalization of social policies in eighteen Western OECD countries, which of course is important. However, remember that this is only about 10 percent of the countries in the world, comprising less than 15 percent of the world's population. According to all cross-country empirical indicators that measure quality of government, the eighteen Western OECD countries that have been the focus of the PRT have comparatively high levels of QoG (cf. Samanni et al. 2008).

While the results show that the QoG theory serves as a necessary complement to the PRT for these developed countries, it seems reasonable to argue that the importance of QoG for establishing an encompassing welfare state would increase as we move to countries in other regions of the world, such as Latin America or sub-Saharan Africa. Given the rampant corruption and clientelism in countries like Brazil, it is unlikely we will see the enactment of a northern European type of welfare state, even if they were to have leftist governments for an extended period (Sorj and Martuccelli 2008; Weyland 1996). As Nita Rudra states it, politicians in these countries are inclined to use the welfare systems for patronage politics "by appointing teachers, health and social workers in exchange for political support" (Rudra 2004, 699). The same can be said for several countries in sub-Saharan Africa (Adésínà 2007; Samson 2002). Thus, I presume that as the two theories travel farther from the eighteen developed countries, the quality of government theory will become more important than the power resource theory for explaining variations in social protection through the welfare state.

CHAPTER SEVEN

The Low Trust–Corruption–Inequality Trap

Social Capital and the Nordic Puzzle

With the publication of Robert Putnam's *Making Democracy Work* in 1993 and his *Bowling Alone* in 2000, social capital has become a huge research industry. Defined as a combination of interpersonal generalized (social) trust and networks based on reciprocity, social capital is seen as a major asset for individuals as well as groups and societies (Rothstein 2005). Although, as he readily admits, Putnam was not the first social scientist to put forward the importance of social capital, it was clearly he who showed how it could be used in important (and ingeniously designed) empirical research. Putnam's work came largely to be interpreted as putting the civil society and voluntary associations on the agenda. By being active in voluntary associations, citizens would learn to develop social trust and understand the importance of reciprocity. For many, this gave arguments for a political agenda in which the state's responsibilities for social welfare should be scaled back and replaced by an emphasis on the importance of voluntary associations. It was argued that one could expect that with "big government" we would see a "crowding out" effect. The expansion of the responsibilities of the state would, it was claimed, be detrimental to the development of a vibrant civil society (Ostrom 2000). Moreover, it was argued that in a society where the government takes on responsibility for a large number of social needs, people do not have to develop and maintain trusting relations and invest in social networks. Social capital research has been used by several governments and policy organizations to send people a message that the bad things in their society are caused by too little volunteering (cf. Putnam and Feldstein 2003).[1]

However, when the social capital and social trust research agenda went comparative, it came as a surprise to many that when this concept was being empirically researched the Nordic countries came out on top irrespective of what measures were used. Much can be said about the Nordic countries, but not that they have small and noninterventionist governments. All available empirical studies I have come across show that interpersonal generalized trust is highest in the Nordic countries and that citizens in these countries are among the most active in voluntary associations (Rothstein 2005, chap. 4). Moreover, the Nordic countries also have among the highest levels of QoG and are among the most egalitarian in the world. In this chapter I will deal with how to understand this equilibrium and its counterpart. Thus, while the argument in chapter 6 was based on a standard linear logic in the social sciences, where causes are thought to precede effects, the argument presented in this chapter is inspired by the ideas introduced in chapter 5 about "feedback mechanism" and "path dependency," where causation over time to a large extent blurs the distinction between "independent" and "dependent" variables (Hall 2003; Pierson 2000). In this type of research, the ambition is not to determine linear causality but to understand how variables (such as corruption, inequality, and lack of trust) reinforce one another so that whole systems stabilize in different equilibriums—in plain language, to understand why some societies are stuck in vicious circles and others in virtuous circles.

The Importance of Social Trust

One reason for the strong interest in social trust is that, as measured in surveys, it correlates with a number of other variables that most people consider highly desirable normatively. At the individual level, people who believe most other people in their society can generally be trusted

1. See, for example, the reports from the Irish Government, *The Policy Implications of Social Capital*, published by the National Economic and Social Forum (2003); and from the Swedish government 2000 *En uthållig demokrati!* (Demokratiutredningen 2000). On Australia, see Winter (2002). The World Bank has also been very active in this area; see Woolcock and Narayan (2000).

are also more inclined to have a positive view of their democratic institutions, participate more in politics, and be more active in civic organizations. They are also more tolerant toward minorities and toward people who are not like themselves. Trusting people also have a more optimistic view of their possibilities for influencing their own life chances and, not least important, tend to be happier with how their lives are going (Helliwell and Huang 2008; Uslaner 2002; Delhey and Newton 2003).

The same positive pattern exists at the societal level. Cities, regions, and countries with more trusting people are likely to have better working democratic institutions, more open economies, greater economic growth, and less crime and corruption (Bjørnskov 2004; Putnam 1993; Uslaner 2002, 242–45; Zak and Knack 2001). At both the individual level and the societal level, many things that are normatively desirable seem connected to social trust and social capital. The issue of causality is admittedly a different question from the statistical correlations, but so many correlations point in the same direction that social scientists from many disciplines have begun to pay a lot of attention to the issue of trust.

As I argued above, social trust varies widely across nations. In Norway, Denmark, and the Netherlands, about 60 percent of people state in surveys that they believe most other people can be trusted, while in Brazil, the Philippines, and Turkey, about 10 percent say they think people in general can be trusted (Rothstein and Uslaner 2005). A lot of discussion has taken place about what this general trust question measures, and if it measures anything of interest (Cook, Hardin, and Levi 2005). My viewpoint is that since social trust correlates so systematically with a great number of other variables, it is difficult not to believe it captures something that is important for individuals as well as societies. As I stated in chapter 5, for the interpretation of what the survey question about social trust measures, I have come to support the idea launched by Jan Delhey and Kenneth Newton (2004), who argue that when people say whether they think that "most other people can be trusted," this can be understood as their evaluation of the moral standard of their society. This implies that trust can be seen as an informal institution, as argued by North, and therefore as a source of social solidarity, creating a system of beliefs asserting that the various groups in society have a shared responsibility to provide public goods and also to provide possibilities for those who happen to be endowed with fewer resources (Uslaner 2002, chap. 7).

The theoretical reason trust is important comes from "the problem

with many names" in the social sciences. Among these names are social dilemmas, the problem of collective action, the provision of public
goods, the tragedy of the commons, the danger of social traps, the prisoner's dilemma, and several others (cf. Ostrom 1998). Behind all these
metaphors lies a problem that can be described as follows: A group of
agents know that if they can collaborate they will all gain. However, this
collaboration is not costless, but carries economic burdens for all involved. Without the contribution from (almost) all agents, the good will
not be produced. It makes no sense for the individual agent to contribute if she or he does not trust that (almost) everyone else will also contribute. Moreover, what is going to be produced is by definition a public good and so can be consumed by everyone regardless of whether this
agent has contributed. There is thus always a risk that agents will act op-
portunistically (free ride), hoping they can reap the benefits of the good
without contributing. Without trust that most other agents will refrain
from such treacherous behavior, most agents will not contribute to the
good in question. The result of this lack of trust is that everyone in the
group stands to lose, though they know that if they could trust each other
they would all be better off.

Examples of this problem are endless. It makes no sense to be the
only one who recycles the garbage, pays taxes, does not abuse the social insurance system, follows the rule of law, abstains from corruption,
does not overuse the group's shared natural resources, or shows up well
prepared to the academic department's research seminar. Since trust is
a psychologically delicate thing that is hard to repair once it has truly
become damaged, I prefer the metaphor "social traps," since agents in
a group that have lost trust in one another cannot easily mimic or fab-
ricate the level of trust needed to ensure collaboration even if they all
know they would benefit if they could (Ostrom 1998; Rothstein 2005).

But How Is Social Trust Generated?

The problem with this research approach is that in the abundance of
positive associations between generalized trust, social capital, and various desired social and political outcomes, the *sources* of social trust have
remained undertheorized and empirically unexplored. Simply put, if social capital is such an important societal resource, we need to know more
about how it is generated and maintained.

As I pointed out in the introduction to this chapter, the social capital literature is strongly divided on causes and origins of social trust. On the one side there are scholars who argue that variations in the amount of social trust can be explained primarily by *society-centered approaches* (Fukuyama 1995). In this Tocquevillian approach, the capacity of a society to produce social capital among its citizens is determined by its long-term experience of social organization, anchored in historical and cultural experiences that can be traced back over long periods. The society-centered approach views regular social interaction, preferably through activity in voluntary associations, as the most important mechanism for generating social capital. Following the Tocquevillian tradition, formal and informal associations and networks are seen as creators of social capital because of their socializing effects on democratic and co-operative values and norms.

A number of studies carried out in democratic countries over the past decade have called into question the effect that participating in many voluntary associations directed toward benevolent purposes has on social trust and on the willingness to cooperate outside the specific group. While it is true that people who are "joiners" also generally trust others more, this seems to be an effect of *self-selection*. People who—for some other reason—score high on the social ability to trust and cooperate with others join voluntary associations disproportionately. However, activity in such organizations does not add much to these desired traits, at least not for adults. Members become more trusting of their fellow members only, and they cooperate more only for group purposes (Stolle 2003; Uslaner 2002). Thus the idea that adults' membership in associations *creates* social capital that can be used in the wider society simply does not hold (Armony 2004; Delhey and Newton 2003; Claiborn and Martin 2000; Herreros 2004; Kuenzi 2004; Letki 2006; Theiss-Morse and Hibbing 2005; Dinesen 2006; Uslaner 2002; Wollebæck and Selle 2002). To take one example, one large-scale empirical study aimed at explaining variations in social trust based on the World Values Study surveys and covering no fewer than sixty countries concludes that "perhaps most important and most surprising, none of the four measures of voluntary activity stood up to statistical tests, in spite of the importance attached to them in a large body of writing, from de Tocqueville onwards" (Delhey and Newton 2004, 27).

Other types of social interactions might do the job, yet a second problem arises. Even if we accept the importance of voluntary engagement, not all associations serve a normatively desirable purpose. In fact, many associations are established to create distrust. Sheri Berman (1997) has argued that the Nazis in Weimar Germany used existing voluntary associations as vehicles for their *Machtübername*, "takeover of power." Far from such extreme cases, some voluntary associations may use their power, for example, as producer organizations, to extract resources from society in a way that comes close to blackmail, giving undue or disproportionate advantages to their members to the detriment of the rest of society.

As a response to the society-centered approach's failure to produce good empirical indicators for its claims about how the causal mechanisms generating social trust operate, the *institution-centered* accounts of social capital theory claim that, to flourish, social trust needs to be embedded in and linked to the political context as well as formal political and legal institutions (Berman 1997; Encarnación 2003; Levi 1998b; Rothstein 2005; Rothstein and Uslaner 2005; Kumlin and Rothstein 2005, 2010; Delhey and Newton 2005). According to this group of scholars, who base their research on historical case studies or large-*n* survey data (or both), seeing trustworthy, incorrupt, honest, impartial government institutions exercise public power and implement policies is what creates social trust and social capital. Delhey and Newton concluded from their study mentioned above that "government, especially corruption free and democratic government, seems to set a structure in which individuals are able to act in a trustworthy manner and not suffer, and in which they can reasonably expect that most others will generally do the same" (2004, 28). Using survey data from twenty-nine European countries, Bjørnskov (2004) concluded that a high level of social trust is strongly correlated with a low level of corruption. Using survey data from Sweden, Kumlin and Rothstein (2005) found that citizens who have contact with selective (needs-testing) welfare institutions (which, they argue, operate in more opaque and less impartial ways owing to the problem of assessing individual needs) have less trust than individuals who have contacts only with universal (non-needs-assessing) welfare institutions, such as universal child allowances. They also showed that this negative impact on social trust from "untrustworthy" government institutions remains statistically significant after controlling for a number of other variables such as education, social class, income, employment status, political leanings, activity in voluntary associations, satisfaction with life, and interest in politics.

In addition, these scholars find that social trust is related not to what takes place on the input side of the representational democratic system, but to what happens at the output side. Theoretically, people place different amounts of confidence in these two types of political institutions for these reasons: On the representational side, one of the main roles for political institutions is to be *partisan*. A political party that holds government power, or a majority in the Parliament, is supposed to try to implement its ideology in a partisan way. Thus, people who support the ideology of the ruling party (or parties) are likely to have confidence in it, while citizens who oppose its ideology are likely to report a lack of confidence. However, it is less likely that this type of partisan trust or distrust should influence one's generalized trust in other people. There is to my knowledge no plausible causal mechanism linking these two phenomena, and the statistical correlations that come from surveys on these measures are insignificant (Rothstein and Stolle 2008).

What comes out of this research is that the major source of variations in generalized trust is to be found at the other side of the state machinery: the legal and administrative branches of the state responsible for implementing public policies. In several studies, the strongest correlations with social trust are trust in the rule of law institutions, that is, the police and the courts (Rothstein and Stolle 2008; Holmberg and Weibull 2007). A theoretical reason is that, compared with other political institutions that exercise public policy, the courts, the police, and the other legal institutions of the state have a special task—to detect and punish people who, in game theory parlance, use *opportunistic* strategies (I prefer the term *treacherous*). In other words, the rule of law institutions are in the business of taking care of people it is better not to trust. Results from factor analyses of World Values Survey data as well as Swedish survey data largely confirm that people distinguish between trust in different government institutions, and that this creates different dimensions of institutional trust (Rothstein and Stolle 2008).

Social Trust and Equality

I shall argue that there is a causal link between trust in QoG institutions, social trust, and equality, and that there are good theoretical reasons these three variables "hang together." First, social trust is causally related to two different, yet interrelated types of equality: economic equality and equality of opportunity. Second, both these variables rely heavily on the existence of impartial, trustworthy, reasonable, reliable, and competent government institutions.[2] Third, universal social policies have been shown to be much more effective than selective ones in creating economic redistribution. However, such policies are not likely to get enacted in societies where the level of social trust is low or the level of corruption is high.

Theoretically, universal social programs can be thought to increase social trust in three ways. First, they are more redistributive than means-tested programs and thus create more economic equality (Korpi and Palme 1998; Rothstein 1998a). Second, since they are based on the principle of equal treatment and by their administrative logic tend to minimize bureaucratic discretion and intrusion, they are likely to increase the sense of "equality of opportunity" within the population (Kumlin and Rothstein 2005). Third, the opposite of universal programs is means-tested programs, which exacerbate class and often racial divisions within a society, leading to less generalized trust and more in-group trust.

The reason countries with an initially high level of economic inequality are less likely to establish universal social insurance programs and universal social service programs is that such programs are usually based on the idea that all groups in society share a common fate, regardless of their social and economic status. In highly stratified societies, people will place trust only in their own group or class—and those with fewer resources will believe they do not have the same opportunities as people with greater resources. The rich got rich through unfair advantages, people will reason (Csepeli et al. 2004). People with fewer resources will thus demand radical redistribution from the rich to the poor and will seek to exclude those with greater resources from receiving benefits from the state or society. The unfortunate irony is that when you make people prove they are poor to get government benefits, you

2. There is a huge discussion in political philosophy of how "equality of opportunity" should be conceptualized (cf. Andersen 1999). It is certainly hard to imagine a society that would, in reality, create equal opportunities for all its citizens. Here I employ a narrower definition that focuses on the establishment of public policies intended to create equal conditions for citizens regardless of their income, ethnic/religious background, and sex/gender, in areas such as health care, education, social security, and legal protection ("equality before the law"). Thus what is central for the following argument is not "equality of opportunity" in general, but whether the state promotes equal opportunity in its specific interactions with citizens.

create resentment, stigma, and distrust rather than empowerment, social inclusion, and social trust. In addition, such "means-tested" policies fail to alleviate inequality and to increase trust in fellow citizens. Policies designed to reduce poverty by means-tested programs instead create a trap of high inequality, less optimism for the future, less trust in others, less trust in government institutions, greater in-group identification, and persistent inequities in the distribution of wealth. The trap of inequality, corruption, and low social trust can be described as follows: Countries with an initial level of high inequality or with a dishonest, clientelist, or corrupt government are less likely to establish universal social programs because citizens will not entrust such governments with resources (that is, pay taxes) at the level needed to establish such programs. Universal social programs demand high taxes because "all" citizens or very broad groups of the population are going to receive benefits. Citizens in countries with a corrupt or clientelist public administration are also less likely to believe that other citizens will "play by the rules" in paying for such programs and will abstain from abusing (or "overusing") the benefits they produce, since citizens who do not follow the rules can get out of harm's way by bribes or through personal/clientelist contacts.

One could argue that advocates for low-income groups in societies with high inequality would opt for universal social programs because they would realize such programs would be most beneficial for their groups. Historically, this has seldom been the case (Katz 1986; cf. Gilens 1999). First, the logic for why universal programs are more redistributive than programs directed specifically to "the poor" is complex and difficult to understand. Many well-known political philosophers who have ventured into the discussion about social justice have failed to grasp this logic (for examples, see Rothstein 1998a, chap. 6). Because these redistributive effects are so difficult to explain, it is hard to get support for such programs from underprivileged groups. Second, universal programs benefit the more well-to-do groups as well, and in a society with an initially high inequality, advocates for underprivileged groups will have an uphill battle convincing their followers that scarce public resources should also go to middle-class people.

It is probably impossible to say whether it is equality, trust, or the quality of government that stands at the beginning of this causal chain. The reinforcing effects of equality and high QoG on trust and social policy—and the "feedback" to greater trust and less inequality—lead to a positive equilibrium for societies that initially took the steps to adopt universalist social welfare policies. But logic seems to lead to a negative equilibrium for countries with high or increasing inequality and corrupt governments. Distrust breeds distrust, leading to a social trap. Generalized trust both depends on a foundation of economic and social equality and contributes to the development of a more egalitarian society. As social trust links us to people who are different from ourselves, it reflects a concern for others, especially people who have faced discrimination and thus have fewer resources (Uslaner 2002). In societies with high levels of economic inequality and with few (or inefficient) policies in place for increasing equality of opportunity, there is less concern for people of different backgrounds. The rich and the poor in a country with a highly unequal distribution of wealth, such as Brazil, may live next to each other, but their lives do not intersect. Their children attend different schools, they use different health care services and other public facilities, and in many cases the poor cannot afford any of these services. The rich are protected by both the police and private guards, whom the poor see as their natural enemies. In such societies, neither the rich nor the poor have a sense of sharing a fate with the other group. Generalized trust is low, while particularized (or in-group) trust will be high. In turn, each group looks out for its own interests and is likely to see the other's demands as at variance with its own well-being. Society is seen as a zero-sum game between conflicting groups.

Equality of opportunity focuses on the chance for economic progress in the future—even if the society is highly stratified now. Even in cases when governments cannot reduce economic inequality between groups, they can enact policies that offer greater *opportunities* for economic equality. For example, spending on universal programs for education promises long-term opportunities for greater equality of results as higher education opens up opportunities for economic advancement. Education is also one of the strongest determinants of generalized trust (Brehm and Rahn 1997; Uslaner 2002, chap. 4).

A perception of general social solidarity depends heavily on both types of equality. Seligman (1997, 36–37, 41) argues that widespread social trust *cannot* take root in a hierarchical culture. Such societies have rigid social orders marked by strong class divisions that persist across generations. Feudal systems and societies based on caste dictate what people can and cannot do based on the circumstances of their birth. When economic resources are stratified—or when people believe that others have unfair advantages—trust will not develop, and the benefits of trust, including policies that reduce further inequalities, will be elusive. The assumption that others share your beliefs is illusory, since strict class divisions make it unlikely that people in different classes actually have the same values.

The omission of both these dimensions of equality in the social capital and social trust literature is peculiar for several reasons. One is that the countries that score the highest on social trust also rank the highest on economic equality—the Nordic countries, the Netherlands, and Canada. Social distrust and inequality are strongly related across countries without a legacy of communist rule (Uslaner 2002, 228–31; Rothstein and Uslaner 2005). The Nordic countries have put a lot of effort into creating equality of opportunity, not least in regard to their policies for public education, the labor market, and (more recently) gender equality. One can certainly debate whether these policies have been as successful as was hoped, but comparatively these governments have been ambitious in launching policies and programs in these areas (Huber and Stephens 2001). I argue that by establishing universal social programs, governments send signals that are important for creating citizen solidarity and social trust.

The omission of equality from the literature on social capital and social trust is something of a mystery. While Putnam points to the importance of economic inequality in his analysis of the decline of social capital in the United States, it is not mentioned in his conclusion, "What Killed Civic Engagement?" (2000, 359–61, and chap. 15). Among his seven policy prescriptions for increasing social capital in the United States, none touches on increasing any form of equality (Putnam 2000, chap. 24). This is all the more surprising since the decline of social capital that Putnam finds in the United States since the 1970s seems suspiciously related in time to a dramatic increase in economic inequality (Neckerman 2004; cf. Skocpol 2003). Inequality has increased in the United States at the same time as its welfare state has become smaller since the 1980s (Hacker 2004).

The same strange omission can be seen in the Russell Sage Foundation's large project on trust: among the forty-one chapters in the three edited volumes, none is about economic inequality, and none of the volumes has an index entry on equality or inequality (Braithwaite and Levi 1998; Cook 2001; Ostrom and Walker 2003). The same goes for the three monographs this project has produced (Hardin 2002; Tyler and Huo 2002; Cook, Hardin, and Levi 2005). While political scientists and sociologists largely have neglected the importance of equality for creating social trust, economists have been more interested. Among these are Stephen Knack and Paul Zak (2003) at the World Bank (but in a way that seems mandatory for economists, they add that they worry about the economic inefficiencies they believe such redistribution can cause). However, North, Wallis, and Weingast (2009) argue that social insurance programs should be seen not as a burden for the economy but as a necessary condition for acquiring political support and legitimacy for a prospering market-based "open access" economic system. Simply put, I argue that the low levels of trust and social capital that trouble many countries are caused by too little government action to reduce inequality.

Enter Quality of Government

A reasonably high QoG is important to the enactment of universal social welfare programs for three reasons. First, corruption is based on loyalty to the in-group and *not* to the larger society (Gambetta 1993), which means that universal social welfare policies are anathema to dishonest governments. Corrupt societies reflect patron-client relationships, and corrupt leaders reward only those who show loyalty to them rather than to the entire society (Mungiu-Pippidi 2006). Second, universal policies require higher taxes than means-tested programs, and low-quality governments will have fewer resources to spend on public programs. Corruption transfers resources from the mass public to the elites–and generally from the poor to the rich (Tanzi 1998; Devarajan and Reinikka 2004). It acts as an extra tax on citizens, leaving less money for public expenditures (Mauro 1995). Corrupt governments have less money to spend on their own projects, pushing down the salaries of public employees. In turn, these lower-level staff members will be more likely to extort funds from the public purse. Government employees in corrupt societies will thus spend more time lining their own pockets than serving the public. When political leaders extract money and engage in corrupt or clientelist practices, not only will there be fewer resources to spend on social programs, but the public will have less confidence in government, and people will pay high taxes only if they believe they will get a reasonable value back in services and benefits (Hanousek and Palda 2004).

Third, while universal social welfare policies promote generalized trust, they are unlikely to be adopted in a society that initially ranks low on QoG. Corruption will exacerbate inequality and mistrust and lead to social conflicts that militate against universal social welfare policies. While most Westerners believe wealth stems from hard work, 80 percent of Bulgarians, Hungarians, and Russians say that high incomes reflect dishonesty (Kluegel and Mason 2000, 167; cf. Orkeny 2000, 109)—in direct contrast to Westerners, who are more likely to say that success comes from individual initiative (Csepeli et al. 2004). Orkeney (2000) presents data showing that people in transition countries are far less likely than citizens in Western nations to believe that people have equal opportunities to succeed, are rewarded for their own efforts, and get what they need; instead, they believe that clientelist or corrupt connections and dishonesty are the principal factors that make people wealthy. When people think the only route to prosperity is through dishonesty and corruption, this heightens social tensions between those at the top and the people who have less (Csepeli et al. 2004). This is likely to create a political situation in which most ordinary citizens reject universal welfare programs and instead call for redistribution of income away from the rich. In Romania, belief in widespread corruption, personal experiences of corruption (enforced "gift payments" to public officials or the courts), and perceptions of rising inequality lead to demands for a limit to the income of the rich (Uslaner and Badescu 2005). Where there is a dearth of social solidarity owing to class envy, the social bonds of generalized trust will be weak, and so will the propensity (especially of the middle class) to consent to high taxes. People will identify more with their class or ethnic group (or both) than with members of the larger society. And they will not trust the government to distribute resources in a fair and impartial way.

In low-trust societies with a high degree of economic inequality, universal programs are likely to fail owing to lack of political support. Even if such policies were to be adopted, there is a strong possibility that they would fail in the implementation. Education, health care, and social insurance benefits (as well as the police and the courts) may very well become commodities for sale because corruption is pervasive. Parents "buy" their children's way into good schools, especially universities, and then pay even more for good grades. Extra "gift payments" to doctors are routine in countries with high levels of economic inequality. Police will stop drivers for invented traffic infractions and pedestrians for attempting to cross in the middle of traffic and demand payment to avoid a ticket. Each of these actions subverts trust in government and belies the notion that it could implement universal social policies in a fair and equal way. Instead, suspicion that bureaucrats will give extra advantages to those willing and able to make the "extra" payment is likely to be pervasive (Kornai 2000).

The Paradox of Redistribution

That universal welfare policies fare much better in reducing inequality is a paradox, because one would assume that targeted social policies that tax the rich and give to the poor would be the most efficient way to reduce poverty, while universal policies that give everyone the same services or benefits (e.g., universal child allowances or universal health care) would not have a redistributive effect. But the facts are exactly the opposite (Swank 2002). The technical reason universal systems are more efficient in reducing economic inequality is that taxes are usually proportional or progressive, but services or benefits are nominal—you get a certain sum or a certain type of service (Åberg 1989; Moene and Wallerstein 2003).

People do not get more out of the system because they earn more. The net effect of proportional (or progressive) taxes and nominal services/benefits is a considerable redistribution from the rich to the poor. The political reason universal policies are more effective in alleviating poverty is that if a state is going to tax the rich and give to the poor, the rich (especially the middle class) will not consent to high taxes because they perceive that they do not get enough back (Korpi and Palme 1998; Åberg 1989). They will perceive such programs as policies only for "the poor," and especially members of the middle class (who are also the "swing voters") will turn away from political parties that argue for increasing taxes and social policies (Rothstein 1998a; Swank 2002).

Additionally, the implementation of universal policies follows two important equality principles. First, these programs treat everyone in the same situation equally. Second, because benefits are given without means testing, universal programs do not have to organize a large bureaucracy to decide eligibility. Selective welfare programs often stigmatize recipients as "welfare clients." They demarcate the rich and the poor, and those at the bottom are made to feel less worthy, not least because of the bureaucratic intrusion during implementation (Kumlin and

Rothstein 2005). Universal programs are connected to citizens' rights, while selective welfare programs have trouble with legitimacy because they have to single out the "deserving" poor from among the "undeserving" poor. This will always imply discretionary decisions by street-level bureaucrats, who may intrude on clients' personal integrity.

People who receive selective welfare benefits often feel demeaned and apart from others in society. Recipients of means-tested benefits—for example, Aid to Families with Dependent Children (AFDC) in the United States—are more likely to believe that the government is distant and unresponsive, and that their efforts to participate in the political process would be futile. In the United States, recipients of benefits that are *not* means-tested, such as, for example, disability insurance under Social Security, do not differ from the broader population that received no government benefits (Soss 1999). Soss (2000, 46) writes of means-tested benefits in the United States through AFDC: "The act of welfare claiming, especially in a public assistance program, can be mortifying. The degraded identity it conveys can effectively strip individuals of full and equal community membership."

One AFDC recipient describes how degraded she felt when applying for benefits (Soss 2000, 99): "They're the cowboys and you're a cow. . . . You go all the way through this line to do this, and then this time to do that. It's like a cattle prod. . . . I felt like I was in a prison system. . . . these people are like, 'I'm helping you. This is something I'm doing for you. So just be quiet and follow your line.'"

People who receive Social Security disability benefits in the United States, a universal program, are not required to answer detailed questions about their personal lives, do not feel threatened with loss of benefits, and believe that their caseworkers treat them with respect—and they are not alienated from others (Soss 2000, 144–45, 154). Denigrating recipients of means-tested government programs leads to social strains in two ways: the poor feel stigmatized, and they often perceive that others deem them unworthy. The denigration of welfare recipients feeds on public perceptions that the poor truly are responsible for their own poverty. Neither side sees a shared fate with the other. In contrast, universal programs do not cast aspersions concerning the responsibility of beneficiaries and thus do not destroy trust. When they work well, they can even help to create trust by increasing the feelings of equal treatment and equality of opportunity.

The Stickiness Problem

Trust, inequality, and corruption are all sticky: comparative data from the past twenty-five years show that none of them changes much over time (Rothstein and Uslaner 2005). A closer inspection of the data shows that we are dealing with a problem known as "multiple equilibriums": in the virtuous circle, some countries have low inequality, high trust, high-quality governments, and largely universal social welfare policies. These countries are continually "blessed" as they have been fortunate to begin with a more level playing field and high QoG institutions. In the vicious circle (or equilibrium), countries seem mired in high (or increasing) inequality, low trust, corrupt governments, and demands for more radical redistribution—a policy that will only increase social strains and not accomplish the goal of reducing economic inequality. This is the essence of the inequality trap: it is not easy to make a Brazil into a Sweden or a Finland. Indeed, it is not so easy to make a Brazil into a Portugal, or a United States into a Sweden or even a Canada.

The political logic can look something like this. Perceptions of inequality lead the poor to demand redistribution and the rich to reject those demands. We see this inequality trap very clearly in Central and Eastern Europe, where countries are making the transition from communism to democracy, although the story is likely to be much the same in other developing countries with high levels of poverty and inequality as well as low levels of trust (Miller, Grødeland, and Koshechkina 2001). The growth of a market economy has meant displacement of many former state workers who used to be guaranteed employment and a living wage. Communism had already depressed the levels of generalized trust. Overcoming poverty as well as low levels of trust looms large on the political agenda of these countries—but there has been little support for the universal policies that might create a more vibrant economy and society. Instead, there seems to be backing for a more radical redistribution of income that would exacerbate tensions and make the transition more difficult. As inequality rises, we see a clear link between perceptions of growing inequality and the belief that the only way to prosper is to be corrupt (Miller, Grødeland, and Koshechkina 2001). As an example, Petr Mateju (1997, 4–5) argues:

> The long-lasting presence of an egalitarian socialist ideology and a functioning "nomenclature system" associated with various social and economic priv-

ileges mean that those countries undergoing the post-communist transformation will show a low tolerance for the growth of inequality. . . . individuals who feel that life chances for their group or class are declining in relation to those of other groups or classes may tend to consider such changes as the result of social injustice.

This pessimism about personal control over your own life leads to lower levels of generalized trust in societies as diverse as the United States and Romania (Uslaner 2002, chaps. 4, 6; Uslaner 2003; cf. Rose-Ackerman 2004b). Transition societies are already low in trust. As inequality increases, there are more demands for redistribution of wealth and confiscation of the fortunes of the newly rich.

The best policy response to growing inequality is to enact universalist social welfare programs. However, the social strains stemming from increased inequality make it almost impossible to enact such policies. Demands for redistribution will thus lead to inefficient poverty reduction strategies—and ever increasing social strains. Starting from a base of relative equality, the transition states had a golden opportunity to enact universalist social welfare policies. Yet these states also had corrupt governments with widespread tax evasion and little public confidence. Transition states had only one of the key elements (relative equality) for the enactment of universalist policies. Lacking the other (high-quality government), they have been unable to stem the growing inequality and increased social strains that follow from it. Many transition states *had* universalist social welfare policies under communist regimes, and most still do as official policy, but the implementation of such policies in transition has focused more on targeted benefits, and health care often depends on the ability to pay for insurance (European Commission for Employment and Social Affairs 2003, 114–15, 217). Most transition countries have alternated right-wing and left-wing governments in search of economic stability. Such political instability, veering from one pole to the other, reflects the lack of a social consensus on finding a common ground.

Some Hard Conclusions

If social trust is generated by the two types of equality that I have pointed out here, and if universal social policies are the best way to increase these types of equality, then many countries with low levels of social trust and social capital may be stuck in a social trap (Rothstein 2005). The logic of such a situation is this: social trust will not increase because massive social inequality prevails, but the public policies that could remedy this situation cannot be established because there is a lack of trust. This lack of trust concerns both "other people" and the government institutions needed to implement universal policies. Since social trust is an important intrinsic value (personal happiness, optimism about the future) and also has a political value (support for fair institutions, minority rights, tolerance, etc.) and an economic value (its positive relation to individual earnings and aggregate economic growth), it may be that dysfunctional government institutions are the worst social ill of all.

Poor countries may thus find themselves trapped in continuing inequality and mistrust. High levels of inequality contribute to lower levels of trust, lessening the political and societal support for the state to collect resources for launching and implementing universal welfare programs in an incorrupt and nondiscriminatory way. Highly corrupt societies find themselves trapped in a continuous cycle of inequality and low trust in others and the government, and with policies that do little to reduce the gap between the rich and the poor and thus to create a sense of equal opportunity. Demands for radical redistribution, as we see in many of the transition countries, are likely to exacerbate social tensions rather than relieving them.

There will be no political support for universal programs, since the rich benefit from high-level corruption and see the poor as "undeserving." The poor see almost *all* success in the market economy as evidence of dishonest behavior and believe that those who are well-off have already taken more than enough from the state. From this perspective, the idea that the better-off should also have access to public services and benefits seems awkward. Moreover, even if you could generate enough political support to enact universal programs, people may not have enough confidence in government institutions to deliver the programs fairly and without corruption. Persistent petty corruption may make "gift payments" seem like rational responses to an unresponsive service sector: You may feel more secure knowing that you can buy your children's way into a good school and to good grades rather than risking more neutral assignment and grading criteria. You may well prefer to make an extra payment at the doctor's office rather than wait your turn. Corruption feeds on economic inequality, low trust, and poor government performance. But it generates alternative ways of coping that may inhibit the adoption of programs that might alleviate inequality.

This message is admittedly a pessimistic one. Given the stickiness over time of inequality, corruption, and low levels of social trust, there unfortunately are reasons for this pessimism. Too many of the policy prescriptions that have come out of the social capital agenda have been too optimistic, believing that if people just got more active in voluntary associations, things would improve. There are three reasons I think that approach is wrong. First, the evidence that generalized trust is created by joining associations is simply not there. Second, it relieves governments of their responsibility for dysfunctional public institutions and unfair or ineffective public policies. Third, governments and the political elite can use this demand for increased participation in civic groups to blame the victims in society.

To end on a more optimistic note, if I had a choice, governments in high inequality/low social trust/high corruption societies could opt for universal education programs, maybe under the auspices of international aid organizations. There are several reasons for this focus on education. One is that universal public education both creates a sense of equal opportunity and generates more economic equality. Second, it should give parents a sense of optimism for their children's future, and since optimism is strongly connected to social trust, this would have positive effects. Third, there is a wealth of data showing that at the individual level, education spurs social trust (Uslaner 2002). Fourth, in contrast to large infrastructure investments, schools are low-tech operations that do not rely on the complicated contracts that often come with public procurement and that are known to drive corruption. Empirical research shows that with rather modest forms of institutionalized transparency, corruption in the school sector can be minimized even in highly corrupt societies (Reinikka and Svensson 2005). Fifth, once the children get to school, they can be provided not only with education but also with food, clothing, basic health care, and immunizations. And last, such programs would bring together children and young people from different ethnic, religious, and social groups. Results from social psychology show that this is one important generator of social trust (Yamagishi 2001).

CHAPTER EIGHT

Quality of Government and Social Trust: Two Experiments

How Do We Really Know How the World Works?

The social sciences are strongly divided on issues of ontology and epistemology. Scholars in the social sciences do not agree on how social causality operates and how we can gain scientific knowledge about it. The unfortunate implication is that there are fundamental disagreements about the proper way to conduct social inquiries that relate both to different opinions on how the world works (ontology) and the proper way to establish knowledge about this (epistemology). Leaving aside the postmodernist approach (which is not much used in the type of research dealing with the QoG agenda), a clear division exists in the QoG research field between scholars who work within the instrumental positivist[1] methodology and researchers who take what is called the *scientific realist* approach (Shapiro 2005, chap. 1; MacDonald 2003). To make a long story short, the instrumental positivists accept theories based on their predictive capacity while downplaying how the causal mechanisms within the theory operate. The specificity of the causal logic between the variables in the model is of little interest to them as long as the theory predicts better than competing theories. A case in point is the well-known "public choice" theory, which holds that agents in markets as well as in politics are motivated by rational self-interest. A researcher taking the instrumental positivist approach may very well agree that in real life many agents in many situations do not use such a template, but

---

1. Also called "instrumentalist empiricism" or "logical empiricism."

they may still apply this because the theory predicts better than alternative theories (MacDonald 2003). For example, if such a theory predicts 80 percent of all behavior we want to explain, then we should be content and treat the remaining 20 percent as mere "noise," because few theories reach this level of predictive capacity.

Starting in the late 1970s, the instrumental positivist approach has been challenged by a different metatheory known as *scientific realism*. In this approach, the goal is to produce theories that accurately depict how the causality between the main variables in the models operates. Thus one wants to know, if variable X changes when variable Y changes, what mechanism "makes it happen" (McDermott 2002, 38; cf. Brady and Collier 2004). This mechanism may, for the specific theory, very well be "unobservable," such as power, recognition, information, consent, or rational self-interest (Shapiro 2005, 14–15). The main goal is that the theory depict the causality as it operates in the real world. Since many of the most important mechanisms in the social sciences cannot readily be measured by direct observation, this is admittedly a tall order. Nevertheless, scientific realism, which I should say has guided this study, "places a premium on the design and construction of theories that attempt an accurate description of the process" (MacDonald 2003, 555).

Realists also hold that scientific enterprises should be driven by problems and questions rather than by specific methods (like regressions of large-*n* observables), allowing for a plethora of methods for analyzing the problem or question at hand. Francis Fukuyama (1995, chap. 1) has provided us with a fruitful way to understand the difference between scientific realism and instrumental positivism: compare trying to create a theory for how bridges should be constructed. In his book *Trust: The Social Virtues and the Creation of Prosperity*, Fukuyama readily admits (and I tend to agree) that the standard neoclassical economist may be right that self-interest accounts for as much as 80 percent of human behavior. This 80 percent, he argues, may be thought of as the roadway on the bridge, which admittedly is the major part of the construction. However, according to Fukuyama, the remaining 20 percent should not be disregarded as "noise," because this may comprise the two abutments connecting the bridge to the land at both ends. Metaphorically, this part of the bridge can be seen as the equivalent of trust-based reciprocal behavior or, I would add, of behavior based on some other ethical standard, such as impartiality. If we are going to work out how to construct bridges that work properly (read, high-quality institutions), and if we base the construction on a theory that works only for the roadway, we will have a bridge with no working connection to the two landmasses it is supposed to connect. The point is that the instrumental positivists' idea that we should be content with a theory that predicts even 80 percent of the variation we want to explain may be disastrous if the theory is going to work in practice. What is left out, even if it is a minor part of the story, may be what Jon Elster (1989), in his analysis of the importance of social norms, poignantly has called "the cement of society." A bridge without the proper "cement" connecting the roadway to the land will not work, nor will a society that is constructed from theories that disregard everything except utility-based self-interest.[2] Let me add that Elinor Ostrom, the 2009 Nobel laureate in economics, in her presidential address to the American Political Science Association in 1998, already presented us with a stern warning: "We are producing generations of cynical citizens with little trust in one another, much less in their governments. Given the central role of trust in solving social dilemmas, we may be creating the very conditions that undermine our own democratic ways of life" (Ostrom 1998, 20).

If we work within an epistemological approach that allows us to treat social norms like trust, reciprocity, and impartiality as just "noise," it may have serious implications for our ability to understand, explain, and maybe one day give accurate policy advice on how to create high QoG. However, as Ian Shapiro (2005) has argued, most social scientists go on doing their research without paying much (if any) attention to these metatheoretical questions. Shapiro, as well as Peter Hall, has argued that this comes at a price, since our understanding of "how the world works" (that is, how we understand social causality) largely has outrun the type of methodological tools that are standard in much of the research dealing with the issues raised in this book. Both Hall (2003) and Shapiro (2005, chap. 1), as well as John Gerring (2007, 3), point to the discrepancy between how we now tend to think about the logic of social causality and the standard type of statistical regression models that are used in much comparative study. Among the more problematic issues in the standard regression models are theoretically identifying and specifying the causal mechanism(s) and arriving at an adequate specification of the theoretical model, given the magnitude of possible causal variables not used in the model at hand (Gerring 2007, 3; see also George 1979; Brady

---

2. This argument will be further developed in the final chapter.

and Collier 2004; Tarrow 2004). This criticism of the standard regression model has reintroduced the historical case study as a way to handle these problems through careful process tracing (Hall 2003), something I tried out in chapter 5. However, Gerring also argues that one reason for using case studies is to try, in the social sciences, to approximate the ideal scientific method—*the controlled experiment.* In particular, the comparative case method can be thought of as a sort of "natural" experiment, but it is of course not a controlled one. Although Gerring argues for an increased use of experiments in the social sciences, he also states that while the virtues of the experimental method are generally accepted, its uses have been quite limited. He furthermore states that "the general assumption remains that because experimental work is impossible in most research settings, the experimental ideal is of little consequence" for most practicing political scientists, economists, and sociologists[3] (Gerring 2007, 11).

This is not the place for a lengthy recapitulation of these interesting metatheoretical and methodological discussions that now have become central in political science (cf. Brady and Collier 2004; Gerring and Ysenowitz 2006). However, I bring from this discussion three central themes. One is the argument from the scientific realist approach about the importance of using models that can explain the causal mechanisms central to the theory, especially the importance of getting a handle on "unobservables." The second is Gerring's call for using controlled experiments in this type of research. The third is the importance of understanding how the causal mechanism between social trust–the cement of society–and QoG operates.

Social Trust as an Informal Institution

I should perhaps emphasize (again) that I am interested in social trust, not personal or particularized trust. The latter is based on personal knowledge of another individual's moral orientation, incentives, or both. The number of people one can have this information about is by nature very limited and is therefore irrelevant for explaining differences in the amount of beneficial reciprocity and cooperation in settings such as large organizations and whole societies (Cook, Hardin, and Levi 2005, 2).

---

3. The exception being the psychologists.

Social trust (or generalized trust) is different from personal trust in that it can be understood as a "mental model" of what can be expected when dealing with people for whom you do not have this personalized information (Denzau and North 1994). As I showed in chapter 5, social trust can be seen as an example of the informal institutions in a society, which are established systems of beliefs about the behavior of others (North 1998a, 1998b; cf. Denzau and North 1994). An informal institution such as social trust can have effects like these: In a group (or society) where most agents' default position is that most people can generally be trusted, transaction costs will be lower and many forms of mutually beneficial cooperation will take place that would not have been possible if social trust were lacking (Svendsen and Svendsen 2003). For example, in economic relations, lack of social trust will limit transactions between economic agents to people of the same ethnic clan or tribe while excluding members of disfavored or unknown groups, thus hindering economic efficiency (Rose-Ackerman 2004a, 194).

Moreover, as I will develop further in the final chapter, social trust as an informal institution is essential if groups or societies are to establish socially efficient formal institutions like the rule of law, impartial civil services, and incorrupt public administrations. Such formal institutions are "second order" public goods and thereby prone to the standard problems of free riding as well as opportunistic and treacherous behavior. It is in these ways that social trust can be seen as a collective asset, as *social capital* (Coleman 1990, 99). This implies that the outcome of social and economic interactions depends on how the real-life context has constructed the agents' mutual expectations about what kind of reciprocity to expect and whether the other agents can be trusted (Fehr and Fischbacher 2005). As has been argued from the perspective of evolutionary game theory, people cannot be expected to base their decisions about "how to play" in social dilemmas on perfect information about others, because such information is impossible to get. Instead, they will try to make inferences from others' "history of play" (Young 1998, 5). Moreover, economic competition between rational agents will not weed out agents with low trust and replace them with high-trust agents. On the contrary, as Douglass North has argued, "The rational choice paradigm assumes that people know what is in their self-interest and act accordingly, or at the very least that competition will weed out those who make incorrect choices and reward those who make correct choices. But it is impossible to reconcile this argument with the historical and contemporary record" (North 1998b, 493).

I thus agree with Gary Miller that the major lesson we should take from game theory for this discussion is not about choice, strategy, or individual rationality; it is that we have good reason to expect "dysfunctional results from individual rationality" (Miller 2000, 540; for similar arguments see Hechter 1992; Lichbach 1997; Molander 1994). However, as the huge variation in the level of social trust and levels of QoG between countries shows, the type of theory we need is not a general (more or less functionalist) one, starting from some universal notion of human behavior. The reason is simple: such a theory cannot explain the huge variation that exists (unless one argues that there are genetic variations in the ability to make rational choices or develop social trust). Similarly, the theories we need are not ones that explain why all societies end up with efficient (or dysfunctional) institutions. Rather, we need the sort of theory that can explain the huge variation in social trust and levels of QoG that exists in the world today. Or in plain language, Why, for instance, is corruption in Denmark lower than in Nigeria, why is social trust so much higher in Finland than in Romania, and why are the informal social institutions that embed market relations in Mexico different from those in Canada? A theory that manages to provide answers to such questions should be grounded in some form of empirical knowledge about how the causal mechanism between social trust and QoG operates. Since there is no guarantee that individuals or groups who need to establish an efficient informal institution such as social trust will do so, this theory cannot rest on some functionalist or universal notion of human behavior. Instead, it must be rooted in an empirically verified microfoundation about what causes individuals in different societies to develop (or not develop) social trust. This is where the controlled experimental method comes in. As I demonstrated in chapters 6 and 7, my colleagues and I have been able to show, using survey data, that there are reasonably good empirical indications for saying that social trust is causally related to the level of QoG (Rothstein and Uslaner 2005; Kumlin and Rothstein 2005; Rothstein and Stolle 2008). The problem is, How can we be sure that a person's or a group's social trust is not caused by some totally different variable that is not captured by the survey questions we have been using? Yes, the results have come in fairly well, and I would argue that we have presented a set of convincing theories for why the causality should be the one I argue for. But without a controlled experiment, we cannot be sure our findings actually depict the causal logic. In other words, we cannot be certain our institutional theory of social trust has the type of microfoundation we believe it has. Bear in mind that we are dealing with a complicated matter, how one sort of perception (about the trustworthiness, fairness, and impartiality of government institutions) affects another type of perception (how trustworthy people in general are in one's society). The only way to be sure there is a causal link between these two perceptions, and if so, in what direction the causality operates, is to carry out a controlled experiment. The reason is well known: in a controlled experiment, using a rigorous protocol, one can manipulate precisely the variables one wants to study while the experimental setting makes it possible to hold *all other* variables constant (McDermott 2002).

The Experiments: A Short Background

When I realized I would need to carry out experimental work for this project, my first idea was to send my Swedish students to public health clinics and see how the health care personnel would react if they tried to bribe them so they could cut in line and get to the doctor at once. The idea was to measure the students' social trust before and after and see what effect experiencing untrustworthy and corrupt behavior by public officials would have. When I approached the Swedish Research Council about funding for such a project, I was promptly told by their ethics committee that this would go against the Research Council's ethical standards. In no way could I be allowed to carry out experiments without informing the health care personnel in advance that they would be part of such an experiment.[4] My explanation that such information would ruin the experiment was disregarded. Somewhat disheartened, I turned to my colleagues at the Gothenburg Department of Psychology for advice and was lucky to get in contact with Daniel Eek, one of their postdoctoral students, with whom I started the collaboration that led to the two experiments I will describe below. One of the experiments was carried out in high trust/low corruption Sweden, with Swedish university students

---

4. I could have used actors instead of health care personnel, but that idea unfortunately did not occur to me then.

using the Swedish language in the experiment. The parallel experiment was carried out in low trust/high corruption Romania, with Romanian university students using the Romanian language.

The first thing we realized was that we should do what the experimental literature calls scenario experiments (also known as "judgment experiments"; Aronson, Wilson, and Brewer 1998; cf. de Cremer, Tyler, and den Ouden 2005). These are experiments in which the participants are faced with hypothetical scenarios and state their opinions (judgments) about what takes place in them. Unlike "impact experiments," participants are not asked to act on the "manipulated variable." Instead, the variables one wants to research are measured before and after the participants have experienced the scenario. This method is preferable if one wants to minimize the impact from the participants' everyday life experiences (Hoffman and Hurst 1990). Since Swedish students are unaccustomed to being asked for bribes by public officials, while the opposite is true for Romanian students, the scenario experiment is the preferred method in this case. We do not want to get at what takes place in Romania or Sweden, but rather to determine if persons with these different backgrounds react in similar or different ways when confronted with corruption. The choice of this "most different" research design reflects an ambition to analyze whether the same causal mechanisms for explaining variation in social trust exist in a high trust/low corruption country (Sweden) as in a low trust/high corruption country (Romania). To give some numbers for these differences, the mean for the percentage of people answering yes to the question "Generally speaking, would you say that most people can be trusted?" in the four waves of the World Values Study carried out between 1989 and 2006 was about 60 percent for Sweden (which places the country at the very top, together with the other Nordic countries). In Romania only 16 percent agreed that "most people can be trusted," which is one of the lower scores. Moreover, according to the Corruption Perception Index issued by Transparency International, Romania scores a low 3 on its scale of 0 to 10 (where 10 is least and 0 most corrupt), which ranks the country 85th of the 130 countries surveyed, just below Lebanon and Rwanda (but above Armenia and Benin). Sweden scores 9, which places the country as the sixth least corrupt in the world, just above Switzerland and below Singapore. Thus it seems fair to state that we carried out the experiments with people who live in countries that are very different both in social trust and in the level of corruption.

The Theory: Why Corruption and Low QoG Break Social Trust

As I described above, the scientific realism approach puts great weight on constructing theories about how the "unobservables" in the causal mechanisms operate (MacDonald 2003). A great deal of research in social psychology has shown the importance of social trust for achieving an optimal outcome for social dilemmas (Dawes and Messick 2000; Sally 1995). There is also a lot of research in social psychology showing that procedural fairness has a positive impact on individuals' willingness to accept outcomes that are substantially negative (Lind and Tyler 1997). However, as de Cremer and his colleagues have argued, "although behavioral consequences as a function of procedural fairness . . . seem logical from a theoretical point of view–amazingly little effort has been done to understand why such an effect could occur" (de Cremer, Tyler, and den Ouden 2005, 395). The results they present in their study (also using scenario experiments) show that "fair procedures" increase cooperation. This seems to be based on the following causality: institutions that are perceived to be fair increase group identity and affiliation so that the goal of the group merges with the goal of the individuals. "Being treated fairly and respectful will instill among group members a feeling of inclusiveness" from which also follows increased social trust (ibid., 402). This is in line with the experimental results from the "horizontal trust game," showing that individuals who sense a higher affiliation to the group also have more trust that others in the group will reciprocate pecuniarily (Ostrom 2005, 74).

It is not self-evident that people who live in low QoG societies should have low social trust. One could make the opposite argument, that to make life bearable in a very corrupt or clientelist society, ordinary citizens have to develop a lot of social contacts they can trust. But this does not seem to be so. Instead, they seem to develop mistrust, envy, pessimism, and cynicism toward "people in general" (Csepeli et al. 2004; Sztompka 1998). The type of trust they may develop is what Uslaner (2002) calls "particularized" trust, in which one trusts only very close friends and relatives and is distrustful of people outside one's closed circle. As Uslaner showed, this is the opposite of social trust, which entails having an optimistic outlook and giving people you do not know the benefit of the doubt.

The theory I will present starts from the presumption that in establishing beliefs about social trust, people *make inferences* from the behavior they encounter from public officials. Because it is impossible to know the trustworthiness of "most people" in a society, people must rely on "imperfect information" when they form their beliefs about social trust. Since, as I said above, social trust can be interpreted as people's moral evaluation of their society, it makes sense that the behavior of public officials is one important device they use when forming beliefs about how far people in general can be trusted. In experimental noncooperative game theory, this is known as "heuristics," which can be understood as the kind of clues people who lack perfect information use when they have to decide if they should or should not trust others they have to deal with (cf. Ostrom 2005, 98). The *corruption trust theory* I want to present consists of two interrelated causal mechanisms:

1. The inference from public officials. If public officials in a society are known for being corrupt, partial, or untrustworthy, citizens will believe that even people whom the law requires to act in the service of the public cannot be trusted. From this, *they will make an inference that most other people cannot be trusted either.*

2. The inference from people in general. Citizens will be able to see that most people in a society with corrupt officials must take part in corruption and similar practices in order to obtain what they feel their due. *They will therefore make an inference that most other people cannot be trusted.*[5]

The causal mechanisms specified here assume that individuals make inferences from the information they have about how society works, which is to a considerable extent based on how they perceive the actions of public officials. This information does not need to be correct, of course, and does not have to be related to personal experiences. Hearsay, rumors, collective memories, and the like are part of this story. Simply put, individuals have no choice other than to form their system of beliefs from the imperfect information available to them.

The first mechanism assumes that individuals reason something like this: "If I cannot trust the local policemen, judges, teachers, and doctors,

---

5. One could maybe add a third inference: Since the individual will realize that to get by in such a society, he will himself have to take part in corrupt or clientelistic practices. Thus, the self being an untrustworthy person leads to the same inference as in 1 and 2, that "most people cannot be trusted."

then whom in this society can I trust?" The ethics of public officials become central here, not only how they do their jobs, but also the signals they send to citizens about what kind of "game" is being played in the society. The following mechanism is a logical outcome of the first. People draw personal conclusions from the actions they observe in others–and they also draw conclusions in the other direction: "To know oneself is to know others."

The Experiments

When the scenarios are constructed in experiments of this type, it is imperative that they provide a situation the persons taking part can think of as realistic. Since Swedish students, especially, hardly ever come across corrupt practices in their dealings with public officials, creating realistic scenarios was a challenge. Our solution was based on the idea that nowadays students travel to foreign countries much more commonly than only fifteen years ago (the "backpacker generation"). In Sweden it is very common for students, before going to college or the university, to spend an extended time traveling to faraway countries. Thus, in constructing the scenarios we consulted popular travel guides that give information on what to expect in various countries in situations like the ones we describe below. To give just one example, this is how the *Lonely Planet* guidebook from 2002 describes the police force on the Yucatán Peninsula in Mexico:

> The police are hopelessly corrupt, do not contact them if not absolutely necessary. If you have to contact them for getting a statement for your insurance company that something has been stolen from you, expect to pay bribes. If the police stop you for speeding, just pay even if you are absolutely certain that you have not violated the speeding limit. If you don't pay, the risk is that they will plant illegal drugs in the backseat of your car and then you are in real trouble. Women who get sexually assaulted should not go to the police because there is a clear risk that they will see the perpetrators in uniform at the police station.

From this type of information, Daniel Eek and I constructed scenarios in the experiments describing situations we deemed realistic for students of the twenty-first century: that they are traveling in an unfamiliar country and need immediate assistance from a local authority. The authorities we chose were the police and the health care system. In this particular situation, the scenario is constructed so that they cannot get immediate help, since there are other people already waiting. Still, the participants are informed that another person (the "generalized other," that is, someone representing "people in general" who lives in this "unknown country") considers his own needs too severe to wait in line. The way the experiments tap the effect of corruption on trust can be summarized as follows:

What will happen to people's social trust (and trust in the authorities) if this "generalized other" for some morally dubious reason should be offered immediate assistance before the participant (and all the others who need help) without waiting in line? The participants in the experiments were exposed to the experience that it is possible for people in this "unknown country" to bribe a policeman (or a public health doctor) to cut in line and get immediate help. Or they can see that the policemen or doctors demand bribes for immediate assistance. The outcome can also vary, meaning that the doctor or policeman declines the bribe or the "generalized other" living in the "unknown country" refuses the official's demand for a bribe.

Note that we do not think a situation like the one described affects the social trust of people who already have an established system of beliefs about how far others can be trusted. Thus, when it is "common knowledge" whether others can be trusted, it is unlikely that isolated events such as these will have any effect on social trust in the social setting where the person lives (Uslaner 2002). However, should the situation take place in an unfamiliar country where visitors are uncertain about "common practice," it is reasonable to believe that events like these serve as a "heuristic" on how the country's informal institutions operate.

In the experiment, different factors were manipulated to capture how trust and mistrust are established. First, since *not* receiving immediate help can have different consequences depending on the kind of assistance called for, we assumed that the type of need is important for measuring people's trust. For instance, if the other person received immediate assistance, we expected people's trust to decrease less if the person was seriously ill rather than just in a hurry.

Second, since the theory presented above assumes that trust in others is negatively correlated with corruption, we expected that being asked to pay a bribe to get immediate help would have a negative effect not only on trust in the authorities but, following the corruption trust theory, also on people's social trust.

Third, we expected people's trust would be affected by whether the authority or the person in need suggests preferential treatment (with or without corruption). Here we expected different effects on social trust and on trust in the authorities. For instance, should the authority take the initiative (e.g., demand a bribe), then trust in the authorities should decrease more than social trust. On the other hand, should the person needing help take the initiative, then social trust should decrease more than trust in the authorities.

Another element of potential importance is the outcome of the situation—whether the demand for or offer of a bribe is successful. This has been analyzed as if the two types described above are of equal importance should the person's request for immediate assistance (e.g., in exchange for a bribe) *not* be approved. If such a request is declined, trust in the authorities should increase, since that signals that government officials are honest and impartial. For the same reason, social trust should decrease less when the doctor or policeman's request for a bribe is declined than when it is approved.

In sum, the design of the scenario assumes that four factors are important for social trust when people see another person in need of help try to get immediate assistance without waiting in line. We manipulated one of these factors between subjects: type of authority (policeman/doctor). Thus, half of the participants read encounters taking place at a doctor's office and the other half read encounters at a police station. The remaining three factors were manipulated within subjects. These were bribe or no bribe, who initiates corruption (the other person or the policeman/doctor), and outcome (successful or not). Since experiments of this kind are very rare in political science, and because the validity of the results comes directly from the specific way the experiments have been carried out, I will provide a detailed and at times fairly technical description of methods and results below (readers not interested in this are hereby given permission to jump directly to the concluding section of this chapter). Another reason for this level of detail is that Daniel Eek and I hope colleagues in other countries will be interested in replicating the two experiments.

Method

PARTICIPANTS.   The experiment in Sweden was carried out at the University of Gothenburg, and the one in Romania was carried out at the Babes-Bolyai University in Cluj Napoca. In the Swedish sample sixty-four undergraduates from different educational programs participated in the experiment. Thirty-three were men with a mean age of 26.2 years (standard deviation [SD] = 4.2), and thirty-one were women with a mean age of 29.8 (SD = 10.9). Participants were promised SEK 50 (approximately US$6.50) for participating, and they were randomly assigned to one of two between-subjects conditions where the type of authority was manipulated. One of these groups consisted of fourteen male and eighteen female participants, and the other consisted of nineteen males and thirteen females.

In the Romanian sample eighty-two undergraduates from different educational programs participated in the experiment. Thirty-eight were men with a mean age of 21.7 years (SD = 1.4), and forty-four were women with a mean age of 21.5 (SD = 2.1). Participants were promised ROL (old Romanian leu) 200,000 (approximately US$6.50) for participating and were randomly assigned to one of the two between-subjects conditions. Both groups consisted of nineteen male and twenty-two female participants. The protocol was translated from Swedish into Romanian by Kristina Iosivas, a Romanian undergraduate student at the University of Gothenburg, and we are grateful for her assistance in carrying out the experiment in Romania.

PROCEDURE AND MATERIALS.   In Sweden, we telephoned participants from an available pool of volunteers and invited them to be part of a study about decision making. When they arrived at the laboratory, they were met by a male experimenter and seated in private booths, where they were asked to complete the experimental materials. In Romania, we telephoned contacts at Babes-Bolyai University from Sweden. In a subsequent visit to Cluj Napoca, we collected data during two days at Babes-Bolyai University, using a procedure similar to the one adopted in Sweden.

Each participant was asked to complete a ten-page questionnaire. The first page said that on the next page they would be asked to complete two tasks. The first task was to answer several questions about how far they believed other people could be trusted. The second task was to imagine they were in a strange city in a foreign country and to answer several questions about different scenarios. At the bottom of the first page the participants were asked their age and sex and were told that their responses in the questionnaire would be anonymous.

To get a more complete and nuanced measure of participants' degree of social trust, we did not confine ourselves to the single standard question used in the World Values Survey studies. Instead, on the second page the participants completed a slightly revised version of a more elaborate trust scale developed by Yamagishi (Yamagishi and Sato 1986). The scale consists of six items measuring social trust: "Most people are basically honest," "Most people are trustworthy," "Most people trust a person if the person trusts them," "Most people are basically good-natured and kind," "Most people trust others," and "Generally, I trust others." The following five *caution items* were also included: "People always think about their own gain";[6] "In today's society, if you are not careful, people will use you"; "In today's society, we do not have to worry about being used by someone"; "Most people really do not like to make the effort to help others"; and "If we assume everyone has the capacity to be malicious, we will not be in trouble." Participants responded to each of the items on separate seven-point Likert scales, where 1 corresponded to "strongly disagree" and 7 corresponded to "strongly agree." Subsequently, on each of the eight following pages in the questionnaire participants read the following scenarios (here translated into English from Swedish and Romanian):

> Imagine that you are in a strange city in a foreign country. You wake up one morning and feel very ill and need to see a doctor. In the elevator up to the doctor's office you meet a man who is also on his way there. The man tells you that he is also feeling very ill. When you arrive at the doctor's office there are already several people in the waiting room. You go up to the receptionist and then sit down in the waiting room. You see the man from the elevator approach the doctor and hear him say he feels very ill. The doctor says that he still has to wait in line. The man continues to appeal to the doctor.

6. Participants' responses to items marked with an asterisk were reversed in the analyses. Thus, the higher the participants' values are on the trust scales, the greater the level of trust they put in others and society.

This first paragraph was identical for each of the eight scenarios. The second paragraph varied the three within-subject factors *bribe*, *initiator of offering/requesting immediate assistance*, and *outcome*. Each of these factors varied on two levels, resulting in eight unique scenarios, where all participants completed them all. Thus, whereas a bribe was used to get immediate assistance from the authority in half of the scenarios, a bribe was not used in the other half. Similarly, in half of the scenarios, the man from the elevator (henceforth "the elevator man") took the initiative, and in the other half the authority took the initiative. Finally, in half of the scenarios, the elevator man's request was approved, and thus he received immediate assistance, and for the other half his request was declined and he had to wait in line. As an example, in the scenario condition where a bribe was used to get immediate assistance, the elevator man was the initiator, and the request was approved, the scenario read: "The man from the elevator takes the doctor aside, but you can still hear him whisper and offer the doctor the equivalent of SEK500 [for the Swedish experiment and €50 for the Romanian; approximately US$66] for immediate assistance. The doctor accepts the offer, and the man gets immediate help." (See the appendix to this chapter for a description of all the scenarios.)

As I noted above, the type of authority was the between-subjects factor that varied on two levels. For half of the participants, the authority was a doctor (as in the scenarios described above), and for the other half the authority was a police officer. In the between-subjects condition with a police officer, the first paragraph of the scenarios read:

> Imagine that you are in a strange city in a foreign country. One morning you find that someone has broken into your car. You go to the police station to report the break-in. You are in a hurry. In the elevator up to the reception desk, you meet a man who is also about to report a car break-in. He tells you he too is in a hurry. When you arrive at reception there are already several people in the waiting room. You see the man from the elevator approach a police officer and say that he wants to report a car break-in and is in a hurry. The police officer says the man still has to wait in line. The man continues to appeal to the police officer.

The second paragraphs for these scenarios were the same as in the scenarios where the authority was a doctor, except that the word "doctor" was replaced with "police officer."

MEASUREMENT OF THE DEPENDENT VARIABLES. Following each scenario, participants were asked to answer the following six questions on seven-point Likert scales: How high or low trust they put in (1) the authority's way of handling his work, (2) the authority's way of helping people, (3) authority in general (i.e., doctors or police officers) in this city, (4) the authority as a fellow person, (5) the elevator man,[7] and (6) people in general in this city. The endpoints of these scales were defined as "very low trust" and "very high trust."

In sum, all participants completed eight scenarios. For half of the participants the authority was a doctor, and for the other half it was a police officer. In the scenarios, we varied whether a bribe was used, who took the initiative, and whether or not the request was approved. Participants' levels of trust in the authority and in other people in general, which constitute our main dependent variables, were measured after each scenario. Completing the questionnaire took about thirty minutes, after which participants were paid and debriefed.

Results

INITIAL TRUST LEVELS. For the initial trust levels, the analyses of participants' responses to Yamagishi's trust scale revealed a satisfactory level of reliability for the six items measuring social trust (Cronbach's $\alpha = .803$) and an acceptable level for the five items measuring caution (Cronbach's $\alpha = .689$). To test the effects of our between-subjects factors as well as the sex of participants, we calculated the means of the items measuring *social trust* and *caution* and submitted them to an analysis of variance (ANOVA). Crucial for our aim of testing the effects of *outcome, initiator,* and *bribe* on trust in both high-trust and low-trust cultures was a significant effect of *culture* (Swedish vs. Romanian). We also included the between-subject factor *type of authority* (doctor vs. policeman) to ensure that the two between-subjects groups did not differ in their general propensity to trust others. Similarly, since the number of men and women was not equally balanced between the two groups, the analysis also included *sex* as a factor. Thus, a 2 (culture: Swedish vs.

7. For lack of space, I do not present the analysis of this question. It did not contribute anything in addition to the analyses of the other questions. As expected, the effects were the same, but stronger, as those presented for social trust (trust in people in general in this city).

Romanian) $\times$ 2 (type of authority: doctor vs. policeman) $\times$ 2 (sex: male vs. female) $\times$ 2 (item: trust vs. caution) ANOVA with repeated measures on the last factor was performed on participants' mean ratings on Yamagishi's trust scale.

The main effect of the *trust-caution item* was significant, $F(1, 138) = 76.02, p < .001, \eta_p^2 = .36$, and indicated that participants generally scored higher on the items measuring social trust (M = 4.42, SD = 1.09) than on items measuring caution (M = 3.62, SD = 1.12). The significant main effect of *culture*, $F(1, 138) = 63.44, p < .001, \eta_p^2 = .32$, was qualified by a significant two-way interaction between *culture* and the *trust-caution item*, $F(1, 138) = 4.87, p < .05, \eta_p^2 = .03$. As hypothesized, the Swedish sample scored higher on the scale measuring social trust (M = 4.91, SD = 1.03) than the Romanian sample did (M = 4.03, SD = .98), and the difference between the samples was even larger for the scale measuring caution (M = 4.33, SD = .93 for the Swedish sample; M = 3.06, SD = .93 for the Romanian sample). No other effects in the analysis were significant. Thus—important for the main aim of the present research—the differences found between the two samples in initial trust levels permit us to treat the Swedish sample as a high-trust culture and the Romanian sample as a low-trust culture, which is in line with the findings in the four World Values Survey studies. Furthermore, participants assigned to the doctor condition in the scenarios did not differ in initial trust from participants assigned to the police condition.

VERTICAL TRUST (TRUST IN THE AUTHORITIES). Several ANOVAs with repeated measures on the within-subject factors *outcome* (approved vs. declined), *initiator* (authority vs. elevator man), and *bribe* (bribe vs. no bribe) and the between-subjects factors *culture* (Swedish vs. Romanian) and *type of authority* (doctor vs. policeman) were performed to test the hypotheses regarding effects on vertical and social trust.[8] When the ANOVAs revealed significant interaction effects, those were illuminated with follow-up Bonferroni-corrected *t*-tests at $p = .05$, controlling for multiple comparisons by correcting the probability level ($\propto$) for making

8. Participants' sex was included as a factor in all initial ANOVAs. No significant main effects of sex were found in any of the analyses. Apart from a significant three-way interaction between sex, outcome, and initiator, $F(1, 135) = 4.84, p < .05, \eta_p^2 = .04$, on participants' trust in the elevator man, no substantial interaction effects including sex were found. Thus since our objective did not include sex, the analyses we report exclude sex as a factor.

TABLE 8.1. **Mean ratings of vertical trust related to type of culture, authority, initiator, outcome, and bribe**

			Outcome and bribe			
			Approved request		Declined request	
Authority	Culture	Initiator	Bribe	No bribe	Bribe	No bribe
Doctor	Sweden	Authority	2.10	5.42	2.38	4.56
		Elevator man	2.45	4.69	5.71	4.82
	Romania	Authority	2.20	4.99	2.18	4.29
		Elevator man	2.54	4.73	5.33	4.65
Policeman	Sweden	Authority	2.11	4.43	2.20	3.59
		Elevator man	2.57	4.42	5.49	4.81
	Romania	Authority	1.95	3.85	2.43	4.76
		Elevator man	2.22	3.63	5.19	5.08

type I errors. When the interaction effects regarded within-subject factors only, paired-sample t-tests were used. When the interaction effects included both between-subjects and within-subject factors, both paired-sample t-tests and independent sample t-tests were used. In the following, those are all referred to as follow-up t-tests.

Participants' ratings on the three scales measuring different aspects of vertical trust (i.e., trust in the authority's way of handling his work, the authority's way of helping people, and the authority as a fellow person) showed high internal consistency (in the eight within-subject conditions, Cronbach's αs were .72, .85, .74, .85, .84, .90, .72, and .83, respectively). Therefore, means of participants' ratings on these scales were used in the analysis of the effects of the manipulated factors on vertical trust in the specific authority described in the scenarios. Table 8.1 presents these mean ratings.

A 2 (culture: Swedish vs. Romanian) × 2 (type of authority: doctor vs. policeman) × 2 (outcome: approved vs. declined) × 2 (initiator: authority vs. elevator man) × 2 (bribe: bribe vs. no bribe) ANOVA with repeated measures on the three last factors was performed on participants' ratings of vertical trust. The main effect of *type of authority* was significant, $F(1, 140) = 5.81, p < .05, \eta_p^2 = .04$. Overall, participants in the scenarios with doctors showed higher trust in the authority (M = 3.93) than participants in the police scenarios (M = 3.68). Although not expected, this is in line with research indicating that doctors are generally perceived as more trustworthy than police officers (Holmberg and Weibull 2004).

As hypothesized, the main effect of *outcome* was significant, $F(1, 140)$ = 89.09, $p < .001$, $\eta_p^2 = .39$. This effect indicated that vertical trust was higher when the request was declined ($M = 4.23$) than when it was approved ($M = 3.36$). This effect was qualified by a significant two-way interaction effect between *outcome* and the between-subjects factor *type of authority*, $F(1, 140) = 6.56$, $p = .01$, $\eta_p^2 = .04$, and a significant three-way interaction between *outcome, type of authority,* and *culture,* $F(1, 140) = 8.47$, $p < .01$, $\eta_p^2 = .06$. The follow-up *t*-tests revealed first and foremost that the hypothesized effect of outcome on vertical trust was significant in both cultures and in both types of authority groups. However, in the Romanian sample, there was also an effect of *type of authority* when the request was approved, suggesting that trust in the doctor was then higher ($M = 3.61$) than trust in the police ($M = 2.91$).

The main effect of *initiator* was significant, $F(1, 140) = 253.19$, $p < .001$, $\eta_p^2 = .64$, and indicated as hypothesized that vertical trust was lower when the authority was the initiator ($M = 3.34$) than when the elevator man was the initiator ($M = 4.26$). The three-way interaction between *initiator, culture,* and *type of authority* was significant, $F(1, 140) = 5.52$, $p < .05$, $\eta_p^2 = .04$. However, the effect was so weak that in the follow-up *t*-tests the only significant mean comparisons were those referring to the main effect of initiator, which was highly significant in both cultures and both type of authority groups.

The significant main effect of *bribe,* $F(1, 140) = 472.75$, $p < .001$, $\eta_p^2 = .77$, indicated, as expected, that vertical trust was higher when no bribe was used ($M = 4.54$) than when a bribe was used ($M = 3.07$). This effect was qualified by a significant two-way interaction effect between *bribe* and the between-subjects factor *type of authority,* $F(1, 140) = 6.81$, $p = .01$, $\eta_p^2 = .05$. The follow-up *t*-tests revealed that the difference in vertical trust between the two groups was not significant when a bribe was used ($M = 3.10$ for doctor as authority and $M = 3.01$ for the police as authority), but when a bribe was not used, vertical trust was significantly higher for the doctor ($M = 4.75$) than for the police ($M = 4.32$).

The two-way interaction effect between *outcome* and *initiator* was significant, $F(1, 140) = 189.95$, $p < .001$, $\eta_p^2 = .58$. The follow-up *t*-tests showed that when the elevator man was the initiator and asked for immediate help, vertical trust was significantly higher when the request was declined ($M = 5.14$) than when it was approved ($M = 3.38$). Similarly, when the authority was the initiator and the request was declined, vertical trust was significantly lower ($M = 3.32$) than when the elevator man was the initiator (M = 5.14). However, when the request was approved, vertical trust did not differ depending on whether immediate assistance was offered by the authority (M = 3.35) or requested by the elevator man (M = 3.38). Similarly, when the authority was the initiator, vertical trust did not differ depending on outcome (M = 3.35 for approved request; M = 3.32 for declined request).

The two-way interaction between *outcome* and *bribe* was also signifi-cant, $F(1, 140) = 128.18, p < .001, \eta_p^2 = .48$. The follow-up t-tests showed that, irrespective of whether the request was approved or declined, ver-tical trust was significantly higher when no bribe was offered than when a bribe was offered. However, whereas vertical trust was significantly higher in scenarios where a bribe was used and the request declined (M = 3.85) than when a bribe was used and the request was approved (M = 2.26), there was no difference in vertical trust in the no-bribe con-ditions (M = 4.60 for declined request; M = 4.46 for approved request). This effect was qualified by a significant three-way interaction between outcome, bribe, and culture, $F(1, 140) = 7.94, p < .01, \eta_p^2 = .05$. How-ever, the effect was so weak that in the follow-up t-tests, the only signifi-cant mean comparisons were those referring to the two-way interaction between outcome and bribe. The two-way interaction effect was also qualified by a significant three-way interaction between *outcome*, *bribe*, and *type of authority*, $F(1, 140) = 9.23, p < .01, \eta_p^2 = .06$. Follow-up t-tests showed that in the doctor condition, there was no effect of out-come when a bribe was not used, whereas participants in the police con-dition showed higher vertical trust in the no-bribe condition where the request was declined (M = 4.61) than where it was approved (M = 4.04).

The two-way interaction between *initiator* and *bribe* was also signifi-cant, $F(1, 140) = 200.95, p < .001, \eta_p^2 = .59$. The follow-up t-tests showed that, irrespective of whether the authority or the elevator man was the initiator, vertical trust was significantly higher when no bribe was of-fered than when a bribe was offered. However, whereas vertical trust was significantly higher in scenarios where a bribe was offered by the eleva-tor man (M = 3.92) than when a bribe was requested by the authority (M = 2.18), there was no difference in vertical trust in the no-bribe con-ditions (M = 4.50 when authority was the initiator; M = 4.59 when the el-evator man was the initiator). The three-way interaction between *initia-tor*, *bribe*, and *type of authority* also reached significance, $F(1, 140) = 5.17, p < .05, \eta_p^2 = .04$. However, the effect was so weak that in the follow-up *t*-tests, the only significant mean comparisons were those referring to the two-way interaction between initiator and bribe.

Finally, the hypothesized three-way interaction between *outcome*, *initiator*, and *bribe* was also significant, $F(1, 140) = 85.00, p < .001, \eta_p^2 = .38$. In line with what was expected, this effect showed that vertical trust was highest when the elevator man offered the authority a bribe for immediate assistance and this offer was turned down. The lowest vertical trust was observed when the authority offered the elevator man immediate assistance in exchange for a bribe and the elevator man accepted the offer (see table 8.1).

In sum, the results of the ANOVA on participants' vertical trust verified the hypothesized effects of outcome, initiator, and bribe. Note also that the effects with no exceptions were the same in both the high-trust culture and the low-trust culture. Thus, participants' initial "true" levels of trust did not matter for the effects of outcome, initiator, and bribe. One important question relates to whether participants infer the trustworthiness of the type of authority in general based on the specific encounters they observe. One way to test this is to analyze whether trust in the type of authority in general is affected by the independent factors in the same way as trust in the specific authority described in the scenarios. In table 8.2, means of the second measure of vertical trust—trust in the authority (police officers or doctors) in general—are presented.

A closer look at tables 8.1 and 8.2 reveals two things. First, participants' trust toward the specific authority described in the scenarios extends to their trust in the type of authority in general in the "foreign country." Thus, the mean differences between the different scenarios are similar in both tables. Second, the differences are less pronounced for vertical trust in the type of authority in general (table 8.2) than for vertical trust in the specific authority (table 8.1).

These patterns were confirmed in a parallel 2 (culture: Swedish vs. Romanian) × 2 (type of authority: doctor vs. policeman) × 2 (outcome: approved vs. declined) × 2 (initiator: authority vs. elevator man) × 2 (bribe: bribe vs. no bribe) ANOVA with repeated measures on the last three factors. All main effects from the analysis on trust in the specific authority were replicated. The two-way interaction effect between the factors *bribe* and *type of authority* did not reach significance owing to the less pronounced differences. Otherwise, all two-way interaction effects were replicated. Moreover, the three-way interaction effects in the

TABLE 8.2. **Mean ratings of trust in authority in general related to type of culture, authority, initiator, outcome, and bribe**

			Outcome and bribe			
			Approved request		Declined request	
Authority	Culture	Initiator	Bribe	No bribe	Bribe	No bribe
Doctor	Sweden	Authority	3.94	5.19	3.68	4.97
		Elevator man	4.03	4.77	5.35	5.00
	Romania	Authority	3.69	4.62	3.69	4.26
		Elevator man	3.77	4.72	4.77	4.31
Policeman	Sweden	Authority	3.12	4.12	3.47	4.16
		Elevator man	3.28	4.09	4.78	4.66
	Romania	Authority	2.93	3.71	3.22	4.51
		Elevator man	3.07	3.78	4.85	4.66

previous ANOVA that were too weak for a reliable interpretation did not reach significance in the ANOVA on authority in general. The only significant effect of culture in the ANOVA on trust in authority in general was that, in contrast to the ANOVA on trust in the specific authority, the four-way interaction effect between *culture*, *type of authority*, *initiator*, and *bribe*, $F(1, 139) = 5.07$, $p < .05$, $\eta_p^2 = .04$, was significant. It is interesting that only one mean comparison was significant between the two cultures when looking at the different combinations of initiator and bribe: when the authority took the initiative without offering a bribe, trust in doctors in general was significantly higher in the Swedish sample (M = 5.11) than in the Romanian sample (M = 4.44). Trust in the police showed no such differences (M = 4.14 for the Swedish sample; M = 4.11 for the Romanian sample). Furthermore, both samples responded similarly when a bribe was offered or requested.

SOCIAL TRUST. From the previous two ANOVAs, we can draw two major conclusions. Trust in the specific authority was strongly affected by the manipulated factors, in line with what was expected. This means that participants, based on the observed encounter between the elevator man and the specific authority, put lower trust in the authority when he accepted (as compared with did not accept) a bribe, when he was offered (as compared with was not offered) a bribe, and when he gave immediate assistance to the elevator man (as compared with leaving him waiting in line). Even more interesting is that these effects were the same in high trust/low corruption Sweden and low trust/high corruption Romania.

Furthermore, note that it seems as if the effects were not isolated to the specific situation described. Instead, as expected, *participants seemed to infer the trustworthiness of authorities in general based on their observations of what took place in the scenarios.* Thus the manipulated factors affected not only participants' judgments of the trustworthiness of the authority that they observed, but also their judgments of how far authorities in general in the "unknown" society can be trusted. One question to be answered is to what extent trust in other people in the society also was affected by the manipulated factors. Therefore, the participants also rated how far they believed that other people in general in this "strange city/country" could be trusted. Should trust in other people in general in this strange city/country, who clearly are without responsibility for what is happening in the specific encounters, be influenced by the manipulated factors? If so, this would suggest the existence of a causal relation from trust in government officials to trust in "people in general" in the society where the corrupt behavior is taking place.

Table 8.3 provides means of participants' trust in other people in general in the strange city related to the manipulated variables. This is the main measure of social trust, given that it relates to trust in people who are clearly not involved in the situations described. Instead, this measure should be regarded as how much trust in others in general is influenced by trust put in the people involved in the situation (the authority and the elevator man). A 2 (culture: Swedish vs. Romanian) × 2 (type of authority: doctor vs. policeman) × 2 (outcome: approved vs. declined) × 2 (initiator: authority vs. elevator man) × 2 (bribe: bribe vs. no bribe)

TABLE 8.3. **Mean ratings of social trust related to type of culture, authority, initiator, outcome, and bribe**

			Outcome and bribe			
			Approved request		Declined request	
Authority	Culture	Initiator	Bribe	No bribe	Bribe	No bribe
Doctor	Sweden	Authority	4.13	4.61	4.42	4.51
		Elevator man	4.06	4.45	4.71	4.55
	Romania	Authority	3.35	3.78	3.75	3.48
		Elevator man	3.28	3.65	3.50	3.55
Policeman	Sweden	Authority	4.22	4.47	4.50	4.41
		Elevator man	4.28	4.44	4.59	4.47
	Romania	Authority	3.61	3.85	4.15	4.12
		Elevator man	3.61	4.00	3.80	3.85

ANOVA with repeated measures on the three last factors was performed on these ratings. Again, the main effect of *culture* was significant, $F(1, 140) = 16.82$, $p < .001$, $\eta_p^2 = .11$, indicating that the Romanian sample showed lower social trust (M = 3.71) than did the Swedish sample (M = 4.42). The main effect of *outcome* was also significant, $F(1, 140) = 12.48$, $p < .001$, $\eta_p^2 = .08$, indicating higher trust in people in general when the elevator man did not receive immediate assistance (M = 4.10) than when he did (M = 3.94).

The main effect of *bribe* was also significant, $F(1, 140) = 14.35$, $p < .001$, $\eta_p^2 = .09$. When no bribe was present, social trust was higher (M = 4.09) than when a bribe was present (M = 3.95). More interesting, the interaction between *outcome* and *bribe* was significant, $F(1, 140) = 29.03$, $p < .001$, $\eta_p^2 = .17$. The follow-up *t*-tests showed that social trust was significantly lower when immediate assistance was received thanks to a bribe (M = 3.76) than when a request for a bribe, or an offer of one, was turned down (M = 4.13). The tests also revealed that social trust was higher when immediate assistance was approved without a bribe (M = 4.12) than because of a bribe (M = 3.76).

The three-way interaction effect between *culture*, *initiator*, and *outcome* was also significant, $F(1, 140) = 9.00$, $p < .01$, $\eta_p^2 = .06$. This effect indicated that when immediate assistance was approved, there was no difference whether the authority or the elevator man was the initiator in any of the samples (M = 4.35 for authority and M = 4.30 for elevator man in the Swedish sample; M = 3.65 for authority and M = 3.63 for elevator man in the Romanian sample). However, when immediate assistance was declined, social trust in the Romanian sample was significantly higher when the authority was the initiator (M = 3.88) than when the elevator man was the initiator (M = 3.68), whereas there was no such difference in the Swedish sample (M = 4.45 for authority and M = 4.57 for elevator man). Finally, the three-way interaction effect between *type of authority*, *initiator*, and *outcome* was significant, $F(1, 140) = 6.62$, $p < .05$, $\eta_p^2 = .04$. However, the effect was so weak that in the follow-up *t*-tests, no mean comparisons were significant.

In sum, the analysis on trust in people in general showed that participants inferred the trustworthiness of other people, not involved in the situation, based on the observed encounters between an authority and another person. Furthermore, the basic effects were the same for both the Swedish and the Romanian samples.

As a further test of the theory, we also calculated the correlation between the mean of vertical trust and the mean of trust in authority in general ($r = .658$, $p < .0001$), the correlation between the mean of vertical trust and the mean of social trust ($r = .233$, $p < .005$), and the correlation between the mean of trust in authority in general and the mean of social trust ($r = .351$, $p < .0001$). Since the correlations were all positive and significant, the results support the reasoning put forward here: participants made inferences about the trustworthiness of authorities in general from the behavior they observed by the specific authority, and they reasoned from the trustworthiness of authorities in general to social trust.

"The Fish Rots from the Head Down"

Imagine that you are traveling in a strange city and lose your wallet, which contains some personal things and a considerable amount of money (US$100). So the next day you go to the police station and ask if anyone has handed in your wallet, hoping that people in this strange city are honest. According to a much talked about (but fairly unscientific) experiment that was carried out in the mid-1990s, the chance that the police will have your wallet varies greatly between different Western countries.[9] Moreover, this variation seems to covary with the level of generalized trust as measured by the World Values Study surveys. The chance that someone would have handed in your wallet to the police seems to be much greater in the Nordic countries than in a country like Turkey or Romania. However, this variation does not necessarily have anything to do with personal trustworthiness or honesty among the population. People may not hand in a found wallet because they are convinced that the police in their country are thoroughly corrupt and would keep the money. And they may also be convinced that "everyone else" has the same belief about the police and thus that "people in general" would not hand in a wallet to the police. Such an interpretation would be in line with our findings—our result may be interpreted as support for the German proverb "Der Fisch stinkt von Kopf her" (the fish rots from the head down), implying that when things in a system starts going sour, it starts from the top.

9. This "lost wallet experiment" was reported in the *Economist*, June 22, 1996.

Needless to say, experimental results like these should be interpreted with caution, and not until we have replicated the same type of experiment a number of times can firm conclusions be drawn. Still, as far as I know, this is the first experimental evidence showing how social trust and trust in government officials are causally related. To recapitulate, the first main (but not unexpected) result is that corrupt behavior by public authorities clearly influences people's trust in them, in both the Romanian and the Swedish samples. Thus this result seems to confirm the hypothesis that it is not true that people who live in highly corrupt societies come to morally accept corrupt behavior by public officials. On the contrary, as has been shown by Karklins (2005) and Widmalm (2008), people in highly corrupt societies are more likely to argue that while they view corruption as morally wrong, ordinary citizens who participate in corrupt dealings are not to blame, because "the system" forces them to take part. The second main result is that when people experience deceitful behavior by public authorities, they do not lose trust only in the authorities in question. They also come to believe that people in general in such a society are less trustworthy. It should again be underlined that these effects were the same whether people have been brought up in a high trust/low corruption culture such as Sweden or in a low trust/high corruption culture such as Romania.

Finally, establishing how the causality between QoG and social trust operates at the microlevel is an issue that should not concern only academics, since it has implications for policies on alleviating poverty and other social ills. The World Bank and many other international aid organizations have to quite some extent bought the ideas that social trust and social capital are important for economic and social development and also for democratization and that societal assets are generated from activity in voluntary associations, leading them to channel substantial resources to such groups (Bebbington et al. 2004). However, lacking any microlevel evidence for this theory, this may all have been in vain (Bano 2008). As I argued in previous chapters, the empirical support for this theory is almost nonexistent. Thus, like many other forms of international aid, this support to voluntary associations may have been useless and may even have done more harm than good. What if behind a benevolent facade, many of these voluntary associations in developing societies are just camouflaged interests that strive to increase ethnic, social, racial, gender-based, economic, and religious divisions in their countries, thereby destroying the possibility for building generalized trust (Armony 2004; Encarnación 2003)? Concepts like "community" and "civil society" have a nice gentle ring, but behind them may be exclusion, discrimination, spread of mistrust, and manufacture of hatred. The idea of a virtuous path from civil society to social trust to democratization and economic development may simply be wrong and may have led to seriously damaging social outcomes.

Appendix: Scenarios Used in the Different Conditions

Within-subject condition: Bribe, initiated by the elevator man, leading to immediate assistance.   The man from the elevator takes the doctor aside, but you can still hear him whisper and offer the equivalent of SEK 500 to receive immediate assistance. The doctor accepts the offer. The man from the elevator receives immediate assistance.

Within-subject condition: Bribe, initiated by the elevator man, not leading to immediate assistance.   The man from the elevator takes the doctor aside, but you can still hear him whisper and offer the equivalent of SEK 500 to receive immediate assistance. The doctor does not accept the offer. The man from the elevator has to wait in line.

Within-subject condition: Bribe, initiated by the authority, leading to immediate assistance.   The doctor takes the man from the elevator aside, but you can still hear him whisper and tell the man he will not have to wait in line if he gives the doctor the equivalent of SEK 500. The man accepts the offer. The man from the elevator receives immediate assistance.

Within-subject condition: Bribe, initiated by the authority, not leading to immediate assistance.   The doctor takes the man from the elevator aside, but you can still hear him whisper and tell the man he will not have to wait in line if he gives the doctor the equivalent of SEK 500. The man does not accept the offer. The man from the elevator has to wait in line.

Within-subject condition: No bribe, initiated by the elevator man, leading to immediate assistance.   The man from the elevator takes the doctor aside, but you can still hear him whisper that he wants immediate assistance, since he feels very ill. The doctor grants the man's request. The man from the elevator receives immediate assistance.

Within-subject condition: No bribe, initiated by the elevator man, not leading to immediate assistance.   The man from the elevator takes the doctor aside but you can still hear him whisper that he wants immediate assistance since he feels very ill. The doctor does not grant the man's request. The man from the elevator has to wait in line.

Within-subject condition: No bribe, initiated by the authority, leading to immediate assistance.   The doctor takes the man from the elevator aside but you can still hear him whisper and ask the man how ill he feels. The man says that he feels very ill. The man from the elevator receives immediate assistance.

Within-subject condition: No bribe, initiated by the authority, not leading to immediate assistance.   The doctor takes the man from the elevator aside, but you can still hear him whisper and ask the man how ill he feels. The man says he feels very ill. The man from the elevator has to wait in line.

CHAPTER NINE

The Tale of Two Countries: Democratic Jamaica versus High Quality of Government Singapore

Comparing States

In the previous chapter I used the experimental method to show the likelihood of a causal link between low quality of government (QoG) and low social trust. We saw that people who perceive government institutions as corrupt will lose trust not only in government, but also in other people in general in that particular society. Since social trust and QoG have been shown to be central to economic and social development, we should be able to see this relation at the country level. As has been shown in chapters 2, 3, and 7, the empirical support for this proposition that comes out of large-*n* cross-country comparative research is compelling. In this chapter, I intend to investigate whether this can be shown using the comparative case methodology, which makes it possible to trace development over time. Doing so may give a better understanding of how the causality between QoG, social trust, and socioeconomic outcomes operates at the aggregate (societal) level (Hall 2003).

The question that comes up in all studies employing this method is which cases to select. This all depends on the theoretical prepositions the comparison is meant to shed light on. In our case, the challenge is to find two countries that started out from a similar situation in regard to economic prosperity and social well-being but have since developed in different directions. If our theory about the importance of QoG to economic prosperity and social well-being is correct, we should expect to find this varying. The question is whether it is possible to find two such countries to compare and where enough data and country-based research are available for such an investigation. Following a suggestion by Herbert Werlin, the choice has fallen on Jamaica and Singapore (Werlin 2007).

At first glance, Singapore and Jamaica indeed seem an odd couple to compare. The two states are today at opposite ends on most observable data regarding economic prosperity, social well-being, politics, and location on the globe. Still, except for the geography, it has not always been this way. Had we made the same comparison fifty years ago, we would have seen two soon to be former colonies, strikingly similar in many aspects, in the midst of attempting to establish themselves as independent states and, they hoped, as prosperous societies. First, the countries then had nearly the same population size, about 1.8 million. Second, they were almost equally poor. Third, the political climate was relatively healthy, compared with many other newly independent nations that plunged into civil war as soon as the former masters returned to Europe. Fourth, both countries had for a long time been British colonies, and independence came at about the same time (1962 for Jamaica, 1965 for Singapore).

As Werlin (2007) has argued, most social scientists in the early 1960s would have predicted that Jamaica stood a much better chance of fostering social well-being and economic prosperity than Singapore. Jamaica had large natural resources (the most important being bauxite) that were in high demand on the world market. It was also close to one of the world's biggest markets for what its agricultural sector could produce, and with its stunningly beautiful beaches and good climate, it would have been the ideal site for a large tourist industry, especially since neighboring Cuba had just decided to leave that market. Moreover, as I will show in more detail below, the country inherited from Britain a Westminster model of democracy and, important in this context, a relatively honest, impartial, and professional civil service.

In the mid-1960s Singapore was clearly in a worse situation. At the time of independence, the country lacked marketable natural resources. It was farther than Jamaica from the big markets in the United States and Western Europe. Moreover, Singapore was much more divided ethnically than Jamaica and was suffering racial and religious turmoil as a legacy of its separation from Malaysia in 1965. At independence, mass unemployment added to the difficulties. As I will show below, the outcome today is almost exactly the opposite of what could reasonably have been expected in 1965.

One could of course argue that Southeast Asia and the Caribbean are very different in culture and also in which major powers have dominated them in the past and the present. Still, both regions are by many measures among the most internally divergent. Looking at just one example, UNDP's Index of Human Development (UNDP 2009), there seems to be little evidence that the cultures in these two regions make them homogeneous. The Caribbean states range from place 37 (Barbados) to place 149 (Haiti) in this global ranking, with Jamaica as number 100 (second from the bottom in this region), while in Southeast Asia, Singapore is at place 23, in stark contrast to Myanmar at place 138 and neighboring Malaysia at number 66 (UNDP 2009, 143–46). Hence it appears that a nation from either region is not, like Western Europe or sub-Saharan Africa, more or less bound by its location to perform in a certain way regarding human development.

Comparing Economic and Social Performance

Since independence, GDP per capita for Singapore has increased by more than six times, an incredible accomplishment by most standards. It is now (2010) richer than all former colonial powers and has a GDP per capita higher than most countries in the European Union. In comparison, Jamaica has shown a more modest 25 percent increase, all occurring during the first ten years since independence. In fact, Jamaican (real) GDP per capita today is less than it was in 1972.

In social well-being measured as population health, the differences between the countries are staggering, as shown in table 9.1. WHO statistics from 2006 show that the infant mortality rate (probability of dy-

TABLE 9.1. **Adult mortality rates in Jamaica and Singapore for men fifteen to sixty per 1,000 population**

Country/year	1990	2000	2006
Jamaica	175	182	224
Singapore	152	97	83

Source: WHO Statistics 2006.

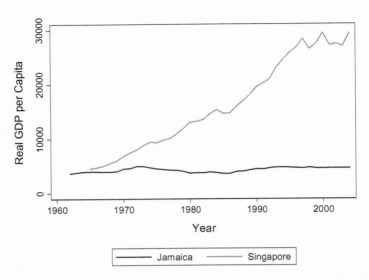

FIGURE 9.1. GDP per capita for Jamaica and Singapore, 1962–2008. Source: QoG Institute time series data bank (Teorell et al. 2010).

ing by age five per 1,000 live births) is eight times higher in Jamaica than in Singapore. Whereas the level of infant mortality has remained constantly high in Jamaica since 1990, during the same period Singapore has managed to cut its rate by more than half and now has one of the lowest levels in the world. When infant mortality is counted as the probability of dying during the first year, the difference between the countries is considerably smaller (five to one), showing that the risk of dying increases for Jamaican children when they are between their first and fifth birthdays, compared with their first year in life. Although overall life expectancy does not differ very much according to the WHO statistics (Jamaica 73.5, Singapore 82), the differences become substantial if broken down by gender and age group.

As the figures show, a male Jamaican between fifteen and sixty years of age has a mortality rate three times that of a male Singaporean. Moreover, this difference has increased dramatically since 1990 as the mortality rate for men in this age group has gone up in Jamaica, while for Singapore it has been cut almost in half. One reason behind this huge difference may be criminal violence. Jamaica has one of the highest homicide rates in the world. Although the data should be treated with some care, the figure from 2006 is 49 per 100,000 inhabitants, more than twice the rate for all the countries in the Caribbean region. Moreover, Jamaica's homicide rate has more than doubled since the early 1980s and has increased five times since 1972. Singapore, on the other hand, has one of the lowest homicide rates in the world, 0.48 per 100,000 inhabitants, according to a report issued jointly by the United Nations Office on Drugs and Crime and the World Bank.[1] Thus the chance of dying from criminal activity is almost exactly one hundred times higher in Jamaica than in Singapore. If Jamaica could reduce its homicide rate to the level of Costa Rica, it would increase its economic growth by 5.4 percent annually (ibid., 10). Jamaica also has one of the highest rates of rape in the world. According to the report cited above, "Due to the high levels of violence in parts of urban Jamaica, residents are afraid to leave their homes and interact less often with friends and family who live elsewhere" (ibid., vi, 15). In the capital, Kingston, one study reports that in the early 1990s, 17 percent of thirteen- and fourteen-year-old girls had been raped or been the victims of attempted rape (ibid., 13). A survey carried out by the World Bank in Jamaica showed that 39 percent of business managers responded that they were unlikely to expand their businesses because of the crime level (ibid., vi). It should come as no surprise that this much violent crime is also likely to have an impact on social trust among Jamaicans and on the possibilities for building a thriving tourist industry.

Two surveys, one from 2006 and one from 2008, show that Jamaicans are one of the least trusting people in the world, with only 15 percent stating that they believe "most people can be trusted," while about 85 percent concur with the statement, "One can't be too careful in dealing with people" (Lyday, O'Donnell, and Munroe 2008; Powell and Lewis 2009). Popular guidebooks issue stern warnings about public safety in Jamaica, especially in Kingston and more generally outside the gated and heavily guarded tourist resorts. *Lonely Planet* states in its recent tourist guidebook for Jamaica: "Many local police are members of the communities they serve and cannot always be trusted to be impartial."

1. Data for Singapore from Statistics Canada, Catalogue no. 85–002-XIE, vol. 26, no. 6. Data for Jamaica and the Caribbean region from the United Nations Office on Drugs and Crime (UNODC), Report 37820 (March 2007), "Crime, Violence, and Development: Trends, Costs, and Policy Options in the Caribbean."

Enter Democracy

Apart from the two states' staggeringly divergent economic and human development since independence, their political histories are also opposite. This will be developed further below, but according to Freedom House's annual democracy rating, it is clear that Jamaica has been a democracy ever since this organization started to measure democracy. In contrast, Singapore is not considered a democracy by Freedom House and has not been democratic since independence. In fact, Jamaica scores as a reasonably well-functioning democracy by most measures. For example, in the Economist Intelligence Unit's index of democracy from 2007, Jamaica scores an impressive 9.17 (out of a maximum of 10) for "electoral process and pluralism," which is at the same level as countries like Canada and Japan and slightly higher than the United States and Mexico. The measure captures issues such as "Are the elections for the national legislature and head of government free?" "Are municipal elections both free and fair?" and "Do opposition parties have a realistic prospect of achieving government?" According to Freedom House's overall score from 2008, Jamaica is deemed a "free" country. Collier (2009, 141–42) reports that in freedom of the press Jamaica has long been ranked as one of the top countries in the world. The country scores an impressive 12 for the democratic quality of its electoral process, which is the top score. Singapore scores a meager 4. Jamaica's score for political pluralism and participation is an equally impressive 14, equaling Mexico and Brazil, while on this item Singapore scores 6, placing the country at about the same level as Morocco, Jordan, Cambodia, and Afghanistan.

There has long been a debate on how to define and measure democracy. According to one definition suggested by Przeworski et al. (2000), a democracy is "a regime in which those who govern are selected through contested elections," where "contested" is defined as the presence of "an opposition that has some chance of winning office." According to this definition, Jamaica is obviously a democracy. Teorell (2010) has convincingly criticized this and other dichotomous (or absolute) measures for democracy and instead argued for a graded definition and measurement strategy. The graded measure of democracy that he has constructed (together with Hadenius) is based on the average scores of political rights and civil liberties reported by Freedom House and the combined autocracy and democracy scores derived from the Polity IV data set (Hadenius and Teorell 2005). This index goes from 0 to 10, where 10 is most

democratic. Hadenius and Teorell (2007) estimate that countries above
7.5 on this scale should count as democratic. The most recent score for
Jamaica in this index is 7.7, and for Singapore it is 4.4.[2] Thus, even in this
finer-grained measure, Jamaica passes the threshold for deserving to be
called a democracy.

To summarize, whichever measure that is used, Singapore fares much
worse than Jamaica and is regularly defined as not being a democracy.
However, by the standard measures used to capture quality of government, Singapore scores very high, usually among the top five countries
in the world. Although not a democracy, Singapore is one of the least
corrupt, most law-abiding countries in the world, with a very high score
on "government effectiveness" as well. Obviously, in terms of economic
prosperity, alleviation of poverty, and standard measures of population
health, the hope that electoral-representative democracy would produce
a good outcome for the social well-being of the population has not been
fulfilled, at least in this comparison. However, although causality is (as
always) a complicated matter, in these terms high QoG Singapore has an
impressive record. How can we account for this unexpected (for many,
including me), undesired, and unwelcome nonexistent relation between
democracy and good social and economic outcomes?

Jamaica: Democracy Goes Clientelist

Since independence, Jamaican politics has been completely dominated
by two competing parties, the People's National Party (PNP) and the Jamaican Labor Party (JLP). The two parties were switching power quite
regularly every ten years from the 1950s to the 1980s. The PNP dominated the office of prime minister during the 1990s and 2000s, although
for the past three years the JLP has been in charge again. Although the
PNP has had a more leftist orientation (especially during the 1970s) and
the JLP has been more neoliberal (at least in the 1980s), these differences are no longer significant, and in most aspects ideology has never
been the driving force in the competition between the parties (Collier
2009, 138).

Going back in time, traditional left-versus-right ideology played a

2. This score is from 2008 and is taken from the QoG data set. See Teorell et al.
(2010).

role in Jamaican politics. Following racial riots in 1938 the working class gained a political awakening and was mobilized as a distinct political force (Edie 1992, 65–69). Around the outbreak of World War II, cousins Alexander Bustamante and Norman Manley (both from the middle class), founded the JLP and the PNP respectively, and together they and their parties would carry Jamaica into sovereign statehood (Collier 2009, 125). At independence in 1962, Jamaica appeared as a relatively stable democracy in the making, having taken great steps away from the shackles of the old plantation society. Collier (2009, 126) argues that by the 1950s, "the professionalized British Colonial Office had reduced corruption to only a minor problem. Jamaica began its first years as a sovereign state with a Jamaican-born civil service that inherited strong values of honesty and probity from its former British colonizers."

The two principal political leaders, Bustamante and Manley, had reputations for strong British democratic values—especially the need for consensus politics—and were considered upstanding politicians whose central concern was the interests of the Jamaican people (Collier 2009, 126). During the first decade after independence, a positive trend was followed with increasing economic prosperity. However, when Norman Manley's son, Michael, assumed power in 1972, it was the start of a shift in the relationship between the two parties, as the new Manley regime, in an "act of political revenge" (ibid., 127), commissioned an inquiry regarding corrupt practices of the previous JLP government. While the report indeed revealed mismanagement, Manley Jr. did not bother taking legal action; rather, he used his political power to strengthen his hold on the state machinery. This eventually climaxed in the state of emergency of 1976–77, when, under the pretense of quelling political gang violence, Manley imprisoned many key members of the opposition while embarking on a short-lived and failed attempt to socialize the economy. In the increasingly polarized and violent political landscape, politically affiliated gangs and organized crime flourished, political murders increased, and poor inner-city communities became impenetrable "garrisons" for the two parties, even today. Supporters of one of the political parties still usually avoid going into areas of Kingston dominated by the other party (Harriot 2008, 61–63). And it is from this point in time, the mid-1970s, that Jamaica's economy stops growing.

Following the JLP's resuming power under Edward Seaga in 1980, the political violence between the JLP and the PNP continued. In this highly ranked democracy, hundreds of politically motivated murders occur every year, "with the numbers peaking each election year" (Collier 2009, 129). Although they have declined somewhat since the late 1990s, violent acts spurred by political motives are still commonplace (Collier 2009, 129; Werlin 2003, 335–36).

Tied into this political polarization, the two parties have shown no scruples about using the civil service to attain their own goals. As Carlene Edie has stated, "In contrast to Weber's rational, impartial model of bureaucratic conduct, all relationships are highly personalized and politicized, even those related to the most trivial administrative procedure" (1992, 65). From the 1970s onward the situation rapidly started to remind ordinary Jamaicans of the time before 1938, as patron-client-relations again became the main modus operandi for getting things done. An intricate clientelist system has developed between members of parliament, civil servants, political brokers, and various criminal or semicriminal local "councilors" in which citizens exchange their political support for various personal favors (Edie 1992, 17). Civil society in Jamaica is strong but is not really a factor that creates social bridges and trust between the various factions.

These structures have now taken root in Jamaican society, and the Bustamante/Manley Sr. era now seems like a historical parenthesis. According to most authors, political violence and corruption have arrested the development of the country yet have also made the situation somewhat stable and self-sustaining, since neither party has been able to permanently gain the upper hand (Lyday, O'Donnell, and Munroe 2008). Clientelism has become the glue that holds the fragile system together. Werlin notes that the state indeed has maintained its vigorous Westminster-style two-party system. However, he adds: "Both political parties regularly employ criminal gangs (assisted to some extent by police and civil servants) to mobilize political support, distribute favors, and intimidate opposition" (Werlin 2007, 335).

The result is that citizens have lost confidence in the public administration and the legal institutions. Inadequate pay in the public bodies is said to be supplemented by income from criminal activity, mostly related to drugs (Lyday, O'Donnell, and Munroe 2008). Harriot also focuses his analysis of Jamaica's problems on the violent and criminal nature of Jamaican politics: "The successful use of both violence and corruption for political purposes is made possible by corrupt networks that extend into the state bureaucracy. These methods encourage party permeation of the state and undermine good governance. The process is made easy by

weak state institutions that are not very resistant to party permeation"
(Harriot 2008, 9).

In the recent measures of level of corruption published by Transparency International, Jamaica has dropped dramatically from place 61 in 2006 to place 84 in 2007 and yet further down to place 99 in 2009. A recent report to the United States Agency for International Development concludes that corruption has been allowed "to infect politics and economics to such an extent that it now threatens the viability of both state and society" (Lyday, O'Donnell, and Munroe 2008, 5). Another recent large-scale survey project comparing twenty-two Latin American and Caribbean countries found that in Jamaica, "citizens' perception that corruption is widespread in the public sphere is exceptionally high in absolute as well as in comparative terms." Moreover, this study also found that Jamaica is "the country with the highest level of citizens' lack of confidence in the integrity of elected and other public officials in the Region" (Powell and Lewis 2009, xxiii).

In May 2010 a week of intensive fighting in Kingston between security forces and one of the best-known criminal gangs, when about eighty people were killed, made world news and forced the government to declare a state of emergency. This small-scale civil war was caused by United States demands that Jamaica extradite a gang leader on charges of drugs and arms dealing. Reports in the media revealed strong connections between the gang leader and the prime minister.[3]

To summarize what the available research says about Jamaica since independence: A relatively stable, peaceful, and "good natured" democracy started to go astray in the 1970s. A political confrontation between the two parties that escalated out of control drove Jamaica into a vicious circle of corruption, favoritism, clientelism, and organized crime. The Jamaican case shows that in developing countries, unchecked democratic competition can destroy a civil service and a law enforcement sector of relatively high quality by politicizing them for clientelist purposes. While the country has many of the features that result in high scores on measures of democracy applied by various international organizations (regular and free elections, free media, etc.), all these measures are on the input side of the system and relate to how democratic the access to power

3. *New York Times*, May 25, 2010; *Washington Post*, May 26, 2010; *Guardian*, May 25, 2010.

is. Measures about the exercise of power show a dramatically different and less encouraging picture, as do most measures of social well-being. That Jamaica had more than a decade of relatively high QoG, reasonably consensual democracy, and considerable economic growth speaks against the argument launched by Elliot and Palmer (2008) that the current problems with highly dysfunctional institutions can be traced back in history to the plantation economy.

Singapore: Autocracy Goes Quality of Government

As I said above, in contrast to Jamaica, by the usual measures and standards Singapore is clearly an undemocratic country (Hadenius and Teorell 2005). However, the country boasts some curious and unusual traits for an autocracy, such as a well-run and incorrupt civil service, and a high degree of rule of law as well as government effectiveness. According to these measures, Singapore's scores are among the five best in the world. While elections are formally free and regular, the ruling party's complete dominance over institutions and society in general makes a shift in power all but impossible.

Lee Kuan Yew, the country's leader from independence to 1991 (when he became "senior minister"; currently he holds the position of "minister mentor"), has also been a somewhat different autocratic leader than most long-sitting dictators. He has never built his authority on personalist ties or pretended to be a charismatic leader, to use Weberian terminology. In contrast to many other autocratic countries, Singapore has no traits of a personality cult (Mauzy and Milne 2002, 6). This does not mean that the top political leadership has taken a backseat. The Singaporean state is to all intents and purposes the state of the ruling political party (the People's Action Party, henceforth PAP). And for the past fifty years the PAP has been heavily dependent on Lee Kuan Yew.

With its focus on, and pride in, meritocracy, Singapore is highly elitist. This founding principle for the PAP version of the state has applied ever since its inception during the 1950s and 1960s. The system can be described as a combination of elitism and managerialism. Recruitment to top positions in the party and state bureaucracy is not geared toward rewarding people according to the patron-client logic. Instead, meritocracy has been the central factor leading to recruitment of top university graduates to the party-state system, and such positions have been highly attractive, not least because of high salaries (Trocki 2006; Mauzy and Milne 2002, 7).

In tandem with the strong emphasis on meritocracy, anticorruption is also central to both Lee Kuan Yew and to the Singaporean state ideology in general. This seems to have come from the top. According to two observers, Lee Kuan Yew's views about corruption and bribery have been very strong: "He is appalled by some third world leaders' acquisition on a vast scale of wealth for their families and themselves. He has called this the 'bane' of the Third World, and examples in the region abound, former Presidents Marcos and Suharto being among the most notorious" (Mauzy and Milne 2002, 7).

However, note that "clean government" has not always been the order of the day in Singapore. On the contrary, until the 1960s, corruption was deeply rooted in Singaporean society, and organized crime had a clear impact on business and on people's lives (Quah 2001). PAP leader Lee Kuan Yew and his entourage seem to have been determined to break this system, a policy that started in the 1960s. As summarized by Uslaner (2008, 204), Singapore "battled corruption largely through political will and strong leadership." In a comparative perspective, Singapore's success story in combating corruption, together with the case of Hong Kong, is as dramatic as it is rare.

I should add that Singapore is far from the neoliberal dream of a minimalist state that does not intervene in business or take an active part in ensuring social well-being among its citizens. Singapore under PAP can best be described as a developmental state that has played a very active role both in the development of the economy and in ensuring the social welfare of its population, not least as to housing (Root 2006; Kwon 2009; Lee 2006).

Civil society and voluntary organizations have not been well thought of by the PAP regime. Its strictly elitist and meritocratic view of politics and the state has given little room for such a sector, which this political regime understands as supporting political factions. As one observer notes, "The main political project of the period between 1959 and 1975, and thereafter, has been the elimination of all forms of civil society" (Trocki 2006, 131). Interest groups, which are central actors in the framework of Western liberal democracies, have in Singapore been something of a "bad word" (Sikorski 1996, 825).

One could argue that the success of creating high quality of government in Singapore would be related to historically inherited cultural values. Such a proposition, however, flies in the face of the fact that Singapore's governance and economic situation appear unique in the region. Looking at Southeast Asia, though most nations have experienced great growth over the past decades, there is little homogeneity in wealth, democracy, or government effectiveness.

Conclusion

Unlike the connection in the Western world, the link between democracy, on the one hand, and high QoG, economic growth, and social well-being on the other is evidently not to be seen in Jamaica and Singapore. As I reported in chapter 2, a lengthy discussion has taken place in political economy circles about whether democracy promotes economic growth and social well-being. Most of this discussion has been based on cross-country large-n analyses, and so far the results seem inconclusive. The two cases analyzed in this chapter provide a clear answer to this issue—that electoral representative democracy as such does not guarantee good social outcomes. Instead, these two cases give strong support to the existence of a causal relation between QoG and social well-being. For example, if population health should be the main indicator for what counts as a "successful society," as argued by Hall and Lamont (2009), high QoG is more important than representative democracy. To recapitulate Larry Diamond's (2007) warning, democratization, while globally a huge success story, is haunted by a ghost named "bad governance." If the democratic process becomes entangled in clientelism, corruption, and similar practices, democracy as such will not improve the social well-being of the population. It would be great if all good things went together, but this is obviously not the case. The stark optimism that many international aid organizations embrace concerning the role that democratization can have in alleviating poverty in many developing countries unfortunately seems unfounded, like the hope that civil society organizations in general will have a positive impact.

What accounts for the exceptional development of Singapore can certainly be debated at length. Many observers have pointed to the importance of the policies against corruption and clientelism launched by Lee Kuan Yew. To present such an idiosyncratic explanation is probably not very helpful from a policy perspective. Moreover, this type of explanation does not really count in the social sciences. Yet even scholars who work with formal econometric models and use advanced statistical analyses to come up with nomothetic "covering laws" in this area have been seen to fall back on "exceptional individual" explanations. A case in point is Botswana's remarkable success in building a relatively incorrupt and nonclientelist state and managing economic growth at a considerable pace, which Acemoglu, Johnson, and Robinson (2003, 78) explain in part by referring to "a number of important and farsighted decisions by the post-independence political leaders, in particular Seretse Khama and Quett Masire." This may very well be true, but then one has to come up with an explanation for why this type of far-sighted political leadership seems so rare in most developing countries, as illustrated not least by the political leadership in Jamaica.

What goes on in the minds of political leaders like these and what motivates their behavior are certainly tricky questions to answer, especially if the ambition is to present a general explanation for such processes. Another explanation for cases like contemporary Singapore, Hong Kong, and Botswana, which have successfully built high quality of government, as well as nineteenth-century Denmark and Sweden, would be that these are all relatively (or very) small states that changed during a period of severe external threat. As I argued in chapter 5, there are reasonably good theoretical arguments and empirical support for claiming that external threats foster group solidarity. It is not too fanciful to imagine that leaders like these could have used such an external threat to convince various factions in their societies that they must make the complicated and difficult move from inefficient to efficient government institutions.

CHAPTER TEN

Preventing Societies from Self-Destructing

There are two features that I think deserve to be pointed out. One is that the financial system as we know it actually collapsed. . . . The other feature is that the financial system collapsed of its own weight. That contradicted the prevailing view about financial markets, namely that they tend toward equilibrium, and that equilibrium is disturbed by extraneous forces, outside shocks. Those disturbances were supposed to occur in a random fashion. Markets were seen basically as self-correcting. That paradigm has proven to be false. So we are dealing not only with a collapse of a financial system, but also with the collapse of a world view. — George Soros, *New York Review of Books*, June 11, 2009

Is There Such a Thing as Legal Corruption?

In his "farewell lecture" on December 9, 2008, former leading World Bank economist Daniel Kaufmann introduced the concept of *legal corruption*. The term certainly seems like an oxymoron, but Kaufmann justifies it by arguing that corruption should be redefined to include "how elites collude and purchase, or unduly influence the rules of the game, shape the institutions, the policies and regulations and the laws for their own private benefits." According to Kaufmann, whether this is done illegally, as in the traditional use of the term corruption, or legally is of minor interest from the viewpoint of economic and social efficiency. The term legal corruption covers situations when public policy is thwarted or "captured" by various private interests instead of serving the common or public interest, and thus applies to all forms of "privatization of public policy." Kaufmann's case in point is the background to the financial and economic crisis that hit the world economy in the fall of 2008, and he points out how powerful agents in the United States financial sector used their influence to "relax regulatory oversight and capital requirements."[1] By this important theoretical move, Kaufmann makes it possible to connect the study of corruption to the analysis of special interest politics, also known as neocorporatism. He claims that the current financial crisis leads to the following conclusion: "If anybody thought that the governance and corruption challenge was a monopoly of the developing world . . . that notion has been disposed [of] completely."[2]

In this concluding chapter I will present four interrelated arguments based on the results from the previous chapters that sum to a theory about the relation between social and economic efficiency and quality of government. The first, and least controversial, is that competitive markets with a certain set of characteristics are the hitherto most efficient organizational form for creating utilitarian-based economic efficiency for the production of most goods and services. Such characteristics include free entry, low transaction costs, reasonably reliable and readily available information, goods that are not by their very nature collective, low external effects, and efficient protection of contracts and property rights.[3] Without such an economic system, poor countries are likely to remain poor. The second argument is that in order to reach this utilitarian-based (or "Pareto efficiency," but henceforth social efficiency) market, economies need a large set of encompassing and complicated in-

---

1. Kaufmann points to a meeting held in April 2004 when the CEOs of the (then) five big investment banks on Wall Street persuaded the U.S. Securities and Exchange Commission to relax the regulation that stipulated their need for financial reserves. See also Stephen Labaton, "Agency's '04 Rule Let Banks Pile Up New Debt," *New York Times*, October 3, 2008.

2. Kaufmann has headed the World Bank Institute's work on "Governance Issues." His farewell lecture can be found at http://info.worldbank.org/etools/bspan/PresentationView .asp?PID=2363&EID=1056.

3. Such markets need not entail what is known as the domination of capitalist power in the relations of production. In a market economy, capital can hire labor, implying that capital will be more powerful than labor in organizing the production process. However, labor can also hire capital (e.g., a group of workers or professionals can start a cooperative and take loans or issue bonds on the securities market), in which case the employees can elect (and hold responsible) a board that employs managers. Moreover, a third party (usually a group of managers or an entrepreneur) can hire both labor and capital, in which case this third party will have the most power in the production process. The common understanding in Marxist and well as non-Marxist theories of the relation between power in the production process and market economy has no logical underpinning. See Ellerman (1992) and Rothstein (1992b). Contrary to Marxian thoughts, it is the nature of the hiring contract, not the market economy as such, that entails power in a market-based production process.

stitutions, both formal and informal. It is the quality of these institutions that determines whether markets will create economic prosperity. Since high-quality institutions will in the long run make all market agents better off, they can be labelled *socially efficient institutions*. The third argument is that we have little reason to expect such institutions to be created endogenously by economic agents. Instead, we should expect such agents to act in a way that will prevent such institutions from being established. If they are established, self-interested agents will try to destroy them. To use a metaphor from evolutionary biology, we have very little reason to expect that efficient institutions will evolve by any selection mechanism that is generated from the sum of economic agency in a society. Instead, I argue that, left to themselves, markets are endogenously self-destructive. The fourth argument is that markets can reach social efficiency only if the agents that reproduce the necessary institutions act according to a logic different from the logic that market agents use when operating on the market. In short, I hope to make the case for the existence of a paradox in social organization: that *you can have a market for anything as long as you do not have a market for everything*. The idea that efficient markets can rest on self-interested agents is refuted not only theoretically by the problems of collective action and provision of public goods but, as has been shown in the previous chapters, also by the facts about the prevalence and persistence of low QoG. Recent experimental research carried out on fifteen local populations in third world countries (mostly hunter-gatherers) shows that the more such a small-scale society is dependent on market transactions, the stronger are the norms about fairness and the less people act according to standards associated with rational self-interest (Henrich et al. 2010).

The argument about the social efficiency of markets should be understood in a relative sense. Markets cannot be seen as efficient in an absolute sense because market agents cannot be presumed to be in possession of anything close to perfect information or to be unboundedly rational, nor are transaction costs instantaneous and costless (Menard and Shirley 2005). On the contrary, empirical research about how market agents act shows the opposite. Agents are often myopic; they rarely have perfect information; they make computational mistakes when calculating costs versus benefits; even if the value/risk is the same, they are more likely to avoid losses than to opt for gains; their beliefs can often be manipulated; transactions have sometimes large costs, and so forth (Frohlich and Oppenheimer 2006; Jones 1999; Loewenstein, Rabin, and

Camerer 2004; Ostrom 1998). It is only in very rare cases that markets can be expected to reach what economists call Pareto efficiency, because agents cannot be expected to meet the assumptions made in the standard welfare economics theorem. As stated by Joseph Stiglitz, "A closer look at those assumptions, however, suggests that the theorem is of limited relevance to modern industrial economics" (Stiglitz 2002, 43). My argument for markets as efficient is based on the much more mundane argument that so far, for most goods and services, the alternatives to democratically regulated competitive markets have not delivered. Neither systems of central planning nor "market socialism" have lived up to the expectations of creating reasonable efficiency or anything close to social or economic equality. For most goods and services, competitive markets are more efficient than known or tried alternative forms of production. This is also a central lesson from much of development studies (Bigsten and Fosu 2004). In addition, markets seem to have important advantages when it comes to innovation and to furthering a Schumpeterian "creative destruction."

Institutions and Change

The main argument in this book has been that the quality of the institutions that exercise political power in a society is central to the social well-being of its population. The causality is both direct from such formally established impartial institutions and indirect, since such impartial institutions increase social trust and social equality. In the previous chapters, I have tried to present a definition of such quality of government (QoG) institutions and to estimate their effects on different social and economic outcomes. Moreover, I have tried to compare the effects of QoG with the effects of representative democracy on various social goods and systems of beliefs such as social trust. One question remains, though: how to differentiate between types of institutions and to answer questions about why in particular "QoGish" institutions seem difficult to establish. If such institutions are as important as shown by the empirical indicators presented in this study and in many others, then why not just go ahead and create them? International aid organizations could make establishing such institutions a condition for economic support to developing countries. Obviously this issue is much more complicated and problematic. To be able to understand, it is necessary to move upward on the ladder of abstractions.

As argued by Algan (2009), a central problem for the approach in economics based on Douglass North's work is that the definitions of what should count as an institution are very vague. For example, according to the definition presented in *The Handbook of Institutional Economics*, "Institutions are the written and unwritten rules, norms and constraints that humans devise to reduce uncertainty and control the environment" (Menard and Shirley 2005, 1). The implication of such a broad definition is that institutions can come in many *forms*—from constitutional laws to what have become known as "standard operating procedures" (Hall 1986) or "work rules" (Ostrom 1990), which are known and generally agreed upon but are unwritten. The problem is that with this definition, corruption, clientelism, organized crime, and low social trust are to be defined as institutions. Although this is not what North and other scholars in this approach have in mind, unfortunately it is so. Obviously we need to be able to distinguish conceptually between institutions that are likely to produce economic growth and social well-being and those that are not likely to have such effects.

That institutions include not only formal but also informal rules makes it difficult to distinguish them from a society's basic cultural traits. From a policy perspective this is problematic, because even though it is possible to change written rules and "standard operating procedures/work rules," for example, through a democratic process, this is much more difficult with things like "shared mental models" (Denzau and North 1994) and other generally held basic beliefs that are rooted in a society's historically established culture. In any case, as a first distinction for understanding the possibilities for change, we can differentiate two basic forms: *formal and informal institutions*. The interplay between formal and informal institutions is thus the second issue we have to understand.

A third problem is that not all institutions are difficult to change. While the problem of institutional inertia and self-reinforcing suboptimal equilibriums is the central theme of the institutional approach to the study of developing nations (Bardhan 1997; Acemoglu and Robinson 2008; Persson 2008), in several recent studies of the rich welfare states the picture is very different. Here change of important institutions occurs almost constantly, in a mostly incremental process. This can occur either because agents are able to find compromises and viable solutions to common problems or as a result of power struggles. Adaptation to new circumstances such as increased international competition for goods and services, globalization of financial markets, and new technologies in the production process may not always be easy in these societies and may be the outcome of difficult political disputes and hard-won compromises (Hall and Thelen 2009; Mahoney and Thelen 2009; Steinmo 2010). Still, the general picture is that in this type of (rich) society, political and economic elites are, after some initial difficulties, usually able to gradually alter central institutions according to their interests for change in the distribution of resources and power that they believe will follow from their ideas of new institutional designs. An example is how Scandinavians' model of high taxes/high spending in universal welfare states has been able to successfully adapt their systems to the increased international globalization of financial and other markets (Steinmo 2010). Another example is the system of industrial relations and vocational training in Germany that change following the changes in the balance of power the main agents command (Thelen 2009). A third example is how the "Bismarckian" welfare state has managed to change and adapt to new economic and social circumstances (Palier and Martin 2008).

A problem for our understanding of institutional change is that these two research approaches about institutions hardly ever communicate their theories, problems, or results. We have to ask why it is that in some (rich capitalist) societies, the political and economic elites usually manage to change institutions so that their societies will remain competitive in the globalized economy or become even more so while other (poor developmental) societies seem stuck with formal as well as informal institutions that are fundamentally detrimental to their needs for economic growth and improvement of social well-being. One reason for this apparent paradox may be that these approaches to institutional change are dealing with institutions that are fundamentally different. Obviously, in addition to the fact that not all institutions are causally related to good social outcomes, some institutions are easier to change than others.

Institutions versus Institutions: The Theory

To make these three distinctions between the myriad institutions that exist in every society, I will rely on a dichotomy presented (for a very different purpose) by George Tsebelis (1990), between "redistributive" and "efficient" institutions. A redistributive institution is simply a (formal or informal) rule that moves resources or power from one group of agents to another. Familiar examples of such a formal redistributive institution would be most social insurance and tax systems, slavery, and industrial relations laws. Informal redistributive institutions would be systems known as patron-client relations, solidarity within ethnically defined local groups, various forms of corruption, organizational cultures, kinship relations, and familism.

The existence of redistributive institutions and changes in them are in general not difficult to explain using standard assumptions about the consequences of allocating various power resources in societies, organizations, or groups. For example, as shown in chapter 6, variation in the extension and coverage of different social insurance systems can to a large extent be explained by the variation in the political mobilization of class-based power resources (Korpi and Palme 2003). Another example is the study of the power of political elites. In general one would expect that in a group, organization, or society, those with power will establish institutions that make it easier and more profitable for them to continue in power. Agents that profit from clientelist or corrupt systems of exchange are likely to keep such systems working, since they of course have no incentive to do away with such practices.

A classic case of establishing redistributive institutions is when economically powerful market agents try to establish rules that will limit competition in their market segment. In electoral politics, gerrymandering is another typical example. There are, however, also instances when social norms about moral obligations and appropriateness play a role (Elster 1989; March and Olsen 1989). One example is the recent strengthening in many Western countries of legal norms about how to treat animals. However, the general assumption here is that agents, when trying to establish or change a redistributive institution, will act according to a "logic of exchange" and maximize their material gains, positions, or power.

Efficient institutions, on the other hand, have quite the opposite character, since their effect is to improve the welfare of all actors in a specific system of exchange. As such, they are genuinely collective (or public) goods and therefore, as I will discuss further below, are difficult to explain from standard assumptions about human behavior in neoclassical economics. Seen in the light of noncooperative game theory, these are institutions that make it possible to avoid situations such as suboptimal outcomes in n-persons prisoner's dilemma games. In the closely related theory about social dilemmas, efficient institutions make it possible for agents to avoid ending up in "social traps" (Rothstein 2005). To repeat the discussion from chapter 5, these are situations in which the agents know they would all be better off if they could collaborate to establish a common set of institutions; but lacking trust that the other agents will adhere by the rules or contribute to the costs of establishing and running the institution, the individual agent has no incentive to collaborate, since the (socially efficient) institutions will not come about unless (almost) all others collaborate/contribute as well. This lack of trust makes all agents worse off. For example, corrupt doctors in a public health system may realize that they would all gain by ending corruption, but it becomes meaningless for individual doctors to stop taking bribes if they cannot trust that most other doctors would do the same. Similarly, it makes little sense for single judges or police officers to stop taking bribes without trusting that (almost) all their colleagues will also refrain. In an emerging democracy, it makes little sense to be the only political party that does not tamper with ballot boxes or engage in clientelist exchanges with voters. The list of examples illustrating this problem is endless.

For market agents, socially efficient institutions would be those that secure property rights and produce reliable information about the solvency and credit record of firms, as well as an incorrupt and impartial judiciary, a state government operating by the "rule of law," and antitrust legislation that can secure fair competition. For most citizens, an honest, impartial, and reasonably efficient public administration would also be counted in this category of efficient institutions. In short, the type of "good governance" or "quality of government" institutions that were defined in chapter 1 are in this context to be seen as socially efficient (formal) institutions.

The best-known example of informal efficient institutions is when generalized trust and social capital are widespread among the population. Informal institutions like generalized social trust increase the likelihood that other economic agents will not use opportunist or treacherous strategies when dealing with you but will follow contracts in a benevolent way. Generalized trust, understood as the belief that you live in a society (or act in an environment) where the moral standards of the other agents in general are high, leads to a decrease in transaction costs (Keefer and

Knack 2005; Svendsen and Svendsen 2004). Theoretically, efficient institutions increase the likelihood that agents who are exchanging values will trust that the other agents will not behave treacherously (Levi 1998a, 1998b, 2006). Thus, efficient institutions change agents' choice of strategy by increasing the likelihood that they will believe most other agents cooperate honestly, which in turn will make it more rational for the individual agent to reciprocate benevolently.

The paradox that scholars studying the rich democracies and scholars studying developing countries have come to such different conclusions about the possibility for institutional change thus comes down to their studying fundamentally different types of institutions. The first group usually concentrates on redistributive institutions for which the analysis of (very often complicated) power constellations explains change. The latter group studies the lack of socially efficient institutions, which are difficult to establish because they are "second order" public goods (Ostrom 1998). According to Acemoglu and Robinson (2008), the problem is that there is currently no generally accepted theory about how to establish socially efficient institutions or about why they are reproduced. As I will argue below, following standard assumptions about self-interested rational agency used in neoclassic economics, socially efficient institutions of the type described above would not exist, and poor countries that lack them would not be able to change from inefficient to efficient institutions.

I should add that the distinction between "socially efficient" and "redistributive" institutions is a theoretical ideal construct. In real life, many efficient institutions have some redistributive effects and vice versa (Tsebelis 1990). However, for theoretical simplification, I will distinguish between these two *types* of institutions (redistributive and effective) and forms of institutions (informal and formal). If the two institutional forms and the two institutional types we have identified are cross-tabulated, the following typology and examples come out.

I am not arguing that redistributive institutions in general produce normatively bad outcomes. This is an ideological issue. Most people would think that taking care of one's family members is a good thing, but they may think otherwise when this extends to nepotism. Some people think a steeply progressive tax system is the height of social justice, while others disagree. However, socially efficient institutions are preferable for the whole group, organization, or society because they will by definition make everyone better off.

Form of institution

		Formal	Informal
		Impartial state	**Generalized Trust**
	Effective	**adm.**	**Social Capital**
Type of		**Rule of Law**	**Civil Service Ethics**
institution		**Audit system**	
	Redistri-	**Tax systems**	**Familism**
	butive	**Industrial rel. laws**	**Corruption**
		Welfare programs	**Business networks**

FIGURE 10.1. Institutional forms and types: examples.

As shown in chapters 6 and 7, these forms and types are strongly correlated empirically. For example, high levels of corruption correlate with
low levels of generalized trust, and high levels of "rule of law" correlate
with high levels of generalized trust (Rothstein and Stolle 2008; Rothstein and Uslaner 2005). Using the experimental method, it was also possible to show a causal link between low QoG and low social trust. However, determining how the causality works over longer time sequences
is admittedly more complicated. The most plausible explanation is that
formal and informal efficient institutions are mutually reinforcing enti-
ties in which causality operates with a considerable amount of feedback
over time. A good example is the analysis by Farrell and Knight of how
firms in a certain district in northern Italy use trust-based collaboration
to strengthen their market position as a collective while also competing
in the very same market segment. They show that the formal efficient
types of institutions work, so to say, behind the scenes as a last resort for
agents to deal with opportunist/treacherous behavior, while it is the informal trust-based relations that create the system of mutually beneficial cooperation (Farrell and Knight 2003). Using large-*n* cross-country
statistics, Bergren and Jordahl (2006, 161) conclude that "legal structure
and security of property rights has a large, statistically significant and
possibly causal effect on trust." Other studies show that informal and

formal efficient institutions can be functional substitutes (Ahlerup, Olsson, and Yanagizawa 2008; Widmalm 2008).

The Difficult Art of Supplying Efficient Institutions

The central claim from the "new institutional" approach in economics is that efficient formal institutions are necessary for creating economic efficiency and economic growth, especially in poverty-stricken third world countries (Acemoglu, Johnson, and Robinson 2005; Eggertsson 2005; Menard and Shirley 2005; Bergren and Jordahl 2006; Rodrik 2007). It has also been claimed that such institutions explain the "miraculous" economic growth in Western Europe that started in the late seventeenth century (North 1990).

The problem of supplying socially efficient institutions is often labeled as creating "credible commitments" between agents when they enter into contracts in a market (Keefer and Knack 2005). Without institutions establishing credible assurances that treacherous[4] agents who violate or renege on contracts will be punished (or ostracized), so as to establish a general belief among most agents that such behavior is uncommon, transaction costs will skyrocket and people will not be inclined to make productive investments in physical or human capital. Many otherwise profitable economic exchanges or investments in skills and education thus will not come about because the agents will not trust one another to fulfill obligations, promises, and contracts. If dishonest and treacherous behavior becomes generally expected ("common knowledge"), then almost all agents will be losers, since they will either refrain from mutually advantageous forms of cooperation or have to invest heavily to monitor and detect treacherous behavior. Moreover, once generalized trust is broken, it becomes hard to mend, for a number of psychological reasons. Because of this, agents that otherwise would have much to gain from cooperation can be "trapped" in a situation of mutual distrust (like the two warring political parties in Jamaica, described in the previous chapter).

In sum, we face two interrelated problems. The first is that socially efficient institutions as they have been defined here are a genuine public good; and as with all such goods, though they are collectively rational,

---

4. Economists often use "opportunistic" to describe such behavior, which I think is too nice a term for this type of agency.

contributing to them may be irrational for the individual agent. Given standard assumptions about the operational logic of economic agents, we cannot assume they will provide such institutions in any organic or functionalist way.

Second, if efficient institutions have been established, we should expect economic agents to try to make them redistributive. Again, the politicizing of the civil service and the law enforcement agencies in Jamaica is a case in point. In more established democracies, economic agents are likely to use various forms of lobbying to change the general rules (laws, regulations) to favor them at the expense of their competitors, as described by Daniel Kaufmann at the beginning of this chapter.[5] When it comes to the specific implementation of general rules, economic agents are likely to use bribes or take part in similar forms of corruption or clientelism. One need only take a quick look at the indexes of corruption provided by organizations such as Transparency International and the World Bank Research Institute to conclude that systemic or semisystemic corruption is the rule around the world, not the exception. As Mary Shirley states: "The vast majority of humans today live in countries that have failed to create or sustain strong institutions to foster exchange and protect persons and property" (Shirley 2005, 612). In sum, as Douglass North has put it, "Institutions are not necessarily or even usually created to be socially efficient" (North 1998a, 249). The earlier idea in economics that market agents would create efficient institutions by a sort of functionalist trial-and-error is simply not credible given the historical record (Bendor and Swistak 2004).

The Problem Is Failures in Sustaining Markets, Not Market Failures

The argument presented here is different from the standard "market failure" argument in neoclassical economics, which has a long history dating back to Adam Smith's famous statement that "people of the same trade

5. Joseph Stiglitz, winner of the prize in economics to the memory of Alfred Nobel, recalls that when he was the chair of the Council of Economic Advisers under former United States president Bill Clinton, CEOs of major U.S. companies regularly came to his office stating their support for the free-market principle that governments should not interfere in the market. However, as a rule they told Stiglitz that their particular industry was a special case that needed strong support from the government (from Block 2007, 12).

seldom meet together, even for merriment and diversion, but the conversation ends in a conspiracy against the public, or in some contrivance to raise prices" (cf. Cowen 1988; Smith 1776). The standard "market failure" theory proposes that there are specific situations or certain types of goods for which markets cannot attain social efficiency, such as when the goods have large costs that are not reflected in the price, when the consumption of them is not exclusive, when their production has large social benefits, or when information problems become too extensive. In such cases, most neoclassical economists argue that there is a need for some form of government intervention or regulation. The argument from neoclassical economics is thus that in general markets will create efficiency if left to themselves, but that a number of special or exceptional circumstances call for government intervention. In contrast, I argue that also for "perfect market goods" with low externalities and when consumption is exclusive and information is (almost) free and perfect, market agents behaving like market agents can generally not be expected to generate efficiency, because we have very little reason to believe they will create the necessary efficient institutions as defined above. This is slowly becoming clear from the new institutionalist research program in economics. For example, Avner Greif argues that such institutions exist only "in a few advanced contemporary countries and only in recent times" (Greif 2005, 737). The same argument has been put forward in a recent book by Douglass North, Joseph Wallis, and Barry Weingast (2009) with the immodest subtitle *A Conceptual Framework for Interpreting Recorded Human History*. As Acemoglu and Robinson recently have put it: "An agreement on the efficient set of institutions is often not forthcoming because . . . groups with political power cannot commit to not using their power to change the distribution of resources in their favour" (Acemoglu and Robinson 2008).

Why can't economic agents be expected to create the efficient institutions they need to create an efficient market?[6] North (1998a, 247) states the problem this way: "Neoclassical theory is simply an inappropriate tool to analyze and prescribe policies that will induce development. It is concerned with markets, not with how markets develop." One

---

6. Cowen (1988) devotes a number of chapters to describing cases when economic agents have been able to overcome the collective action problem and produce public goods. The cases are all interesting, but they are clearly exceptions bordering on the anecdotal. This is largely "make-believe" economics.

problem is that if political leaders create a state that is administratively strong enough to protect property rights, they will also have access to an administrative machine that can violate those rights (North 1990, 59). If those in control of the state are the type of actors assumed by the utility-maximizing neoclassical model, they will also exploit that power to enrich themselves at the expense of the people (Weingast 1993, 287). This is amply shown by the situation in the many "failed states" in Africa as described by Robert Bates: "The civil service assumes the role of a specialist in violence, using its command over the bureaucracy to redistribute income from the citizens to themselves" (Bates 2008, 29). In so doing, they inevitably create distrust of the state as an institution, constructing a barrier to the willingness to invest or take other economic risks. But as is well known, there are exceptions. Research on neocorporatism shows that in some cases market agents (for example, employers' federations, trade unions, or trade organizations) have been able to establish efficient institutions through negotiation. Note that in almost all cases this has been carried out either in close collaboration with government agents or under the threat that if economic agents cannot establish such institutions through some form of compromise, the government would step in (Katzenstein 1994; Lewin 1994; Scharpf 1997).

The other main exception to the general rule that economic agents are unable to create efficient institutions is the work on "common pool resource problems" by Elinor Ostrom. She has shown that groups of economic agents who all depend on a local natural resource can create (efficient) institutions to prevent extraction by free riders that would be detrimental to the sustainability of the resource. Finding out that, if left to themselves without government interference, economic agents can overcome the famous "tragedy of the commons" problem is a major achievement, and her research has rightfully gained a lot of attention (Ostrom 1990). Other studies—for example, of water control systems in the Netherlands during the seventeenth and eighteenth centuries—have confirmed her results (Kaijser 2002).

However, there are a number of arguments for the position that Ostrom's findings are not generalizable to large-scale modern societies. First, in all her cases, the group in question has developed strong social bonds and mutual trust over a very long time. Second, the groups are socially and ethnically homogeneous, something that other scholars have put forward as critical. For example, a recent paper reviewing the literature concludes that "the negative association between ethnic heterogeneity and public goods provision is widely accepted" (Habyarimana et al. 2006). Other scholars contend that the negative relation between ethnic heterogeneity and production of public goods is "one of the most powerful hypotheses in political economy" (Banerjee, Somanathan, and Iyer 2005). They add that this is true not only in obvious and extreme cases like civil wars, but also in "normal" times. Third, success depends on the opportunity for the group to enforce strict rules about who has the right to use the resource in question, which implies that a cartel-like situation already exists. Fourth, Ostrom reports a number of cases where such local regulations have failed for a number of reasons, mostly related to the agents' failure to enter into what should be called a deliberative democratic process. Last, even while the state is far away, it seems to be present in the shadows. For example, in her famous case about water regulation in Southern California, Ostrom notes that it is government institutions that provide the forum for discussions and decisions. In her conclusion, she states that "most of the institutional arrangements used in the success stories were rich mixtures of public and private instrumentalities" (Ostrom 1990, 182).

Another well-known case dealing with the problem of producing efficient institutions has been examined by Paul Milgrom, Douglass C. North, and Barry Weingast (1990) in an often-cited paper. Their example illuminates how merchants of a certain region in fourteenth-century Europe could develop legal praxis that greased the wheels of trade despite the lack of credible state institutions. They faced the problem of managing contractual disputes between merchants—how they should handle the deceptive behavior of certain merchants in terms of various kinds of breach of contract. The situation may be likened to a classic social trap: all merchants have a vested interest in everyone's behaving honestly, but there is no point in being the only honest actor if everyone else is engaged in trickery and deceit of one kind or another. If "everyone does it," the financial gains from trade decline significantly, in part because fewer transactions are completed, and in part because the actors are forced to devote considerable resources to protecting themselves from the deceptive actions of others. Merchant A incurs substantial costs in entering into a financial contract with merchant B, who intends to swindle him. Even if the wronged merchant A spreads information that the dishonest merchant B is not to be trusted, merchant B can just say it isn't true. In the absence of credible information institutions, other merchants have little or no means of determining who is in the right.

Milgrom, North, and Weingast report that the merchants' guilds of fourteenth-century France appointed "law merchants" who were empowered to act as judges in disputes between merchants and to publicize information about those who refused to voluntarily accept their verdicts (e.g., by paying compensation to the wronged party). This made deceptive behavior and refusal to comply with the law merchants' verdicts an expensive business, since those who did so gained a reputation for lacking credibility and for being unreliable trading partners. This led to a strong decline in deceptive behavior because it was in the merchants' own interest to avoid getting such a reputation (see chapter 5; in these contexts, the appearance of credibility is a vital asset). Therewith, according to Milgrom and his coauthors, an institution for solving the problem of the social trap had blossomed from the market's own inherent logic. The actors had an interest both in establishing the institution and in accepting its verdicts, which made the institution as such self-reinforcing. According to this analysis, a type of society under the rule of law had sprung up by itself; the problem of the social trap had been resolved by the self-interested utility-maximizing actors on their own volition and with no outside involvement by something like a state or some social norm.

This is a neat and very appealing analysis to be sure, but it is also supremely idealistic, if not naively romantic. Merchants and trading companies are not homogeneous quantities. Market logic dictates that some will eventually become much stronger financially than others. If they are economic rationalists, the large trading houses will use their financial strength to bribe or corrupt the law merchants in one way or another to gain economic advantages. They will also try to get their confidants in corruption installed in those positions in order to render verdicts in favor of their own trading houses. And if the law merchants are also economic rationalists, their integrity will be for sale as long as the price is right and the transaction can be kept secret. Secret interactions are the hallmark of corruption. Such a scenario is a rather apt description of events in Russia after the privatizations of the 1990s. The economic oligarchs seem to have become so strong that they have managed to buy attempts to build universal legal institutions out of existence (Hedlund 1999; Ledeneva 2006).

The paradox is that when well-known scholars in this research tradition try to solve the problem of how to create socially efficient institutions, they introduce a number of noneconomic explanations such as "beliefs," "norms," "legitimacy," and altruistic actors" (Rothstein 2005, chap. 6). These explanations may very well be true, but in light of their utility-based rationalistic models, they are all ad hoc and thereby outside the reach of their theory. As Lichbach (1997) and also Falaschetti and Miller (2001) have shown, within the rationalistic paradigm *there is no solution* to the problem of creating efficient institutions. It is noteworthy that economists who carry out empirical research in this area emphasize the need for public employees to have a strong public interest orientation (Besley and Ghatak 2007; Collier 2007; Miller and Hammond 1994).

An alternative and in many ways more promising approach to keeping societies from falling into "social traps" can be found in the economic sociology literature. The main claim from this approach is that markets are always socially embedded (Block 2007; Dobbin 2004). This approach entails a very relevant critique of the neoclassical models of how markets operate, since it shows that markets are almost never based on a pure utility-maximizing logic but depend on historically established and often "taken for granted" formal and informal institutions that can vary a lot between settings (Fligstein and Dauter 2007). A part of this literature is inspired by Karl Polanyi's theoretical framework developed in his book *The Great Transformation* (1944). Central to Polanyi's claim is also a strong critique of the idea of a "self-adjusting market" (cited in Block 2007, 5).[7] However, the problem with this approach—within the context of this discussion—is that there is no such thing as "efficient" institutions in economic sociology, only different types of what I have labeled here redistributive institutions (Block 2007). Second, the concept of embeddedness lacks precision, since it can be almost anything that surrounds a market. Third, the approach is not well suited to handle variations across time and space, since it does not entail a well-specified theory of why embeddedness differs. In a similar vein, in the influential approach known as the "variety of capitalism" that has emanated from within political science, this problem is not dealt with, probably because the difference between redistributive and efficient institutions is not recognized. In principle, all institutions in this approach are the outcome of differences in social or economic power and thus redistributive (Hall and Soskice 2001).

---

7. Polanyi is not always clear and easy to interpret. My understanding is that he sees markets as exogenously self-destructive; that is, if not properly embedded, they will destroy their external conditions. Understood in this way, he differs from the argument presented here, which is that markets are also endogenously self-destructive.

Standard textbooks in economics regularly refer back to Adam Smith's "invisible hand" from his *Wealth of Nations* as an argument for why markets, if left to themselves, will become efficient. However, thirteen years before the publication of *Wealth of Nations*, Smith published another book titled *A Theory of Moral Sentiments*, which put strong emphasis on things like virtue, self-restraint, and also the role of proper government regulation. There is now a large literature in the "history of ideas" field showing that these books should be seen as a unified theory that can be viewed as supporting the idea that markets can be efficient only if embedded in what have here been conceptualized as (formal and informal) institutions (Brown 1994; Darwall 1999; Griswold 1999; Werhane 1994). What comes out of this research is that only from a superficial understanding of Adam Smith can his work be used to argue that markets can generate economic efficiency endogenously.

A Concluding Illustration

The ever so popular HBO television show *The Sopranos* contains a scene that speaks to the problem of the supply of efficient institutions. In a state of rage, the mob leader himself, Tony Soprano, gun in hand, goes after and kills a low-level gang member who has betrayed him. Usually, of course, he would have used an underling for an operation like this, but this time (owing to his mental instability, which is a central theme of the series) he is so overtaken by emotion that he forgets the golden rule that Mafia bosses should never do any of the dirty work themselves. As it happens, an "ordinary citizen" sees him chasing the victim. This eyewitness goes to the police, not knowing it is the local Mafia leader he has seen. The "ordinary Joe" tells the police he is just sick and tired of all the violence in his neighborhood and that as a law-abiding citizen he wants to help the police clean it up. When the police show him photos of known criminals, he immediately identifies the perpetrator—still not knowing who the person is. After he has left the police station, the police are in a state of joy, since they now seem to have what they need to put Tony Soprano behind bars. In the next scene, the eyewitness is sitting comfortably in what seems to be a middle-class home listening to classical music. A woman his age, probably his wife, is sitting near him reading the newspaper. Suddenly she starts screaming, then shouts that he must read an article in the paper. The article makes it clear to this honest and law-abiding citizen that the person he has identified at the police station is the local Mafia leader Tony Soprano. The law-abiding citizen races to the phone, calls the chief of police, whose direct number he has, and in a terrified voice says he didn't see anything and won't testify. Before his wife showed him the newspaper article, our law-abiding citizen was reading a book. An observant spectator has about one second to see that it is the philosopher Robert Nozick's modern classic *Anarchy, State, and Utopia*—an icon for all ultraliberal, antigovernment, and free-market proponents ever since it was published (Nozick 1974). The message from the people behind *The Sopranos* seems clear: In a "stateless," Robert Nozick society, where everything should be arranged by individual, freely entered contracts, markets will deteriorate into organized crime and corruption. The conclusion is, again, that there can be a market for anything as long as there is not a market for everything. In other words, if everything is for sale, markets will not come close to what should count as economic efficiency, and poor people in poor countries will remain in poverty.

References

Åberg, Rune. 1989. Distributive Mechanisms of the Welfare State—a Formal Analysis and an Empirical Application. *European Sociological Review* 5 (2): 188–214.

Acemoglu, Daron, Simon Johnson, and James A. Robinson. 2003. An African Success Story: Botswana. In *In Search of Prosperity: Analytical Narratives of Economic Growth*, edited by D. Rodrik. Princeton, NJ: Princeton University Press.

——. 2005. Institutions as the Fundamental Cause of Long-Run Growth. In *Handbook of Economic Growth*, edited by P. Aghion and S. Durlauf. Amsterdam: Elsevier.

Acemoglu, Daron, and James A. Robinson. 2006. Paths of Economic and Political Development. In *The Oxford Handbook of Political Economy*, edited by Barry A. Weingast and Donald Wittman. Oxford: Oxford University Press.

——. 2008. The Role of Institutions in Growth and Development. Washington, DC: World Bank (on behalf of the Commission on Growth and Development).

Ackerman, Bruce A., and James S. Fishkin. 2004. *Deliberation Day*. New Haven, CT: Yale University Press.

Akçay, Selçuk. 2006. Corruption and Human Development. *Cato Journal* 26 (1): 29–48.

Adésínà, 'Jìmí O. 2007. *Social Policy in Sub-Saharan African Context: In Search of Inclusive Development. Social Policy in a Development Context*. New York: Palgrave Macmillan.

Afrobarometer. 2006. Citizens and the State in Africa. Working Paper 61, Afrobarometer Network.

Ahlerup, Pelle, Ola Olsson, and David Yanagizawa. 2008. Social Capital vs. Institutions in the Growth Process. *European Journal of Political Economy* 25 (1): 1–14.

Aidt, Toke S. 2003. Economic Analysis of Corruption: A Survey. *Economic Journal* 113 (November): 632–52.

———. 2009. Corruption, Institutions, and Economic Development. *Oxford Review of Economic Policy* 25 (2): 271–91.

Alber, Jens. 1984. Government Responses to Challenges of Unemployment. In *The Development of Welfare States in Europe and America*, edited by P. Flora. New Brunswick, NJ: Transaction Books.

———. 2006. Das "Europäische Sozialmodell" und die USA *Leviathan. Berliner Zeitschrift für Sozialwissenschaft* 34 (2): 207–40.

Alence, Rod. 2004. Political Institutions and Developmental Governance in Sub-Saharan Africa. *Journal of Modern African Studies* 42 (2): 163–87.

Alesina, Alberto, and George-Marios Angeletos. 2005. Corruption, Inequality, and Fairness. *Journal of Monetary Economics* 52 (7): 1227–44.

Algan, Yann. 2009. Institutions and Economic Performance. *Economic Journal* 119 (541): 536–41.

Allan, James P., and Lyle Scruggs. 2004. Political Partisanship and Welfare State Reform in Advanced Industrial Societies. *American Journal of Political Science* 48 (3): 496–512.

Alt, James E., and David Dreyer Lassen. 2003. The Political Economy of Institutions and Corruption in American States. *Journal of Theoretical Politics* 15 (3): 341–65.

Anbarci, Nejat, Monica Escaleras, and Charles A. Register. 2009. The Ill Effects of Public Sector Corruption in the Water and Sanitation Sector. *Land Economics* 85 (2): 363–77.

Andersen, Elizabeth S. 1999. What Is the Point of Equality? *Ethics* 109 (2): 287–337.

Anderson, Christopher J., and Yuliya V. Tverdova. 2003. Corruption, Political Allegiances, and Attitudes toward Government in Contemporary Democracies. *American Journal of Political Science* 47 (1): 91–109.

Andrews, Matt. 2008. The Good Governance Agenda: Beyond Indicators without Theory. *Oxford Development Studies* 36 (4): 379–407.

Angell, Marcia. 2009. Drug Companies and Doctors: A Story of Corruption. *New York Review of Books*, February 11.

Arimah, Ben. 2004. Poverty Reduction and Human Development in Africa. *Journal of Human Development* 5 (3): 399–415.

Armingeon, Klaus, Marlène Gerber, Philipp Leimgruber, and Michelle Beyler. 2008. Comparative Political Data Set 1960–2006: Institute of Political Science, University of Berne.

Armony, Ariel C. 2004. *The Dubious Link: Civic Engagement and Democratization*. Stanford, CA: Stanford University Press.

Arneson, Richard. 1998. The Priority of the Right over the Good Rides Again.

In *Impartiality, Neutrality and Justice*, edited by P. Kelly. Edinburgh: Edinburgh University Press.

Arnold, Peri E. 2003. Democracy and Corruption in the 19th Century United States. In *History of Corruption in Central Government*, edited by S. Tiihonen. Amsterdam: IOS Press.

Aronson, Elliot, Timothy D. Wilson, and Marilyn B. Brewer. 1998. Experimentation in Social Psychology. In *Handbook of Social Psychology*. 4th ed., edited by D. T. Gilbert, S. T. Fiske, and G. Lindzey. New York: McGraw-Hill.

Aumann, Robert J., and Jacques H. Dreze. 2005. When All Is Said and Done: How Should You Play and What Should You Expect? Discussion Paper 387, March. Jerusalem: Center for the Study of Rationality, Hebrew University.

Baldacci, Emanuele, Benedict Clements, Sanjev Gupta, and Qiang Cui. 2008. Social Spending, Human Capital, and Growth in Developing Countries. *World Development* 36 (8): 1317–41.

Banerjee, Abhijit, Rohini Somanathan, and Lakshmi Iyer. 2005. History, Social Divisions and Public Goods in Rural India. *Journal of the European Economic Association* 3 (2/3): 639–47.

Bano, Masooda. 2008. Dangerous Correlations: Aid's Impact on NGOs' Performance and Ability to Mobilize Members in Pakistan. *World Development* 36 (11): 2297–2313.

Bardhan, Pranab. 1997. Corruption and Development: A Review of the Issues. *Journal of Economic Literature* 35 (3): 1320–46.

Barr, Nicholas. 2004. *The Economics of the Welfare State*. 4th ed. Oxford: Oxford University Press.

Barrett, Scott, and Kathryn Graddy. 2000. Freedom, Growth, and the Environment. *Environment and Development Economics* 5 (4): 433–56.

Barry, Brian. 1995. *Justice as Impartiality*. Oxford: Oxford University Press.

——. 1998. Something in the Disputation Not Unpleasant. In *Impartiality, Neutrality and Justice*, edited by P. Kelly. Edinburgh: Edinburgh University Press.

Bates, Robert H. 2008. *When Things Fell Apart: State Failure in Late Century Africa*. New York: Cambridge University Press.

Bayliss, Kate. 2003. Utility Privatisation in Sub-Saharan Africa: A Case Study of Water. *Journal of Modern African Studies* 41 (4): 507–31.

Bebbington, Anthony, Scott Guggenheim, Elizabeth Olson, and Michael Woolcock. 2004. Exploring Social Capital Debates at the World Bank. *Journal of Development Studies* 40 (5): 32–62.

Beetham, David. 1991. *The Legitimation of Power*. Basingstoke, UK: Macmillan.

Beevor, Antony. 2006. *The Battle for Spain: The Spanish Civil War, 1936–1939*. London: Weidenfeld and Nicolson.

Bendor, Jonatan, and Piotr Swistak. 2004. The Rational Foundation of Social Institutions. In *Politics from Anarchy to Democracy*, edited by I. L. Morris, J. A. Oppenheimer, and K. E. Soltan. Stanford, CA: Stanford University Press.

Bengtsson, Åsa, and Kimmo Grönlund, eds. 2005. *Den Finlandssvenska Väljaren*. Åbo: Åbo Akademi, Institutet för Finlandssvensk Samhällsforskning.

Bennett, Christopher. 1995. *Yugoslavia's Bloody Collapse: Causes, Course and Consequences*. London: Hurst.

Berman, Sheri. 1997. Civil Society and the Collapse of the Weimar Republic. *World Politics* 49 (3): 401–29.

——. 2007. How Democracies Emerge: Lessons from Europe. *Journal of Democracy* 18 (1): 28–41.

Besley, Timothy, and Maitreesh Ghatak. 2007. Reforming Public Service Delivery. *Journal of African Economies* 16 (suppl. 1): 127–56.

Besley, Timothy, and Masayuki Kudamatsu. 2006. Health and Democracy. *American Economic Review* 96 (2): 313–18.

Bigsten, Arne, and Augustin K. Fosu. 2004. Growth and Poverty in Africa: An Overview. *Journal of African Economies* 13 (suppl. 1): 1–15.

Bjørnskov, Christian. 2004. Social Capital, Political Competition, and Corruption. Aarhus, Denmark: Aarhus School of Business, Aarhus University.

Blaydes, Lisa, and Mark Kayser. 2007. *Counting Calories: Democracy and Distribution in the Developing World*. Paper presented at the annual meeting of the American Political Science Association, Chicago, 2007.

Block, Fred. 2007. Understanding the Diverging Trajectories of the United States and Western Europe: A Neo-Polanyian Analysis. *Politics and Society* 35 (1): 3–33.

Blomkvist, Hans. 2001. Stat och Förvaltning i U-länder. In *Politik som Organisation, 3rd ed.*, edited by B. Rothstein. Stockholm: SNS.

Bloom, David. E., and David Canning. 2000. The Health and Wealth of Nations. *Science* 287 (5456): 1207–9.

Böhringer, Cristoph, and Patrick E. P. Jochem. 2007. Measuring the Immeasurable—a Survey of Sustainability Indices. *Ecological Economics* 63 (1): 1–8.

Boix, Charles, and Daniel N. Posner. 1998. Social Capital: Explaining Its Origins and Effects on Government Performance. *British Journal of Political Science* 28 (4): 686–93.

Bouckaert, Geert, and Steven van de Walle. 2003. Comparing Measures of Citizen Trust and User Satisfaction as Indicators of "Good Governance": Difficulties in Linking Trust and Satisfaction Indicators. *International Review of Administrative Sciences* 69 (3): 329–43.

Brady, Anne-Mary. 2009. Mass Persuasion as a Means of Legitimation and China's Popular Authoritarianism. *American Behavioral Scientist* 53 (3): 434–57.

Brady, Henry E., and David Collier, eds. 2004. *Rethinking Social Inquiry*. Lanham, UK: Rowman and Littlefield.

Braithwaite, Valerie, and Margaret Levi, eds. 1998. *Trust and Governance*. New York: Russell Sage Foundation.

Brand, Donald. 1988. *Corporatism and the Rule of Law*. Ithaca, NY: Cornell University Press.

Bratton, Michael, and Eric C. C. Chang. 2006. State Building and Democratization in Sub-Saharan Africa—Forwards, Backwards, or Together? *Comparative Political Studies* 39 (9): 1059–83.

Bräutigam, Deborah, Odd-Helge Fjeldstad, and Mick Moore. 2008. *Taxation and State-Building in Developing Countries: Capacity and Consent*. Cambridge: Cambridge University Press.

Brehm, John, and Wendy Rahn. 1997. Individual-Level Evidence for the Causes and Consequences of Social Capital. *American Journal of Political Science* 41 (3): 999–1023.

Broadman, Harry G., and Francisca Recanatini. 2001. Seeds of Corruption: Do Market Institutions Matter? *Moct-Most* 11 (4): 359–92.

Brown, Vivienne. 1994. *Adam Smith's Discourse*. London: Routledge.

Bruns, Bryan Randolph, and Ruth S. Meinzen-Dick. 2000. *Negotiating Water Rights*. London: Intermediate Technology.

Buchanan, Allen. 2002. Political Legitimacy and Democracy. *Ethics* 112 (4): 689–719.

Bukovansky, Mlada. 2006. The Hollowness of Anti-corruption Discourse. *Review of International Political Economy* 13 (2): 181–209.

Carnes, Matthew E., and Isabela Mares. 2007. The Welfare State in Global Perspective. In *The Oxford Handbook of Comparative Politics*, edited by C. Boix and S. Stokes. Oxford: Oxford University Press.

Carothers, Thomas. 2007. How Democracies Emerge: The "Sequencing" Fallacy. *Journal of Democracy* 18 (1): 12–28.

Chapman, Richard A., and J. R. Greenaway. 1980. *The Dynamics of Administrative Reform*. London: Croom Helm.

Charron, Nicholas, and Victor Lapuente. 2010. Does Democracy Produce Quality of Government? *European Journal of Political Research* (forthcoming).

Chetwynd Eric, Frances Chetwynd, and Bertram Spector. 2003. Corruption and Poverty: A Review of Recent Literature. Washington, DC: Management Systems International.

Choe, Yonhyok. 1997. *How to Manage Free and Fair Elections: A Comparison of Korea, Sweden and the United Kingdom*. Gothenburg: Department of Political Science, Gothenburg University.

Chong, Alberto, and César Calderón. 2000. Institutional Quality and Poverty Measures in a Cross-Section of Countries. *Economics of Governance* 1 (2): 123–35.

Chong, Alberto, and Mark Gradstein. 2004. Inequality and Institutions. Research Department Working Paper 506. Inter-American Development Bank, New York.

Christiansen, Peter Munk, and Lise Togeby. 2006. Power and Democracy in Denmark: Still a Viable Democracy. *Scandinavian Political Studies* 29 (1): 1–24.

Chung, Haejoo, and Carles Muntaner. 2006. Political and Welfare State Determinants of Infant and Child Health Indicators: An Analysis of Wealthy Countries. *Social Science and Medicine* 63 (3): 829–42.

Clague, Christopher, Philip Keefer, Stephen Knack, and Mancur Olson. 1999. Contract-Intensive Money: Contract Enforcement, Property Rights, and Economic Performance. *Journal of Economic Growth* 4 (2): 185–211.

Claiborn, Michele P., and Paul S. Martin. 2000. Trusting and Joining? An Empirical Test of the Reciprocal Nature of Social Capital. *Political Behavior* 22 (4): 267–91.

Cockcroft Anne, Neil Andersson, Sergio Paredes-Solis, Dawn Caldwell, Steve Mitchell, Deborah Milne, Serge Merhi, Melissa Roche, Elena Konceviciute, and Robert J. Ledogar. 2008. An Inter-country Comparison of Unofficial Payments: Results of a Health Sector Social Audit in the Baltic States. *BMC Health Services Research* 8 (15): 1–12.

Coleman, James S. 1990. *Foundations of Social Theory.* Cambridge, MA: Harvard University Press.

Collier, Michael W. 2009. *Political Corruption in the Caribbean Basin.* London: Routledge.

Collier, Paul. 2007. *The Bottom Billion: Why the Poorest Countries Are Failing and What Can Be Done about It.* Oxford: Oxford University Press.

Cook, Karen S., ed. 2001. *Trust in Society.* New York: Russell Sage Foundation.

Cook, Karen S., Russell Hardin, and Margaret Levi. 2005. *Cooperation without Trust?* Russell Sage Foundation Series on Trust 9. New York: Russell Sage Foundation.

Costa, Antonio Maria. 2008. Rule of Law: A (Missing) Millennium Development Goal That Can Help Reach the Other MDGs. United Nations Commission on Crime Prevention and Criminal Justice, 17th Session, Vienna, April 14.

Cowen, Tyler, ed. 1988. *The Theory of Market Failure.* Fairfax, VA: George Mason University Press.

Csepeli, György, Antal Örkéney, Maria Székelyi, and Ildikó Barna. 2004. Blindness to Success: Social Psychological Objectives along the Way to a Market Economy in Eastern Europe. In *Creating Social Trust in Post-socialist Transition,* edited by János Kornai, Bo Rothstein, and Susan Rose-Ackerman. New York: Palgrave Macmillan.

Cunningham, William P., and Mary Ann Cunningham. 2008. *Environmental Science: A Global Concern.* 10th ed. Boston: McGraw-Hill Higher Education.

Cupit, Geoffrey. 2000. When Does Justice Require Impartiality? Political Studies Association–UK 50th Annual Conference, London, April 10–13.

Dahl, Robert A. 1989. *Democracy and Its Critics.* New Haven, CT: Yale University Press.

——. 2006. *On Political Equality.* New Haven, CT: Yale University Press.

Damania, Richard, Per G. Fredriksson, and John A. List. 2003. Trade Liberalization, Corruption, and Environmental Policy Formation: Theory and Evidence. *Journal of Environmental Economics and Management* 46 (3): 490–512.

Danchev, Alex. 1999. Liddell Hart's Big Idea. *Review of International Studies* 25 (1): 29–48.

Darwall, Stephen. 1999. Sympathetic Liberalism: Recent Work on Adam Smith. *Philosophy and Public Affairs* 28 (2): 139–64.

Davenport, Christian, and David A. Armstrong II. 2004. Democracy and the Violation of Human Rights: A Statistical Analysis from 1976 to 1996. *American Journal of Political Science* 48 (3): 538–54.

Davis, Jennifer. 2004. Corruption in Public Service Delivery: Experience from South Asia's Water and Sanitation Sector. *World Development* 32 (1): 53–71.

Davis, Natalie Zemon. 2000. *The Gift in Sixteenth-Century France.* Madison: University of Wisconsin Press.

Dawes, Robin M., and David M. Messick. 2000. Social Dilemmas. *International Journal of Psychology* 35 (2): 111–16.

de Cremer, David, Tom R. Tyler, and Nathalie den Ouden. 2005. Managing Cooperation via Procedural Fairness: The Mediating Influence of Self-Other Merging. *Journal of Economic Psychology* 26 (3): 393–406.

Deininger, Klaus, and Paul Mpuga. 2005. Does Greater Accountability Improve the Quality of Public Service Delivery? Evidence from Uganda. *World Development* 33 (1): 71–191.

de Jasay, Anthony. 1996. Justice as Something Else. *Cato Journal* 16 (2): 161–74.

Delhey, Jan, and Kenneth Newton. 2003. Who Trusts? The Origins of Social Trust in Seven Societies. *European Societies* 5 (2): 93–137.

——. 2004. *Social Trust: Global Pattern or Nordic Exceptionalism?* Berlin: Wissenschaftszentrum Berlin für Socialforschung.

——. 2005. Predicting Cross-National Levels of Social Trust: Global Pattern or Nordic Exceptionalism? *European Sociological Review* 21 (4): 311–27.

Della Porta, Donatella, and Alberto Vannucci. 1999. *Corrupt Exchanges: Actors, Resources, and Mechanisms of Political Corruption.* New York: Aldine de Gruyter.

——. 2007. Corruption and Anti-corruption: The Political Defeat of "Clean Hands" in Italy. *West European Politics* 30 (4): 830–53.

Demokratiutredningen. 2000. *En uthållig demokrati! Politik för folkstyrelse på 2000-talet: Demokratiutredningens betänkande, Statens offentliga utredningar, 2000:1.* Stockholm: Fritzes Offentliga Publikationer.

Denzau, Arthur T., and Douglas C. North. 1994. Shared Mental Models: Ideologies and Institutions. *Kyklos* 47 (1): 3–31.

de Soto, Hernando. 2000. *The Mystery of Capital: Why Capitalism Triumphs in the West and Fails Everywhere Else*. London: Black Swan.

de Sousa, Luís. 2008. "I Don't Bribe, I Just Pull Strings." Assessing the Fluidity of Social Representations of Corruption in Portuguese Society. *Perspectives on European Politics and Society* 9 (1): 8–23.

Devarajan, Shantayanan, and Ritva Reinikka. 2004. Making Services Work for the Poor. *Journal of African Economies* 13 (suppl. 1): 142–66.

Diamond, Larry. 1999. *Developing Democracy: Toward Consolidation*. Baltimore, MD: Johns Hopkins University Press.

———. 2007. A Quarter-Century of Promoting Democracy. *Journal of Democracy* 18 (4): 118–20.

———. 2008. The Democratic Rollback: The Resurgence of the Predatory State. *Foreign Affairs* 87 (2): 36–48.

Dinesen, Peter Thisted. 2006. *Social Tillid, Civilsamfund og Institutioner—en Empirisk Analyse af Årsager til Social Tillid i Europa*. Aarhus, Denmark: Department of Political Science, Aarhus University.

Di Tella, Rafael, and Robert MacCulloch. 2007. Gross National Happiness as an Answer to the Easterlin Paradox? *Journal of Development Economics* 86 (1): 22–42.

Djankov, Simeon, Rafael La Porta, Florencio Lopez-de-Silanes, and Andrei Shleifer. 2002. The Regulation of Entry. *Quarterly Journal of Economics* 117 (1): 1–37.

Dobbin, Frank. 2004. *The Sociology of the Economy*. New York: Russell Sage Foundation.

Doces, John A., and Gregory S. Sanjian. 2009. Achieving the U.N.'s MDGs. Corruption, Human Development, and Child Mortality. Paper presented at the Annual Meeting of the American Political Science Association, Montreal, September 2–6.

Dogan, Mattei. 2005. Erosion of Confidence in Thirty European Democracies. In *Political Mistrust and the Discrediting of Politicians*, edited by M. Dogan. Leiden: Brill.

Doig, Alan, David Watt, and Robert Williams. 2007. Why Do Developing Country Anti-corruption Commissions Fail to Deal with Corruption? Understanding the Three Dilemmas of Organisational Development, Performance Expectation, and Donor and Government Cycles. *Public Administration and Development* 27 (3): 251–59.

Donahue, John D. 1989. *The Privatization Decision: Public Ends, Private Means*. New York: Basic Books.

Dowding, Keith, Robert E. Goodin, and Carole Pateman, eds. 2004. *Justice and Democracy*. Cambridge: Cambridge University Press.

Dryzek, John S., Anne Phillips, and Bonnie Honig. 2006. *The Oxford Handbook of Political Theory*. Oxford: Oxford University Press.

du Gay, Paul. 2000. *In Praise of Bureaucracy: Weber, Organization and Ethics*. London: Sage.

Dugger, Celia W. 2005. Where a Cuddle with Your Baby Requires a Bribe. *New York Times*, August 30, 2005.

Dunleavy, Patrick. 1991. *Democracy, Bureaucracy and Public Choice: Economic Explanations in Political Science*. New York: Harvester Wheatsheaf.

Dworkin, Ronald. 1977. *Taking Rights Seriously*. London: Duckworth.

Dyck, Joshua J. 2009. Initiated Distrust: Direct Democracy and Trust in Government. *American Politics Research* 37 (4): 539–68.

Easterly, William. 2001. *The Elusive Quest for Growth: Economists' Adventures and Misadventures in the Tropics*. Cambridge, MA: MIT Press.

Easterly, William, and Ross Levine. 2003. Tropics, Germs, and Crops: How Endowments Influence Economic Development. *Journal of Monetary Economics* 50:3–39.

Easterly, William, Jozef Ritzan, and Michael Woolcock. 2006. Social Cohesion, Institutions, and Growth. Working Paper 94. Center for Global Development, Washington, DC.

Economics and the Rule of Law: Order in the Jungle. 2008. *Economist*, March 13.

Edén, Nils, Lennart Berglöf, and Erik Schalling. 1941. *Kammarkollegiets Historia*. Stockholm: Isaac Marcus.

Edie, Carlene J. 1992. *Democracy by Default: Dependency and Clientelism in Jamaica*. Boulder, CO: Lynne Rienner.

Eggertsson, Thráinn. 2005. *Imperfect Institutions: Possibilities and Limits of Reform*. Ann Arbor: University of Michigan Press.

Ellerman, David P. 1992. *Property and Contract in Economics: The Case for Economic Democracy*. Oxford: Blackwell.

Elliott, Dawn. R., and Ransford W. Palmer. 2008. Institutions and Caribbean Economic Performance: Insights from Jamaica. *Studies in Comparative International Development* 43 (2): 181–205.

Elster, Jon. 1989. *The Cement of Society*. Cambridge University Press: Cambridge.

———. 1991. Rationality and Social Norms. *Archives Europennées de Sociologie* 31:233–56.

Encarnación, Omar G. 2003. *The Myth of Civil Society: Social Capital and Democratic Consolidation in Spain and Brazil*. New York: Palgrave Macmillan.

Esaiasson, Peter. 2003. Vad Menas med Folkviljans Förverkligande? In *Demokratins mekanismer*, edited by M. Gilljam and J. Hermansson. Lund: Liber.

———. 2007. Electoral Losers Revisited—Is There Really a Winner-Loser Gap? Paper presented at the annual meeting of the American Political Science Association, Chicago, August 30-September 2.

Esaiasson, Peter, and Sören Holmberg. 1996. *Representation from Above: Members of Parliament and Representative Democracy in Sweden*. Brookfield, VT: Dartmouth.

Esping-Andersen, Gøsta. 1990. *The Three Worlds of Welfare Capitalism*. Cambridge: Polity Press.

Estevez-Abe, Margarita, Torben Iversen, and David Soskice. 2001. Social Protection and the Formation of Skills: A Reinterpretation of the Welfare State. In *Varieties of Capitalism: The Institutional Foundations of Comparative Advantage*, edited by P. A. Hall and D. Soskice. Oxford: Oxford University Press.

Esty, Daniel C., and Michael E. Porter. 2005. National Environmental Performance: An Empirical Analysis of Policy Results and Determinants. *Environment and Development Economics* 10 (4): 391–434.

European Commission for Employment and Social Affairs. 2003. Social Protection in the Thirteen Candidate Countries: A Comparative Analysis, Luxembourg: European Commission Directorate-General for Employment and Social Affairs Unit E.2.

Evans, Peter B. 2005. Harnessing the State: Rebalancing Strategies for Monitoring and Motivation. In *States and Development*, edited by M. Lange and D. Rueschemeyer. New York: Palgrave Macmillan.

———. 2009. Population Health and Development: An Institutional-Cultural Approach to Capability Expansion. In *Successful Societies: How Institutions and Culture Affect Health*, edited by P. A. Hall and M. Lamont. New York: Cambridge University Press.

Evans, Peter B., and James E. Rauch. 1999. Bureaucracy and Growth: A Cross-National Analysis of the Effects of "Weberian" State Structures on Economic Growth. *American Sociological Review* 64 (5): 748–65.

———. 2000. Bureaucratic Structure and Bureaucratic Performance in Less Developed Countries. *Journal of Public Economics* 75 (1): 49–71.

Ewers, Robert M., and Robert J. Smith. 2007. Choice of Index Determines the Relationship between Corruption and Environmental Sustainability. *Ecology and Society* 12 (1): r2.

Falaschetti, Dino, and Gary Miller. 2001. Constraining the Leviathan: Moral Hazard and Credible Commitment in Constitutional Design. *Journal of Theoretical Politics* 13 (4): 389–411.

Fallend, Franz. 1997. The Crisis of the Proporz Governments: Current Political Debates about the Constitutional System of Government in the Austrian Provinces. *Österreichische Zeitschrift für Politikwissenschaft* 26 (1): 23–40.

Farrell, Henry, and Jack Knight. 2003. Trust, Institutions, and Institutional Change: Industrial Districts and the Social Capital Hypothesis. *Politics and Society* 31 (4): 537–66.

Fearon, James D., and David D. Laitin. 2003. Ethnicity, Insurgency, and Civil War. *American Political Science Review* 97 (1): 75–90.

Fedderke Johannes, Klitgaard Robert. 2006. Economic Growth and Social Indicators: An Exploratory Analysis. *Journal of Comparative Policy Analysis* 8 (3): 283–303.

Fehr, Ernst, and Urs Fischbacher. 2005. The Economics of Strong Reciprocity. In *Moral Sentiments and Material Interests: The Foundations for Cooperation in Economic Life*, edited by H. Gintis, S. Bowles, R. Boyd, and E. Fehr. Cambridge, MA: MIT Press.

Fligstein, Neil, and Luke Dauter. 2007. The Sociology of Markets. *Annual Review of Sociology* 33 (1): 105–28.

Forbarth, William E. 1989. *Law and the Shaping of the American Labor Movement*. Cambridge, MA: Harvard University Press.

Fredriksson Per G., and Muthukumara Mani. 2002. *The Rule of Law and the Pattern of Environmental Protection*. IMF Working Paper 02/49. Washington, DC: International Monetary Fund.

Fredriksson, Per G., and Jim R. Wollscheid. 2007. Democratic Institutions versus Autocratic Regimes: The Case of Environmental Policy. *Public Choice* 130 (3–4): 381–93.

Frey, Bruno S., and Alois Stutzer. 2000. Happiness, Economy and Institutions. *Economic Journal* 110 (466): 918–38.

Frisk Jensen, Mette. 2008. *Korruption og Embedsetik: Danske Embedsmænds Korruption i Perioden 1800 til 1886*. Aalborg, Denmark: Aalborg Universitet.

Fritzell, Johan, and Olle Lundberg. 2007. *Health Inequalities and Welfare Resources: Continuity and Change in Sweden*. Bristol, UK: Policy Press.

Frohlich, Norman, and Joe A. Oppenheimer. 2006. Skating on Thin Ice—Cracks in the Public Choice Foundation. *Journal of Theoretical Politics* 18 (3): 235–66.

Frohnert, Per. 1993. *Kronans Skatter och Bondens Bröd: Den Lokala Förvaltningen och Bönderna i Sverige, 1719–1775*. Lund: Rättshistoriskt Bibliotek.

Frum, David, and Richard Norman Perle. 2003. *An End to Evil: How to Win the War on Terror*. New York: Random House.

Fukuyama, Francis. 1995. *Trust: The Social Virtues and the Creation of Prosperity*. New York: Free Press.

Gagnon, Valère P. 2004. *The Myth of Ethnic War: Serbia and Croatia in the 1990s*. Ithaca, NY: Cornell University Press.

Gambetta, Diego. 1993. *The Sicilian Mafia: The Business of Private Protection*. Cambridge, MA: Harvard University Press.

George, Alexander L. 1979. Case Studies and Theory Development: The Method of Structured, Focused Comparisons. In *Diplomacy: New Approaches in History, Theory and Policy*, edited by P. G. Lauren. New York: Free Press.

Gerring, John. 2007. *Case Study Research: Principles and Practices*. New York: Cambridge University Press.

Gerring, John, and Strom C. Thacker. 2005. Do Neoliberal Policies Deter Political Corruption? *International Organization* 59 (1): 233–54.

Gerring, John, Strom C. Thacker, and Rodrigo Alfaro. 2005. Democracy and Human Development. Paper presented at the annual meeting of the American Political Science Association, Washington, DC, September 1–4.

Gerring, John, and Joshua Ysenowitz. 2006. A Normative Turn in Political Science. *Polity* 38 (1): 101–33.

Ghobarah, Hazem A., Paul Huth, and Bruce Russett. 2004. Comparative Public Health: The Political Economy of Human Misery and Well-Being. *International Studies Quarterly* 48 (1): 73–94.

Gierow, Krister. 1971. *Lunds Universitets Historia, 1790–1867*. Lund: Gleerup.

Gilens, Martin. 1999. *Why Americans Hate Welfare: Race, Media, and the Politics of Antipoverty Policy*. Chicago: University of Chicago Press.

Gilley, Bruce. 2006. The Determinants of State Legitimacy: Results for Seventy-two Countries. *International Political Science Review* 27 (1): 47–71.

Gintis, Herbert, Samuel Bowles, Robert Boyd, and Ernst Fehr, eds. 2005. *Moral Sentiments and Material Interests: The Foundations for Cooperation in Economic Life*. Cambridge, MA: MIT Press.

Glaeser, Edward L., Rafael La Porta, Florencio Lopez-de-Silanes, and Andrei Shleifer. 2004. Do Institutions Cause Growth? *Journal of Economic Growth* 9 (3): 271–303.

Glaeser, Edward L., Jose Scheinkman, and Andrei Shleifer. 2003. The Injustice of Inequality. *Journal of Monetary Economics* 50 (1): 199–222.

Golden, Miriam A. 2003. Electoral Connections: The Effects of the Personal Vote on Political Patronage, Bureaucracy and Legislation in Postwar Italy. *British Journal of Political Science* 33 (2): 189–212.

Goldsmith, Arthur A. 2007. Is Governance Reform a Catalyst for Development? *Governance—an International Journal of Policy and Administration* 20 (2): 165–86.

Goodin, Robert E. 2004. Democracy, Justice and Impartiality. In *Justice and Democracy*, edited by K. Dowding, R. E. Goodin, and C. Pateman. Cambridge: Cambridge University Press.

Goodwin-Gill, Guy S. 2006. *Free and Fair Elections*. Geneva: Inter-Parliamentary Union.

Goudie, Andrew W., and David Stasavage. 1998. A Framework for the Analysis of Corruption. *Crime, Law and Social Change* 29 (4): 113–59.

Gow, James. 2003. *The Serbian Project and Its Adversaries: A Strategy of War Crimes*. London: Hurst.

Greif, Avner. 2005. Institutions and the Path to the Modern Economy: Lessons from Medieval Trade. In *Handbook of Institutional Economics*, edited by C. Ménard and M. M. Shirley. Amsterdam: Springer.

Griffith, Winston H. 1987. Can Caricom Countries Replicate the Singapore Experience? *Journal of Development Studies* 24 (1): 60–82.

Grimes, Marcia. 2006. Organizing Consent: The Role of Procedural Fairness in Political Trust and Compliance. *European Journal of Political Research* 45 (2): 285–315.

Grindle, Marilyn S. 2004. Good Enough Governance: Poverty Reduction and Reform in Developing Countries. *Governance—an International Journal of Policy and Administration* 17 (4): 525–48.

Griswold, Charles L., Jr. 1999. *Adam Smith and the Virtues of Enlightenment.* New York: Cambridge University Press.

Gupta, Sanjeev, Hamid R. Davoodi, and Rosa Alonso-Terme. 1998. Does Corruption Affect Income Inequality and Poverty? Working Paper 98/76, International Monetary Fund. Washington, DC.

Gupta, Sanjeev, Hamid R. Davoodi, and Erwin R. Tiongson. 2000. Corruption and the Provision of Health Care and Education Services. Working Paper 00/116, International Monetary Fund, Washington, DC.

Habyarimana, James, Macartan Humphreys, Daniel N. Posner, and Jeremy M. Weinstein. 2006. *Why Does Ethnic Diversity Undermine Public Goods Provision?* Washington, DC: Center for Global Development.

Hacker, Jacob S. 2004. Privatizing Risk without Privatizing the Welfare State: The Hidden Politics of Social Policy Retrenchment in the United States. *American Political Science Review* 98 (2): 243–60.

Hadenius, Axel, and Jan Teorell. 2005. Assessing Alternative Indices of Democracy. Concepts and Methods Working Papers 6, International Political Science Association.

——. 2007. Pathways from Authoritarianism. *Journal of Democracy* 18 (1): 143–56.

Hage, Jerald, and Barbara Foley Meeker. 1988. *Social Causality.* Boston: Unwin and Hyman.

Hall, Peter A. 1986. *Governing the Economy: The Politics of State Intervention in Britain and France.* New York: Oxford University Press.

——. 2003. Aligning Ontology and Methodology in Comparative Politics. In *Comparative Historical Analysis in the Social Sciences,* edited by J. Mahoney and D. Rueschemeyer. New York: Cambridge University Press.

Hall, Peter A., and Michèle Lamont, eds. 2009. *Successful Societies: How Institutions and Culture Affect Health.* New York: Cambridge University Press.

Hall, Peter A., and David Soskice, eds. 2001. *Varieties of Capitalism: The Institutional Foundations of Comparative Advantage.* Oxford: Oxford University Press.

Hall, Peter A., and Rosemary C. R. Taylor. 2009. Health, Social Relations, and Public Policy. In *Successful Societies: How Institutions and Culture Affect*

Health, edited by P. A. Hall and M. Lamont. New York: Cambridge University Press.

Hall, Peter A., and Kathleen Thelen. 2009. Institutional Change in Varieties of Capitalism. *Socio-economic Review* 7 (1): 7–34.

Hall, Robert E., and Charles I. Jones. 1999. Why Do Some Countries Produce So Much More Output per Worker Than Others? *Quarterly Journal of Economics* 114 (1): 83–116.

Halperin, Morton H., Joseph T. Siegle, and Michael M. Weinstein. 2004. *The Democracy Advantage: How Democracies Promote Prosperity and Peace.* New York: Routledge.

Hanousek, Jan, and Filip Palda. 2004. Quality of Government Services and the Civic Duty to Pay Taxes in the Czech and Slovak Republics, and Other Transition Countries. *Kyklos* 57 (2): 237–52.

Hardin, Russell. 1995. *One for All: The Logic of Group Conflict.* Princeton, NJ: Princeton University Press.

——. 1998. Reasonable Agreement: Political Not Normative. In *Impartiality, Neutrality and Justice*, edited by P. Kelly. Edinburgh: Edinburgh University Press.

——. 2002. *Trust and Trustworthiness.* New York: Russell Sage Foundation.

Harling, Philip. 1996. *The Waning of "Old Corruption." The Politics of Economical Reform in Britain, 1779–1846.* Oxford: Clarendon Press.

Harriot, Anthony. 2008. *Organized Crime and Politics in Jamaica.* Kingston: Canoe Press.

Hattam, Victoria Charlotte. 1993. *Labor Visions and State Power: The Origins of Business Unionism in the United States, Princeton Studies in American Politics.* Princeton, NJ: Princeton University Press.

Hechter, Michael. 1992. The Insufficiency of Game Theory for the Resolution of Real-World Collective Action Problems. *Rationality and Society* 4 (1): 33–40.

Heckscher, Gunnar. 1952. *Svensk Statsförvaltning i Arbete.* Stockholm: Norstedt.

Hedlund, Stefan. 1999. *Russia's "Market" Economy: A Bad Case of Predatory Capitalism.* London: UCL Press.

Heidenheimer, Arnold J. 2002. Perspectives on the Perception of Corruption. In *Political Corruption—Concepts and Contexts*, edited by A. J. Heidenheimer and M. Johnston. London: Transaction.

Heinisch, Reinhard. 2002. *Populism, Proporz, Parian: Austria Turns to the Right.* New York: Nova Scotia.

Helliwell, John F. 2006. Well-Being, Social Capital and Public Policy: What's New? *Economic Journal* 116 (510): C34-C45.

Helliwell, John F., and Haifaing F. Huang. 2008. How's Your Government? International Evidence Linking Good Government and Well-Being. *British Journal of Political Science* 38 (4): 595–619.

Helpman, Elhanan, ed. 2008. *Institutions and Economic Performance*. Cambridge, MA: Harvard University Press.

Henrich, Joseph, Jean Ensminger, Richard McElreath, Abigail Barr, Clark Barrett, Alexander Bolyanatz, Juan C. Cardenas, Michael Gurven, Edwins Gwako, Natalie Henrich, Carolyn Lesorogol, Frank Marlowe, David Tracer, and John Ziker. 2010. Markets, Religion, Community Size, and the Evolution of Fairness and Punishment. *Science* 327 (5972): 1480–84.

Herreros, Francisco. 2004. *The Problem of Forming Social Capital: Why Trust?* New York: Palgrave Macmillan.

Heston, Alan, Robert Summers, and Bettina Aten. 2002. Penn World Table, version 6.1. Center for International Comparisons at the University of Pennsylvania (CICUP).

Hildebrand, Emil. 1896. *Svenska Statsförfattningens Historiska Utveckling från Äldsta Tid till Våra Dagar*. Stockholm: Norstedts.

Hodess, Robin, Jessie Banfield, and Toby Wolfe. 2001. *Global Corruption Report 2001*. Berlin: Transparency International.

Hoffman, Curt, and Nancy Hurst. 1990. Gender Stereotypes: Perception or Rationalization? *Journal of Personality and Social Psychology* 58 (2): 197–208.

Holmberg, Sören. 1999a. Collective Policy Congruence. In *Policy Representation in Western Democracies*, edited by W. Miller. Oxford: Oxford University Press.

——. 1999b. Down and Down We Go: Political Trust in Sweden. In *Critical Citizens*, edited by P. Norris. Oxford: Oxford University Press.

——. 1999c. *Representativ Demokrati*. Stockholm: Demokratiutredningen.

——. 2000. *Välja parti*. Stockholm: Norstedts.

——. 2007. The Good Society Index. Working paper 2007:6. Quality of Government Institute, University of Gothenburg.

Holmberg, Sören, Bo Rothstein, and Naghmeh Nasiritousi. 2009. Quality of Government: What You Get. *Annual Review of Political Science* 12 (1): 135–61.

Holmberg, Sören, and Lennart Weibull. 2007. Ökat Förtroende—Bara en Valårseffekt. In *Det Nya Sverige. SOM-undersökningen 2006*, edited by S. Holmberg and L. Weibull. Gothenburg: SOM-Institute, University of Gothenburg.

Hooghe, Marc, and Dietlind Stolle, eds. 2003. *Generating Social Capital: Civil Society and Institutions in a Comparative Perspective*. New York: Palgrave Macmillan.

Hopkin, Jonathan, and Andrés Rodríguez-Pose. 2007. "Grabbing Hand" or "Helping Hand"? Corruption and the Economic Role of the State. *Governance—an International Journal of Policy and Administration* 20 (2): 187–205.

Huber, Evelyne, Charles Ragin, John D. Stephens, Donald Brady, and Jason Beckfield. 2004. Comparative Welfare State Data Set 2004. Northwestern University and University of North Carolina.

Huber, Evelyne, and John D. Stephens. 2001. *Development and Crisis of the Welfare State*. Chicago: University of Chicago Press.

Huther, Jeff, and Anwar Shah. 2005. A Simple Measure of Good Governance. In *Public Services Delivery*, edited by A. Shah. Washington, DC: World Bank.

Ignatieff, Michael. 1993. *Blood and Belonging*. London: BBC; Farrar, Straus and Giroux.

IMF. 2008. World Economic Outlook Database, October 2008 ed. Washington, DC: International Monetary Fund.

Isham, Jonathan, Daniel Kaufmann, and Lant H. Pritchett. 1997. Civil Liberties, Democracy, and the Performance of Government Projects. *World Bank Economic Review* 11 (2): 219–42.

Issacharoff, Samuel. 2007. Fragile Democracies. *Harvard Law Review* 120 (6): 1405–67.

Iversen, Torben. 2005. *Capitalism, Democracy, and Welfare*. Cambridge: Cambridge University Press.

Iversen, Torben, and David Soskice. 2006. Electoral Institutions and the Politics of Coalitions: Why Some Democracies Redistribute More Than Others. *American Political Science Review* 100 (2): 165–81.

Iversen, Torben, and John D. Stephens. 2008. Partisan Politics, the Welfare State, and Three Worlds of Human Capital Formation. *Comparative Political Studies* 41 (4–5): 600–637.

Jansson, Torkel. 1985. *Adertonhundratalets Associatoner*. Uppsala: Almqvist and Wiksell International.

Johnston, Michael. 2005. *Syndromes of Corruption: Wealth, Power, and Democracy*. Cambridge: Cambridge University Press.

——. 2006. From Thucydides to Mayor Daley: Bad Politics, and a Culture of Corruption. *PS, Political Science and Politics* 39 (4): 809–12.

Jones, Bryan D. 1999. Bounded Rationality. *Annual Review of Political Science* 2:297–321.

Jordan, William Chester. 2009. Anti-corruption Campaigns in Thirteenth-Century Europe. *Journal of Medieval History* 35:204–19.

Jordan Smith, Daniel. 2007. *A Culture of Corruption: Everyday Deception and Popular Discontent in Nigeria*. Princeton, NJ: Princeton University Press.

Kaijser, Arne. 2002. System Building from Below: Institutional Change in Dutch Water Control Systems. *Technology and Culture* 43 (3): 521–48.

Karklins, Rasma. 2005. *The System Made Me Do It: Corruption in Post-Communist Societies*. Armonk, NY: Sharpe.

Katz, Michael B. 1986. I*n the Shadow of the Poorhouse: A Social History of Welfare in America*. New York: Basic Books.

Katzenstein, Peter J. 1994. *Corporatism and Change*. Ithaca, NY: Cornell University Press.

Kaufman, Herbert. 1960. *The Forest Ranger: A Study in Administrative Behavior*. Baltimore: Johns Hopkins Press.

Kaufmann, Daniel. 2004. *Human Rights and Governance: The Empirical Challenge*. New York: New York University Law School.

Kaufmann, Daniel, and Art Kraay. 2002. Growth without Governance. *Economia* 3 (1): 169–229.

Kaufmann, Daniel, Art Kraay, and Massimo Mastruzzi. 2004. Governance Matters III: Governance Indicators for 1996–2002. World Bank Policy Research Working Paper 3106. World Bank, Washington, DC.

———. 2007. Governance Matters VI: Governance Indicators for 1996–2006. World Bank Policy Research Working Paper 4280. World Bank, Washington, DC.

Kaufmann, Daniel, Art Kraay, and Pablo Zoido-Lobatón. 1999. Governance Matters. World Bank Policy Research Working Paper 2196. World Bank, Washington, DC.

Kaufmann, Daniel, and Pedro C. Vicente. 2005. Legal Corruption. MPRA Paper 8186. University of Munich.

Keefer, Philip. 2004. A Review of the Political Economy of Governance: From Property Rights to Voice: World Bank Policy Research Working Paper 3315. World Bank, Washington, DC.

Keefer, Philip, and Stephen Knack. 2005. Social Capital, Social Norms and the New Institutional Economics. In *Handbook of New Institutional Economics*, edited by C. Menard and M. M. Shirley. Amsterdam: Springer.

Kenworthy, Lane, and Jonas Pontusson. 2005. Rising Inequality and the Politics of Redistribution in Affluent Countries. *Perspectives on Politics* 3 (3): 449–71.

Khan, Mushtaq H. 1996. The Efficiency Implications of Corruption. *Journal of International Development* 8 (5):683–96.

———. 1998. Patron-Client Networks and the Economic Effects of Corruption in Asia. *European Journal of Development Research*, 10 (1): 15–39.

Klitgaard, Robert. 1997. Cleaning Up and Invigorating the Civil Service. *Public Administration and Development* 17 (5): 487–509.

Klomp, Jeroen, and Jakob de Haan. 2008. Effects of Governance on Health: A Cross-National Analysis of 101 Countries. *Kyklos* 61 (4): 599–614.

Kluegel, James R., and David S. Mason. 2000. Market Justice in Transition. In *Marketing Democracy*, edited by D. S. Mason and J. L. Kluegel. Lanham, MD: Rowman and Littlefield.

Knack, Stephen, and Philip Keefer. 1995. Institutions and Economic Performance: Cross-Country Tests Using Alternative Institutional Measures. *Economics and Politics* 7 (3): 207–27.

———. 1997. Does Social Capital Have an Economic Payoff? A Cross-Country Investigation. *Quarterly Journal of Economics* 112 (4): 1251–88.

244 REFERENCES

Knack, Stephen, and Paul Zak. 2003. Building Trust: Public Policy, Interpersonal Trust and Economic Development. *Supreme Court Economic Review* 10 (Fall): 91–107.

Kornai, János. 2000. Hidden in an Envelope: Gratitude Payments to Medical Doctors in Hungary. Discussion Paper Series 60. Collegium Budapest Institute for Advanced Study, Budapest.

Kornai, János, and Susan Rose-Ackerman, eds. 2004. *Building a Trustworthy State in Post-socialist Transition*. New York: Palgrave Macmillan.

Kornai, János, Bo Rothstein, and Susan Rose-Ackerman, eds. 2004. *Creating Social Trust in Post-socialist Transition*. New York: Palgrave Macmillan.

Korpi, Walter. 1974. Conflict, Power and Relative Deprivation. *American Political Sceince Review* 68 (4): 1569–78.

———. 1983. *The Democratic Class Struggle*. London: Routledge and Kegan Paul.

———. 1988. Power, Politics, and State Autonomy in the Development of Social Citizenship—Social Rights during Sickness in Eighteen OECD Countries since 1930. *American Sociological Review* 54 (3): 309–28.

———. 2001. Contentious Institutions—an Augmented Rational-Action Analysis of the Origins and Path Dependency of Welfare State Institutions in Western Countries. *Rationality and Society* 13 (2): 235–83.

———. 2006. Power Resources and Employer-Centered Approaches in Explanations of Welfare States and Varieties of Capitalism—Protagonists, Consenters, and Antagonists. *World Politics* 58 (2): 167–206.

Korpi, Walter, and Joakim Palme. 1998. The Paradox of Redistribution and Strategies of Equality: Welfare State Institutions, Inequality, and Poverty in the Western Countries. *American Sociological Review* 63 (5): 661–87.

———. 2003. New Politics and Class Politics in the Context of Austerity and Globalization: Welfare State Regress in Eighteen Countries, 1975–95. *American Political Science Review* 97 (3): 425–46.

Kraay, Art. 2004. When Is Growth Pro-Poor? Cross-Country Evidence. IMF Working Paper 04/47. International Monetary Fund, Washington, DC.

Krause, Matthias. 2009. *The Political Economy of Water and Sanitation*. New York: Routledge.

Krishna, Anirudh. 2010. *One Illness Away: Why People Become Poor and How They Escape Poverty*. New York: Oxford University Press.

Krugman, Paul. 2009. How Did Economists Get It So Wrong? *New York Times Mazagine*, September 8.

Kuenzi, Michelle. 2004. Social Capital, Political Trust, and Ethnicity in West Africa. Paper presented at the annual meeting of the American Political Science Association, Chicago, September 2–5.

Kudamatsu, Masayuki. 2006. Has Democratization Reduced Infant Mortality in Africa: Evidence from Micro Data. Unpublished manuscript, London School of Economics.

Kumlin, Staffan. 2004. *The Personal and the Political: How Personal Welfare State Experiences Affect Political Trust and Ideology.* New York: Palgrave Macmillan.

Kumlin, Staffan, and Bo Rothstein. 2005. Making and Breaking Social Capital. The Impact of Welfare State Institutions. *Comparative Political Studies* 38 (4): 339–65.

———. 2010. Questioning the New Liberal Dilemma: Immigrants, Social Networks and Institutional Fairness. *Comparative Politics* 43 (5): 63–80.

Kurer, Oscar. 2005. Corruption: An Alternative Approach to Its Definition and Measurement. *Political Studies* 53 (1): 222–39.

Kurzman, Charles, Regina Werum, and Ross E. Burkhart. 2002. Democracy's Effect on Economic Growth: A Pooled Time-Series Analysis, 1951–1980. *Studies in Comparative International Development* 37 (1): 3–33.

Kwon, Huck-ju. 2009. The Reform of the Developmental Welfare State in East Asia. *International Journal of Social Welfare* 18 (suppl. 1): 12–21.

Lange, Matthew. 2005. The Rule of Law and Development: A Weberian Framework of States and State-Society Relations. In *States and Development*, edited by M. Lange and D. Rueschemeyer. New York: Palgrave Macmillan.

La Porta, Rafael, Florencio Lopez-de-Silanes, Andrei Shleifer, and Robert Vishny. 1999. The Quality of Government. *Journal of Law, Economics and Organization* 15 (1): 222–79.

Lapuente, Victor, and Bo Rothstein. 2010. Civil War Spain versus Swedish Harmony: The Quality of Government Factor. Paper presented at the annual meeting of the American Political Science Association, Washington, DC, August 31–September 3.

Larsen, Christian Albrekt. 2006. *The Institutional Logic of Welfare Attitudes: How Welfare Regimes Influence Public Support.* Burlington, VT: Ashgate.

Lazarova, Emiliya, and Ilaria Mosca. 2008. Does Governance Matter for Aggregate Health Capital? *Applied Economics Letters* 15 (3): 599–614.

Ledeneva, Alena V. 2006. *How Russia Really Works: The Informal Practices That Shaped Post-Soviet Politics and Business, Culture and Society after Socialism.* Ithaca, NY: Cornell University Press.

Lee, Eliza W. Y. 2006. Welfare Restructuring in Asian Newly Industrialised Countries: A Comparison of Hong Kong and Singapore. *Policy and Politics* 34 (3): 453–71.

Lee, Soo-Young, and Andrew B. Whitford. 2008. Government Effectiveness in Comparative Perspective. Paper presented at the annual meeting of the MPSA Annual National Conference, Palmer House Hotel, Hilton, Chicago, April 3.

Letki, Natalia. 2006. Investigating the Roots of Civic Morality: Trust, Social Capital, and Institutional Performance. *Political Behavior* 28 (4): 305–25.

Levi, Margaret. 1998a. A State of Trust. In *Trust and Governance*, edited by V. Braithwaite and M. Levi. New York: Russell Sage Foundation.

——. 1998b. *Consent, Dissent, and Patriotism*. New York: Cambridge University Press.

——. 2006. Why We Need a New Theory of Government. *Perspectives on Politics* 4 (1): 5–19.

Lewin, Leif. 1994. The Rise and Decline of Corporatism: The Case of Sweden. *European Journal of Political Research* 26 (1): 59–79.

Lewis, Colin M., and Peter Lloyd-Sherlock. 2009. Social Policy and Economic Development in South America: An Historical Approach to Social Insurance. *Economy and Society* 38 (1): 109–31.

Lewis, Maureen. 2006. Governance and Corruption in the Public Health Sector. Working Paper 78. Center for Global Development, Washington, DC.

Li, Hongyi, Lyn Squire, and Heng-fu Zou. 1998. Explaining International and Intertemporal Variations in Income Inequality. *Economic Journal* 108 (446): 26–43.

Lichbach, Mark I. 1997. *The Co-operator's Dilemma*. Ann Arbor: University of Michigan Press.

Liddell Hart, Basil Henry. 1967. *Strategy: The Indirect Approach*. 4th ed., rev. and further enl. London: Faber.

Lind, E. Allan, and Tom R. Tyler. 1997. *The Social Psychology of Procedural Justice*. New York: Plenum.

Lindberg, Staffan I. 2006. *Democracy and Elections in Africa*. Baltimore: Johns Hopkins University Press.

——. 2009. *Democratization by Elections: A New Mode of Transition*. Baltimore: Johns Hopkins University Press.

Lindert, Peter H. 2004. *Growing Public: Social Spending and Economic Growth since the Eighteenth Century*. Cambridge: Cambridge University Press.

Lindroth, Sten. 1976. *Uppsala Universitet, 1477–1977*. Uppsala: Uppsala Universitet.

Lindstrom, Martin, and Mohabbat Mohseni. 2009. Social Capital, Political Trust and Self-Reported Psychological Health: A Population-Based Study. *Social Science and Medicine* 68 (3): 436–43.

Loewenstein, George, Matthew Rabin, and Colin Camerer. 2004. *Advances in Behavioral Economics*. Roundtable Series in Behavioral Economics. New York: Russell Sage Foundation.

Lopez, J. Humberto. 2004. Pro-Growth, Pro-Poor: Is There a Tradeoff? World Bank Policy Research Working Paper 3378. World Bank, Washington, DC.

Lopez, Ramon, and Siddharta Mitra. 2000. Corruption, Pollution, and the Kuznets Environment Curve. *Journal of Environmental Economics and Management* 40 (2): 137–50.

Lundquist, Lennart. 1999. *Ämbetsmännen som Demokratins Väktare*. Lund: Studentlitteratur.

Lyday, Corbin, Margaret O'Donnell, and Trevor Munroe. 2008. Corruption Assessment for Jamaica. Report for USAID. Washington, DC: Management Systems International.

MacDonald, Paul K. 2003. Useful Fiction or Miracle Maker: The Competing Epistemological Foundations of Rational Choice Theory. *American Political Science Review* 97 (4): 551–65.

Mackie, Gerry. 2003. *Democracy Defended*. Cambridge: Cambridge University Press.

Mahoney, James, and Kathleen Thelen. 2009. *Explaining Institutional Change: Ambiguity, Agency, and Power in Historical Institutionalism*. New York: Cambridge University Press.

Manin, Bernhard. 1997. *The Principles of Representative Government*. New York: Cambridge University Press.

Mann, Michael. 2005. *The Dark Side of Democracy: Explaining Ethnic Cleansing*. New York: Cambridge University Press.

Mansfield, Edward D., and Jack Snyder. 2005. *Electing to Fight: Why Emerging Democracies Go to War*. Cambridge, MA: MIT Press.

March, James B., and Johan P. Olsen. 1989. *Rediscovering Institutions: The Organizational Basis of Politics*. New York: Basic Books.

Mares, Isabela. 2003. *The Politics of Social Risk: Business and Welfare State Development*. Cambridge Studies in Comparative Politics. Cambridge: Cambridge University Press.

———. 2005. Social Protection Around the World—External Insecurity, State Capacity, and Domestic Political Cleavages. *Comparative Political Studies* 38 (6): 623–51.

Marmot, Michael. 2004. *The Status Syndrome: How Social Standing Affects Our Health and Longevity*. New York: Henry Holt.

Mateju, Petr. 1997. Beliefs about Distributive Justice and Social Change: Czech Republic, 1991–1995. Working Paper Series 6, Socialni Trendy/Social Trends, Prague.

Matthews, Emily, and Gregory Mock. 2003. More Democracy, Better Environment? *World Resources*, 2002–4:32–33.

Mauro, Paolo. 1995. Corruption and Growth. *Quarterly Journal of Economics* 110 (3): 681–712.

Mauzy, Diane K., and R. S. Milne. 2002. *Singapore Politics under the People's Action Party*. London: Routledge.

McDermott, Rose. 2002. Experimental Methods in Political Science. *Annual Review of Political Science* 5:31–61.

McMillan, John, and Pablo Zoido. 2004. How to Subvert Democracy: Montesinos in Peru. *Journal of Economic Perspectives* 18 (4): 69–92.

Meinzen-Dick, Ruth S. 2007. Beyond Panaceas in Water Institutions. *Proceedings of the National Academy of Sciences of the United States of America* 104 (39): 15200–205.

Menard, Claude, and Mary M. Shirley, eds. 2005. *Handbook of New Institutional Economics*. Amsterdam: Springer.

Mendus, Susan. 2002. *Impartiality in Moral and Political Philosophy*. Oxford: Oxford University Press.

Menon-Johansson, Anatole S. 2005. Good Governance and Good Health: The Role of Societal Structures in the Human Immunodeficiency Virus Pandemic. *BMC International Health and Human Rights* 5 (1): 96–111.

Messick, Richard E. 1999. Judicial Reform and Economic Development: A Survey of the Issues. *World Bank Research Observer* 14 (1): 117–36.

Migdal, Joel S. 1988. *Strong Societies and Weak States: State-Society Relations and State Capabilities in the Third World*. Princeton, NJ: Princeton University Press.

Milgrom, Paul R., Douglass C. North, and Barry R. Weingast. 1990. The Role of Institutions in the Revival of Trade: The Medieval Law Merchant, Private Judges and the Champagne Fairs. *Economics and Politics* 2 (1): 1–23.

Mill, John Stuart. 1861/1992. *On Liberty and Utilitarianism*. New York: Knopf Everyman's Library.

Miller, David. 2004. Justice, Democracy and Public Goods. In *Justice and Democracy*, edited by K. Dowding, R. E. Goodin, and C. Pateman. Cambridge: Cambridge University Press.

Miller, Gary J. 2000. Rational Choice and Dysfunctional Institutions. *Governance* 13 (4): 535–47.

Miller, Gary J., and Thomas Hammond. 1994. Why Politics Is More Fundamental Than Economics: Incentive-Compatible Mechanisms Are Not Credible. *Journal of Theoretical Politics* 6 (1): 5–26.

Miller, William L., Åse B. Grødeland, and Tatyana Y. Koshechkina. 2001. *A Culture of Corruption? Coping with Government in Post-Communist Europe*. Budapest: Central European University Press.

Mo, Pak H. 2001. Corruption and Economic Growth. *Journal of Comparative Economics* 29 (1): 66–79.

Moene, Karl-Ove, and Michael Wallerstein. 2003. Earnings Inequality and Welfare Spending—a Disaggregated Analysis. *World Politics* 55 (4): 485–507.

Molander, Per. 1994. *Aqvedukten vid Zaghouan*. Stockholm: Atlantis.

Montinola, Gabriella R, and Robert W. Jackman. 2002. Sources of Corruption: A Cross-Country Study. *British Journal of Political Science* 32 (1): 147–70.

Moran, Michael, Martin Rein, and Robert E. Goodin. 2006. *The Oxford Handbook of Public Policy*. New York: Oxford University Press.

Morris, Stephen D. 2009. *Political Corruption in Mexico*. London: Lynne Reiner.

Morse, Stephen. 2006. Is Corruption Bad for Environmental Sustainability? A Cross-National Analysis. *Ecology and Society* 11 (1): 22–44.

Morse, Stephen, and Evan D. G. Fraser. 2005. Making "Dirty" Nations Look Clean? The Nation State and the Problem of Selecting and Weighting Indices as Tools for Measuring Progress towards Sustainability. *Geoforum* 36 (5): 625–40.

Mungiu-Pippidi, Alina. 2006. Corruption: Diagnosis and Treatment. *Journal of Democracy* 17 (3): 86–99.

Myhrman, Johan. 2003. *Hur Sverige blev Rikt*, 2nd ed. Stockholm: SNS.

Myrberg, Israel. 1922. Bidrag till Tjänsteackordens Historia i Vårt Land. *Från den Svenska Statsförvaltningen* 5–6.

Nannestad, Peter, and Gert T. Svendsen. 2005. Institutions, Culture and Trust. Paper presented at the Quality of Government Institute conference, Gothenburg, November 2005.

National Economic and Social Forum. 2003. *The Policy Implications of Social Capital*. Dublin: Irish Government Publications.

Neckerman, Katherine, ed. 2004. *Social Inequality*. New York: Russell Sage Foundation.

Neumayer, Eric. 2002. Do Democracies Exhibit Stronger International Environmental Commitment? A Cross-Country Analysis. *Journal of Peace Research* 39 (2): 139–64.

Newton, Kenneth. 1997. Social Capital and Democracy. *American Behavioral Scientist* 40 (5): 575–86.

Nilsson, Göran B. 2001. *Grundaren: André Oscar Wallenberg (1816–1886)*. Stockholm: Carlsson.

Norris, Pippa, and Ronald Inglehart. 2004. *Sacred and Secular: Religion and Politics Worldwide*. Cambridge Studies in Social Theory, Religion, and Politics. Cambridge: Cambridge University Press.

North, Douglass C. 1990. *Institutions, Institutional Change and Economic Performance*. Cambridge: Cambridge University Press.

———. 1998a. Economic Performance through Time. In *The New Institutionalism in Sociology*, edited by M. C. Brinton and V. Nee. New York: Russell Sage Foundation.

———. 1998b. Where Have We Been and Where Are We Going? In *Economics, Values and Organization*, edited by A. Ben-Ner and L. Putterman. Cambridge: Cambridge University Press.

———. 2006. What Is Missing from Political Economy. In *The Oxford Handbook of Political Economy*, edited by Barry R. Weingast and Donald Wittman. Oxford: Oxford University Press.

North, Douglass C., John J. Wallis, and Barry R. Weingast. 2009. *Violence and Social Orders: A Conceptual Framework for Interpreting Recorded Human History*. Cambridge: Cambridge University Press.

Nozick, Robert. 1974. *Anarchy, State, and Utopia*. Cambridge, MA: Harvard University Press.

Nye, Joseph S. 1967. Corruption and Political Development: A Cost-Benefit Analysis. *American Political Science Review* 61 (2): 417–27.

Öberg, Magnus, and Erik Melander. 2010. On the Effect of Quality of Government, as Compared to, e.g., Democracy, on Civil War Outbreak. Paper presented at the annual meeting of the American Political Science Association, Washington, DC, August 31–September 3.

Oberschall, Anthony. 2000. The Manipulation of Ethnicity: From Ethnic Cooperation to Violence and War in Yugoslavia. *Ethnic and Racial Studies* 23 (6): 982–1001.

O'Donnell, Guillermo. 2001. Democracy, Law, and Comparative Politics. *Studies in Comparative International Development* 36 (1): 7–26.

——. 2004. Why the Rule of Law Matters. *Journal of Democracy* 15 (4): 32–46.

——. 2007. The Perpetual Crises of Democracy. *Journal of Democracy* 18 (1): 5–9.

OECD. 2006. *Population and Labour Force Statistics*. Vol. 2006, release 02. Paris: Organisation for Economic Co-operation and Development.

——. 2007. *Main Economic Indicators*. Paris: Organisation for Economic Co-operation and Development.

Offe, Claus. 2004. Political Corruption: Conceptual and Practical Issues. In *Building a Trustworthy State in Post-socialist Transition*, edited by Susan Rose-Ackerman and János Kornai. New York: Palgrave Macmillan.

Olivecrona, Knut. 1859. *Om den Juridiska Undervisningen vid Universitetet i Uppsala och om den Juridiska Fakultetens Flyttande till Stockholm*. Uppsala: Juridiska Fakulteten.

Olowu, Dele. 2000. Bureaucracy and Democratic Reform. In *African Perspectives on Governance*, edited by G. Hyden, D. Olowy, and H. W. O. Okoth-Ogendo. Trenton, NJ: Africa World Press.

Olsen, Johan P. 1983. *Organized Democracy: Political Institutions in a Welfare State, the Case of Norway*. New York: Universitetsforlaget; Columbia University Press.

——. 2006. Maybe It Is Time to Rediscover Bureaucracy. *Journal of Public Administration Research and Theory* 16 (1): 1–24.

Olson, Mancur, Jr. 1996. Big Bills Left on the Sidewalk: Why Some Nations Are Rich, and Others Poor. *Journal of Economic Perspectives* 10 (2): 3–24.

Orkeny, Antal. 2000. Trends in Perceptions of Social Inequality in Hungary, 1991–1996. In *Marketing Democracy*, edited by D. S. Mason and J. L. Kluegel. Lanham, MD: Rowman and Littlefield.

Østerud, Øyivind, and Per Selle. 2006. Power and Democracy in Norway: The Transformation of Norwegian Politics. *Scandinavian Political Studies* 29 (1): 25–46.

Ostrom, Elinor. 1990. *Governing the Commons: The Evolution of Institutions for Collective Action*. New York: Cambridge University Press.

———. 1998. A Behavioral Approach to the Rational Choice Theory of Collective Action. *American Political Science Reveiw* 92 (1): 1–23.

———. 2000. Crowding Out Citizenship. *Scandinavian Political Studies* 23 (1): 3–16.

———. 2005. *Understanding Institutional Diversity*. Princeton, NJ: Princeton University Press.

Ostrom, Elinor, and James Walker, eds. 2003. *Trust and Reciprocity: Interdisciplinary Lessons from Experimental Research*. New York: Russell Sage Foundation.

Ott, Jan C. 2010. Good Governance and Happiness in Nations: Technical Quality Precedes Democracy and Quality Beats Size. *Journal of Happiness Studies* 11 (3): 353–68.

Pacek, Alexander C., and Benjamin Radcliff. 2008. Welfare Policy and Subjective Well-Being Across Nations: An Individual-Level Assessment. *Social Indicators Research* 89 (1): 179–91.

Palier, Bruno, and Claude Martin. 2008. *Reforming the Bismarckian Welfare Systems*. Oxford: Blackwell.

Paris, Roland. 2004. *At War's End. Building Peace after Civil Conflict*. Cambridge: Cambridge University Press.

Pasotti, Eleonora. 2010. *Political Branding in Cities*. New York: Cambridge University Press.

Paster, Thomas. 2009. *Choosing Lesser Evils: The Role of Business in the Development of the German Welfare State from the 1880s to the 1990s*. San Domenica di Fiesole, Florence: European University Institute, Department of Political and Social Science.

Payne, Stanley G. 2006. *The Collapse of the Spanish Republic, 1933–1936: Origins of the Civil War*. New Haven, CT: Yale University Press.

Paz-Fuchs, Amir. 2008. *Welfare to Work: Conditional Rights in Social Policy*. Oxford Monographs on Labour Law. Oxford: Oxford University Press.

Persson, Anna. 2008. *The Institutional Sources of Statehood: Assimilation, Multiculturalism, and Taxation*. Göteborg Studies in Politics 111. Gothenburg: University of Gothenburg, Department of Political Science.

Peters, Guy B., and Jon Pierre, eds. 2002. *Handbook of Public Administration*. London: Sage.

Petersson, Olof. 2006. *Mediernas Valmakt. Demokratirådets Rapport, 2006*. Stockholm: SNS.

Pettersson, Lars. 1995. In Search of Respectability: Popular Movements in Scandinavian Democracy. In *Democratization in the Third World*, edited by L. Rudebeck and O. Törnqvist. Uppsala: Uppsala University, Department of Development Studies.

Pharr, Susan J., and Robert D. Putnam, eds. 2000. *Disaffected Democracies? What's Troubling the Trilateral Countries*. Princeton, NJ: Princeton University Press.

Pierson, Paul. 2000. Increasing Returns, Path Dependence, and the Study of Politics. *American Political Science Review* 94 (2): 251–67.

———. 2004. *Politics in Time: History, Institutions, and Social Analysis.* Princeton, NJ: Princeton University Press.

Plesch, Dan. 2005. Neo-conservative Thinking since the Onset of the Iraq War. In *The Iraq War and Democratic Politics*, edited by Alex Danchev and John MacMillan. London: Routledge.

Polanyi, Karl. 1944. *The Great Transformation.* New York: Farrar and Rinehart.

Pontusson, Jonas. 2005. *Inequality and Prosperity: Social Europe vs. Liberal America.* Ithaca, NY: Cornell University Press.

Popov, Vladimir, and Natalia E. Dinello. 2007. *Political Institutions and Development: Failed Expectations and Renewed Hopes.* Cheltenham, UK: Edward Elgar.

Postel, Sandra, and Lisa Mastny. 2005. *Liquid Assets: The Critical Need to Safeguard Freshwater Ecosystems.* Worldwatch Paper 170. Washington, DC: Worldwatch Institute.

Powell, Lawrence, and Balford Lewis. 2009. The Political Culture of Democracy in Jamaica, 2008: The Impact of Governance. In *Latin American Public Opinion Project*, edited by M. A. Seligson. Mona: Center for Leadership and Governance, University of West Indies at Mona.

Przeworski, Adam. 1991. *Democracy and the Market: Political and Economic Reforms in Eastern Europe and Latin America.* Cambridge: Cambridge University Press.

———. 2004. Institutions Matter? *Government and Opposition* 39 (4): 527–40.

Przeworski, Adam, Michael B. Alvarez, José Antonio Cheibub, and Fernando Limongi. 2000. *Democracy and Development: Political Institutions and Well-Being in the World, 1950–1990.* Cambridge Studies in the Theory of Democracy. Cambridge: Cambridge University Press.

Przeworski, Adam, and Fernando Limongi. 1993. Political Regimes and Economic Growth. *Journal of Economic Perspectives* 7 (3): 51–69.

Przeworski, Adam, Susan Stokes, and Bernhard Manin, eds. 1999. *Democracy, Accountability and Representation.* Cambridge: Cambridge University Press.

Putnam, Robert D. 1993. *Making Democracy Work: Civic Traditions in Modern Italy.* Princeton, NJ: Princeton University Press.

———. 2000. *Bowling Alone: The Collapse and Revival of American Community.* New York: Simon and Schuster.

Putnam, Robert D., and Lewis D. Feldstein. 2003. *Better Together: Restoring the American Community.* New York: Simon and Schuster.

Quah, Jon S. T. 2001. Combatting Corruption in Singapore: What Can Be Learned? *Journal of Contingencies and Crisis Management* 91 (1): 29–25.

Quinn, Dennis. 1997. The Correlates of Change in International Financial Regulation. *American Political Sceince Review* 91 (3): 531–51.

Ragaru, Nadège. 2003. Elections, Political Legitimacy and Stability in the Balkans: The Missing Link. *Revue d'Études Comparatives Est-Ouest* 34 (1): 83–101.

Rajkumar, Andrew. S., and Vinaya Swaroop. 2008. Public Spending and Outcomes: Does Governance Matter? *Journal of Development Economics* 86 (1): 96–111.

Rangwala, Glen. 2005. Democratic Transition and Its Limitations. In *The Iraq War and Democratic Politics*, edited by Alex Danchev and John MacMillan. London: Routledge.

Rauch, James E., and Peter B. Evans. 2000. Bureaucratic Structure and Bureaucratic Performance in Less Developed Countries. *Journal of Public Economics* 75 (2): 49–71.

Rawls, John. 1971. *A Theory of Justice*. Oxford: Oxford University Press.

——. 1984. The Right and the Good Contrasted. In *Liberalism and Its Critics*, edited by M. J. Sandel. New York: New York University Press.

——. 2005. *Political Liberalism*. Expanded ed. New York: Columbia University Press.

Reinikka, Ritva, and Jacob Svensson. 2005. Fighting Corruption to Improve Schooling: Evidence from a Newspaper Campaign in Uganda. *Journal of the European Economic Association* 3 (2–3): 259–67.

Resnick, Danielle, and Regina Birner. 2006. Does Good Governance Contribute to Pro-Poor Growth? A Review of the Evidence from Cross-Country Studies. DSGD Discussion Paper 30, International Food Policy Research Institute, Washington, DC.

Rhodes, R. A. W., Sarah A. Binder, and Bert A. Rockman. 2006. *The Oxford Handbook of Political Institutions*. Oxford: Oxford University Press.

Riesco, Manuel, and Sonia M. Draibe, eds. 2007. *Latin America: A New Developmental Welfare State Model in the Making?* New York: Palgrave Macmillan.

Rijsberman, Frank R. 2008. Water for Food: Corruption in Irrigation Systems. In *Global Corruption Report 2008: Corruption in the Water Sector*. Cambridge: Cambridge University Press.

Ringen, Stein. 2004. Wealth and Decay: The Norwegian Study of Power and Democracy. *Times Literary Supplement*, April 8, 2–4.

Robert, Harris. 2003. *Political Corruption in and beyond the Nation State*. London: Routledge.

Rodrik, Dani. 2007. *One Economics, Many Recipes: Globalization, Institutions and Economic Growth*. Princeton, NJ: Princeton University Press.

——. 2008. Goodbye Washington Consensus, Hello Washington Confusion? A Review of the World Bank's Economic Growth in the 1990s: Learning from a Decade of Reform. *Panoeconomicus* 55 (2): 135–56.

Rodrik, Dani, Arvind Subramanian, and Francesco Trebbi. 2004. Institutions Rule: The Primacy of Institutions over Geography and Integration in Economic Development. *Journal of Economic Growth* 9 (2):131–65.

Root, Hilton L. 1996. *Small Countries, Big Lessons: Governance and the Rise of East Asia.* Hong Kong: Oxford University Press.

———. 2006. *Capital and Collusion.* Princeton, NJ: Princeton University Press.

Rose, Jonathan. 2004. The Rule of Law in the Western World: An Overview. *Journal of Social Philosophy* 35 (4): 457–70.

Rose, Richard, and Doh Chull Shin. 2001. Democratization Backwards: The Problem of Third-Wave Democracies. *British Journal of Political Science* 31 (2): 331–54.

Rose-Ackerman, Susan. 2004a. Governance and Corruption. In *Global Crises, Global Solutions*, edited by B. Lomborg. Cambridge: Cambridge University Press.

———. 2004b. Public Participation in Consolidating Democracies: Hungary and Poland. In *Building a Trustworthy State in Post-socialist Transition*, edited by János Kornai and Susan Rose-Ackerman. New York: Palgrave Macmillan.

Ross, Michael. 2006. Is Democracy Good for the Poor? *American Journal of Political Science* 50 (4): 860–74.

Rotberg, Robert I. 2007. On Improving Nation-State Governance. *Daedalus* 136 (1): 152–55.

Rother, Larry. 1999. Where Taxes Aren't So Certain. *New York Times*, March 21.

Rothstein, Bo. 1991. State Structures and Variations in Corporatism: The Swedish Case. *Scandinavian Political Studies* 14 (3): 149–71.

———. 1992a. Labor-Market Institutions and Working-Class Strength. In *Structuring Politics: Historical Institutionalism in a Comparative Perspective*, edited by S. Steinmo, K. Thelen, and F. Longstreth. Cambridge: Cambridge University Press.

———. 1992b. Social Justice and State Capacity. *Politics and Society* 20:101–26.

———. 1996. *The Social Democratic State: The Swedish Model and the Bureaucratic Problem of Social Reforms.* Pittsburgh: University of Pittsburgh Press.

———. 1998a. *Just Institutions Matter: The Moral and Political Logic of the Universal Welfare State.* Cambridge: Cambridge University Press.

———. 1998b. State Building and Capitalism: The Rise of the Swedish Bureaucracy. *Scandinavian Political Studies* 21 (2): 287–306.

———. 2000. Trust, Social Dilemmas and Collective Memories. *Journal of Theoretical Politics* 12 (4): 477–503.

———. 2005. *Social Traps and the Problem of Trust.* Cambridge: Cambridge University Press.

Rothstein, Bo, and Dietlind Stolle. 2003. Social Capital, Impartiality, and the Welfare State: An Institutional Approach. In *Generating Social Capital: The*

Role of Voluntary Associations, Institutions and Government Policy, edited by M. Hooghe and D. Stolle. New York: Palgrave Macmillan.

———. 2008. The State and Social Capital: An Institutional Theory of Generalized Trust. *Comparative Politics* 40 (4): 441–67.

Rothstein, Bo, and Eric M. Uslaner. 2005. All for All: Equality, Corruption and Social Trust. *World Politics* 58 (3): 41–73.

Roy, Indrajit. 2005. Good Governance and the Dilemma of Development: What Lies Beneath? Socio-economic Review 3 (1): 83–116.

Rubinstein, W. D. 1987. *Elites and the Wealthy in Modern British History.* Sussex: Harvester Press.

Rudra, Nita. 2004. Openness, Welfare Spending, and Inequality in the Developing World. *International Studies Quarterly* 48 (3): 683–709.

Rueschemeyer, Dietrich. 2005. Building States—an Argument from Theory. In *States and Development*, edited by M. Lange and D. Rueschemeyer. New York: Palgrave Macmillan.

Sacks, Audrey, and Margaret Levi. 2007. Measuring Government Effectiveness and Its Consequences for Social Welfare. Paper discussed at WGAPE meeting, Stanford, CA, April 20–21.

Sally, David. 1995. Conversation and Cooperation in Social Dilemmas—a Metaanalysis of Experiments from 1958 to 1992. *Rationality and Society* 7 (1): 58–92.

Samanni, Marcus, and Sören Holmberg. 2010. Quality of Government Makes People Happy. Working Paper 2010:1, Quality of Government Institute, University of Gothenburg.

Samanni, Marcus, Jan Teorell, Staffan Kumlin, and Bo Rothstein. 2008. The QoG Social Policy Data Set, version 4. Quality of Government Institute, University of Gothenburg.

Samson, Michael J. 2002. The Social, Economic and Fiscal Impact of Comprehensive Social Security Reform for South Africa. *Social Dynamics—a Journal of the Centre for African Studies, University of Cape Town* 28 (2): 69–97.

Sarsfield, Rudolfo, and Fabián Echegaray. 2006. Opening the Black Box: How Satisfaction with Democracy and Its Perceived Efficacy Affect Regime Preference in Latin America. *International Journal of Public Opinion Research* 18 (2): 153–73.

Savedoff, William D., and Karen Hussmann. 2006. Why Are Health Systems Prone to Corruption? In *Global Corruption Report 2006*, edited by Transparency International. London: Pluto.

Scharpf, Fritz W. 1997. *Games Real Actors Play: Actor-Centered Institutionalism in Policy Research.* Boulder, CO: Westview Press.

Schedler, Andreas. 2002. The Menu of Manipulation. *Journal of Democracy* 13 (2): 36–50.

Schelling, Thomas C. 1998. Social Mechanisms and Social Dynamics. In *Social*

Mechanism: An Analytical Approach to Social Theory, edited by P. Hedström and R. Swedberg. Cambridge: Cambridge University Press.

Schiffbauer, Marc, and Ling Shen. 2010. Democracy vs. Dictatorship. *Economics of Transition* 18 (1): 59–90.

Schmidt, Vivien A. 2002. Does Discourse Matter in the Politics of Welfare State Adjustment? *Comparative Political Studies* 35 (2): 168–93.

———. 2009. Putting the Political Back into Political Economy by Bringing the State Back in Yet Again. *World Politics* 61 (3): 516–46.

Scholz, John T. 1998. Trust, Taxes and Compliance. In *Trust and Governance*, edited by V. Braithwaite and M. Levi. New York: Russell Sage Foundation.

Scholz, John T., and Mark Lubell. 1998. Trust and Taxpaying: Testing the Heuristic Approach to Collective Action. *American Journal of Political Science* 42 (2): 398–417.

Schultz, Jennifer, A. Maureen O'Brien, and Bedassa Tadesse. 2008. Social Capital and Self-Rated Health: Results from the US 2006 Social Capital Survey of One Community. *Social Science and Medicine* 67 (4): 606–17.

Scruggs, Lyle. 2002. The Ghent System and Union Membership in Europe, 1970–1996. *Political Research Quarterly* 55 (2): 275–97.

———. 2006. Welfare State Entitlements Data Set: A Comparative Institutional Analysis of Eighteen Welfare States, version 1.2. University of Connecticut.

———. 2007. Welfare State Generosity Across Space and Time. In *Investigating Welfare State Change*, edited by J. Clasen and N. A. Seigel. Cheltenham, UK: Edward Elgar.

Scruggs, Lyle, and James Allan. 2006. Welfare-State Decommodification in Eighteen OECD Countries: A Replication and Revision. *Journal of European Social Policy* 16 (1): 55–72.

Seligman, Adam B. 1997. *The Problem of Trust*. Princeton, NJ: Princeton University Press.

Seligson, Mitchell A. 2002. The Impact of Corruption on Regime Legitimacy: A Comparative Study of Four Latin American Countries. *Journal of Politics* 64 (2): 408–33.

Selle, Per, and Øyvind Østerud. 2006. The Eroding of Representative Democracy in Norway. *Journal of European Public Policy* 13 (4): 551–68.

Sened, Itai. 1997. *The Political Institution of Private Property*. Theories of Institutional Design. Cambridge: Cambridge University Press.

Shah, Anwar. 2005. Overview. In *Public Services Delivery*, edited by A. Shah. Washington, DC: World Bank.

Shapiro, Ian. 2005. *The Flight from Reality in Human Sciences*. Princeton, NJ: Princeton University Press.

Shepherd, Andrew. 2000. Governance, Good Government and Poverty Reduction. *International Review of Administrative Sciences* 66 (2): 269–84.

Shirley, Mary M. 2005. Institutions and Development. In *Handbook of Insti-*

tutional Economics, edited by C. Menard and M. M. Shirley. Amsterdam: Springer.

Shleifer, Andrei, and Robert W. Vishny. 1993. Corruption. *Quarterly Journal of Economics* 108 (3): 599–617.

Siegrist, Johannes, and Michael Marmot. 2006. *Social Inequalities in Health: New Evidence and Policy Implications*. Oxford: Oxford University Press.

Sikorski, Douglas. 1996. Effective Government in Singapore: Perspective of a Concerned American. *Asian Survey* 36 (18): 818–32.

Silber, Laura, and Allan Little. 1997. *Yugoslavia: Death of a Nation*. New York: Penguin.

Sjöstedt, Martin. 2008. *Thirsting for Credible Commitments: How Secure Land Tenure Affects Access to Drinking Water in Sub-Saharan Africa*. Göteborg Studies in Politics *110*. Gothenburg: Department of Political Science, University of Gothenburg.

Skocpol, Theda. 1987. America's Incomplete Welfare State. The Limits of New Deal Reforms and the Origins of the Present Crisis. In *Stagnation and Renewal in Social Policy*, edited by M. Rein. Armonk, NY: Sharpe.

———. 1992. *Protecting Soldiers and Mothers: The Political Origins of Social Policy in the United States*. Cambridge, MA: Harvard University Press.

———. 2003. *Diminished Democracy: From Membership to Management in American Civic Life*. Norman: University of Oklahoma Press.

Smeeding, Timothy. 2004. Twenty Years of Research on Income Inequality, Poverty and Redistribution in the Developed World: Introduction and Overview. *Socio-economic Review* 2 (2): 149–63.

Smith, Adam. 1776. *An Inquiry into the Nature and Causes of the Wealth of Nations*. London: Strahan and Cadell.

Smith, Brian C. 2007. *Good Governance and Development*. New York: Palgrave Macmillan.

Sohail, Muhammed, and Sue Cavill. 2008. Water for the Poor: Corruption in Water Supply and Sanitation. In *Global Corruption Report 2008: Corruption in the Water Sector*. Cambridge: Cambridge University Press.

Sorj, Bernardo, and Danilo Martuccelli. 2008. *The Latin America Challenge: Social Cohesion and Democracy*. Buenos Aires: Edelstein Center for Social Research.

Soss, Joe. 1999. Lessons of Welfare: Policy Design, Political Learning, and Political Action. *American Political Science Review* 93 (2): 363–80.

———. 2000. *Unwanted Claims: The Politics of Participation in the U.S. Welfare System*. Ann Arbor: University of Michigan Press.

Soss, Joe, and Sanford F. Schram. 2007. A Public Transformed? Welfare Reform as Policy Feedback. *American Political Science Review* 101 (1): 111–27.

Steinmetz, George. 1991. Workers and the Welfare State in Imperial Germany. *International Labor and Working-Class History* 40:18–46.

Steinmo, Sven. 2010. *The Evolution of Modern States: Sweden, Japan, and the United States*. New York: Cambridge University Press.

Stensöta, Helena O. 2010. The Conditions of Care: Reframing the Debate about Public Sector Ethics. *Public Administration Review* 70 (2): 295–303.

Stiglitz, Joseph E. 2002. Keynesian Economics and Critique of First Fundamental Theorem of Welfare Economics. In *Market Failure or Success: The New Debate*, edited by T. Cowen and E. Crampton. Cheltenham, UK: Edward Elgar.

Stockholm International Water Institute. 2006. *Corruption in the Water Sector: Causes, Consequences and Potential Reform*. Stockholm: Stockholm International Water Institute.

Stolle, Dietlind. 2003. The Sources of Social Capital. In *Generating Social Capital: Civil Society and Institutions in a Comparative Perspective*, edited by M. Hooghe and D. Stolle. New York: Palgrave Macmillan.

Stoyanov, Alexander, Maragarita Pavlikianova, Andrej Nontchev, and Galja Krasteva. 2000. Bulgaria: Political and Economic Crisis; Democratic Consolidation. In Marketing Democracy, edited by D. S. Mason, and J. L. Kluegel. Lanham, MD: Rowman and Littlefield.

Streeck, Wolfgang, and Colin Crouch. 2006. *The Diversity of Democracy: Corporatism, Social Order and Political Conflict*. Cheltenham, UK: Edward Elgar.

Strömberg, Håkan. 2000. *Allmän Förvaltningsrätt*. Malmö: Liber.

Stålgren, Patrik. 2006a. Corruption in the Water Sector: Causes, Consequences and Potential Reform. Swedish Water House Policy, Brief 4. Stockholm: Stockholm International Water Institute (SIWI).

——. 2006b. *Worlds of Water: Worlds Apart. How Targeted Domestic Actors Transform International Regimes. Göteborg Studies in Politics 99*. Gothenburg: Department of Political Science, University of Gothenburg.

Sung, Hung-En. 2004. Democracy and Political Corruption: A Cross-National Comparison. *Crime, Law and Social Change* 41 (2): 179–94.

Svallfors, Stefan, ed. 2007. *The Political Sociology of the Welfare State: Institutions, Social Cleavages, and Orientations*. Stanford, CA: Stanford University Press.

Svendsen, Gunnar L. H., and Gert T. Svendsen. 2003. On the Wealth of Nations: Bourdieuconomics and Social Capital. *Theory and Society* 32 (5–6): 607–31.

——. 2004. *The Creation and Destruction of Social Capital: Entrepreneurship, Co-operative Movements, and Institutions*. Cheltenham, UK: Edward Elgar.

Swank, Duane. 2002. *Global Capital, Political Institutions, and Policy Change in Developed Welfare States*. New York: Cambridge University Press.

Swenson, Peter. 2002. *Capitalists Against Markets: The Making of Labor Markets and Welfare States in the United States and Sweden*. New York: Oxford University Press.

Sztompka, Piotr. 1998. Trust, Distrust and Two Paradoxes of Democracy. *European Journal of Social Theory* 1 (1): 19–32.

Talbott, William J. 2005. *Which Rights Should Be Universal?* New York: Oxford University Press.

Tanzi, Vito. 1998. Corruption Around the World: Causes, Consequences, Scope, and Cures. IMF Staff Papers 45:559–94. International Monetary Fund, Washington, DC.

——. 2000. *Policies, Institutions and the Dark Side of Economics.* Northampton, MA: Edward Elgar.

Tarrow, Sidney. 2004. Bridging the Quantitative-Qualitative Divide. In *Rethinking Social Inquiry*, edited by H. E. Brady and D. Collier. Lanham, MD: Rowman and Littlefield.

Tebble, Adam J. 2002. What Is the Politics of Difference. *Political Theory* 30 (2): 259–81.

Teorell, Jan. 1998. *Demokrati eller Fåtalsvälde: Om Beslutsfattande i Partiorganisationer.* Uppsala: Uppsala University.

——. 2007. Corruption as an Institution: Rethinking the Nature and Origins of the Grabbing Hand. Quality of Government Institute Working Paper 2007:5. Quality of Government Institute, University of Gothenburg.

——. 2009. The Impact of Quality of Government as Impartiality: Theory and Evidence. Paper presented at the annual meeting of the American Political Science Association, Montreal, September 2–6.

——. 2010. *Determinants of Democratization: Explaining Regime Change in the World, 1972–2002.* Cambridge: Cambridge University Press.

Teorell, Jan, Nicholas Charron, Marcus Samanni, Sören Holmberg, and Bo Rothstein. 2010. The Quality of Government Dataset, version 27, May 10. Quality of Government Institute, University of Gothenburg.

Theiss-Morse, Elizabeth, and John R. Hibbing. 2005. Citizenship and Civic Engagement. *Annual Review of Political Science* 8 (1): 227–50.

Thelen, Kathleen. 2009. Institutional Change in Advanced Political Economies. *British Journal of Industrial Relations* 47 (3): 471–98.

Thomas, Melissa A. 2009. What Do the Worldwide Governance Indicators Measure? *European Journal of Development Research* 22 (1): 31–54.

Thompson, Dennis F. 2005. *Restoring Responsibility: Ethics in Government, Business, and Healthcare.* New York: Cambridge University Press.

Torpe, Lars. 2003. Social Capital in Denmark: A Deviant Case? *Scandinavian Political Studies* 26 (1): 27–48.

Transparency International. 2006. *Global Corruption Report 2006.* London: Pluto Press.

——. 2008a. *Global Corruption Report 2008: Corruption in the Water Sector.* Cambridge: Cambridge University Press.

——. 2008b. Poverty and Corruption. TI Working Paper 02. Transparency International, Berlin.

Tranvik, Tommy, and Per Selle. 2003. *Farvel til Folkestyret? Nasjonalstaten og de Nye Nettverkene*. Oslo: Gyldendal Akademisk.

Treisman, Daniel. 2000. The Causes of Corruption: A Cross-National Study. *Journal of Public Economics* 76 (3): 399–457.

Trocki, Carl A. 2006. *Singapore: Wealth, Power and the Culture of Control*. London: Routledge.

Trubek, David, and Marc Galanter. 1974. Scholars in Self-Estrangement: Some Reflections on the Crisis in Law and Development Studies in the United States. *Wisconsin Law Review* 54 (4): 1062–1101.

Tsebelis, George. 1990. *Nested Games: Rational Choice in a Comparative Perspective*. New York: Cambridge University Press.

Tyler, Tom R. 1998. Trust and Democratic Governance. In *Trust and Governance*, edited by V. Braithwaite and M. Levi. New York: Russell Sage Foundation.

Tyler, Tom R., and Yuen J. Huo. 2002. *Trust in the Law: Encouraging Public Cooperation with the Police and Courts*. Russell Sage Foundation Series on Trust 5. New York: Russell Sage Foundation.

Udovički, Jasminka, and Ivan Torov. 1997. The Interlude: 1980–1990. In *Burn This House: The Making and Unmaking of Yugoslavia*, edited by J. Udovički and J. Ridgeway. Durham, NC: Duke University Press.

United Nations. 2000. *United Nations Millennium Declaration*. Resolution 55/2, adopted by the General Assembly, September 8.

——. 2004. *The Global Programme Against Corruption*. United Nations Anticorruption Toolkit, 3rd ed. Vienna: United Nations Office on Drugs and Crime.

United Nations Development Program (UNDP). 2002. *Human Development Report 2002: Bosnia and Herzegovina*. New York: United Nation Development Program.

——. 2003. *Human Development Report 2003: Millennium Development Goals: A Compact among Nations to End Human Poverty*. New York: Oxford University Press.

——. 2006. *Human Development Report 2006: Beyond Scarcity: Power, Poverty and the Global Water Crisis*. New York: United Nations Development Program.

——. 2009. *Human Development Report 2009: Overcoming Barriers—Human Mobility and Development*. New York: United National Development Program.

Uslaner, Eric M. 2002. *The Moral Foundations of Trust*. New York: Cambridge University Press.

——. 2003. Trust and Civic Engagement in East and West. In *Social Capital and the Transition to Democracy*, edited by G. Badescu and E. M. Uslaner. London: Routledge.

———. 2004. Trust and Corruption. In *The New Institutional Economics of Corruption*, edited by J. G. Lambsdorf, M. Taube, and M. Schramm. London: Routledge.

———. 2008. *Corruption, Inequality, and the Rule of Law: The Bulging Pocket Makes the Easy Life*. Cambridge: Cambridge University Press.

Uslaner, Eric M., and Gabriel Badescu. 2005. Making the Grade in Transition: Equality, Transparency, Trust, and Fairness. Unpublished manuscript, University of Maryland–College Park.

Wagstaff, Adam, and Mariam Claeson. 2004. *Rising to the Challenge: The Millennium Goals for Health*. Washington, DC: World Bank.

Walzer, Michael. 1983. *Spheres of Justice. A Defense of Pluralism and Justice*. New York: Basic Books.

Weingast, Barry R. 1993. Constitutions as Governance Structures—the Political Foundations of Secure Markets. *Journal of Institutional and Theoretical Economics* 149 (1): 286–311.

———. 1997. The Political Foundations of Democracy and the Rule of Law. *American Political Science Review* 91 (3): 245–63.

Weir, Margaret. 1992. *Politics and Jobs: The Boundaries of Employment Policy in the United States*. Princeton, NJ: Princeton University Press.

Weir, Margaret, and Theda Skocpol. 1985. State Structures and the Possibilities for "Keynesian" Responses to the Great Depression in Sweden, Britain, and the United States. In *Bringing the State Back In*, edited by P. B. Evans, D. Rueschemeyer, and T. Skocpol. Cambridge: Cambridge University Press.

Weis, Eberhard. 2005. *Montgelas—der Architekt des Modernen Bayerischen Staates, 1799–1838*. Munich: Beck.

Welsch, Heinz. 2004. Corruption, Growth, and the Environment: A Cross-Country Analysis. *Environment and Development Economics* 9 (5): 663–93.

Welzel, Christian, and Ronald Inglehart. 2008. The Role of Ordinary People in Democratization. *Journal of Democracy* 19 (1): 126–40.

Werhane, Patricia. 1994. *Adam Smith and His Legacy for Modern Capitalism*. Oxford: Oxford University Press.

Werlin, Herbert H. 2003. Poor Nations, Rich Nations: A Theory of Governance. *Public Administration Review* 63 (3): 329–42.

———. 2007. Corruption and Democracy: Is Lord Acton Right? *Journal of Social, Political and Economic Studies* 32 (3): 359–76.

Westerhult, Bo. 1965. *Kronofogde, Häradsskrivare, Länsman: Den Svenska Fögderiförvaltningen, 1810–1917*. Lund: Gleerup.

Western, Bruce. 2001. Bayesian Thinking about Macrosociology. *American Journal of Sociology* 107 (2): 353–78.

Westerståhl, Jörgen, and Folke Johansson. 1985. *Bilden av Sverige: Studier av Nyheter och Nyhetsideologier i TV, Radio och Dagspress.* Stockholm: SNS.

Weyland, Kurt. 1996. Obstacles to Social Reform in Brazil's New Democracy. *Comparative Politics* 29 (1): 1–22.

Whiteley, Paul F. 1999. The Origins of Social Capital. In *Social Capital and European Democracy*, edited by J. W. van Deth, M. Maraffi, K. Newton, and P. F. Whiteley. London: Routledge.

Widmalm, Sten. 2008. *Decentralisation, Corruption and Social Capital: From India to the West.* Thousand Oaks, CA: Sage.

Wilkinson, Richard G., and Kate Pickett. 2009. *The Spirit Level: Why More Equal Societies Almost Always do Better.* London: Allen Lane.

Winter, Ian, ed. 2002. *Social Capital and Public Policy in Australia.* Melbourne: Australian Institute of Family Studies.

Wittman, Donald. 1995. *The Myth of Democratic Failure.* Chicago: University of Chicago Press.

Wolff, Stefan, ed. 2001. *German Minorities in Europe: Ethnic Identity and Cultural Belonging.* New York: Berghahn Books.

Wollebæck, Dag, and Per Selle. 2002. Does Participation in Voluntary Associations Contribute to Social Capital? The Impact of Intensity, Scope, and Type. *Nonprofit and Voluntary Sector Quarterly* 31 (1): 32–61.

Woodward, Susan L. 1995. *Balkan Tragedy: Chaos and Dissolution after the Cold War.* Washington, DC: Brookings Institution.

Woolcock, M., and D. Narayan. 2000. Social Capital: Implications for Development Theory, Research, and Policy. *World Bank Research Observer* 15 (2): 225–49.

World Bank. 2000. *Anti-corruption in Transition: A Contribution to the Policy Debate.* Washington, DC: World Bank.

———. 2005. World Bank Speak Out: Interview with James D. Wolfensohn on Peace and Poverty: Ten Years at the World Bank, May 25.

———. 2007. *HNPStats: Health, Population and Nutrition Data.* Washington, DC: World Bank.

———. 2010. *Silent and Lethal: How Quiet Corruption Undermines Africa's Development Efforts.* Washington, DC: World Bank.

Wrong, Michela. 2009. *It's Our Turn to Eat: A Story of a Kenyan Whistle Blower.* London: Fourth Estate.

Yamagishi, Toshio. 2001. Trust as a Form of Social Intelligence. In *Trust in Society*, edited by K. S. Cook. New York: Russell Sage Foundation.

Yamagishi, Toshio, and Kaori Sato. 1986. Motivational Bases of the Public Goods Problem. *Journal of Personality and Social Psychology* 50 (1): 67–73.

Years of Plenty? 2003. *Economist*, July 12.

You, Jong-Sung, and Sanjeev Khagram. 2005. A Comparative Study of Inequality and Corruption. *American Sociological Review* 70 (1): 136–57.

Young, H. Peyton. 1998. *Individual Strategy and Social Structure: An Evolutionary Theory of Institutions*. Princeton, NJ: Princeton University Press.

Young, Iris M. 1990. *Justice and the Politics of Difference*. Princeton, NJ: Princeton University Press.

——. 1993. Together in Difference: Transforming the Logic of Group Political Conflict. In *Principled Positions: Postmodernism and the Rediscovery of Value*, edited by J. Squires. London: Lawrence and Wishart.

Zak, Paul J., and Stephen Knack. 2001. Trust and Growth. *Economic Journal* 111 (470): 295–321.

Zakaria, Fareed. 2003. *The Future of Freedom: Illiberal Democracy at Home and Abroad*. New York: Norton.

Zhang, Yan, Liqun Q. Cao, and Michael S. Vaughn. 2009. Social Support and Corruption: Structural Determinants of Corruption in the World. *Australian and New Zealand Journal of Criminology* 42 (2): 204–17.

Zuberi, Dan. 2006. *Differences That Matter: Social Policy and the Working Poor in the United States and Canada*. Ithaca, NY: Cornell University Press.

Index

Note: Page numbers followed by f or t indicate figures or tables, respectively.

274 INDEX

International Monetary Fund (IMF), 7,
105, 134
International Political Science Associa-
tion, 80
Iraq, 77–78, 83
irrigation, 3–4
Issacharoff, Samuel, 80
Italy, 42, 86, 135, 216
Iversen, Torben, 120, 123n1
Iyer, Lakshmi, 221

Jackman, Robert W., 25
Jamaica: agricultural sector of, 194; British
Colonial Office and, 200; Bustamante
and, 200–201; clientelism and, 199–203;
comparative case methodology with
Singapore and, 194–99, 203–6; corruption in, 200–202; criminal gangs of,
202; democracy and, 25, 37, 194–203,
205–6, 217–18; economic/social performance of, 195–97; as former colony,
194–95; as free country, 198; homicide
rate in, 197; Human Development Index (HDI) ranking of, 195; impartiality
in, 197; Manley and, 200–201; mortality rates in, 196–97; natural resources
of, 194; People's National Party (PNP)
and, 199–201; pluralism in, 198; political murders in, 200–201; population
size of, 194; poverty rates in, 194, 199,
205; racial riots in, 200; reforms and,
37; Seaga and, 200; social trust in, 197;
Westminster model of, 194
Jamaican Labor Party (JLP), 199–201
Jansson, Torkel, 117
Japan, 63, 135, 198
Jews, 116
Jochem, Patrick E. P., 51
Johansson, Folke, 82
Johnson, Simon, 206, 217
Johnston, Michael, xii, 10, 41, 99
Jones, Bryan D., 209
Jones, Charles I., 6
Jordahl, 216–17
Jordan, William Chester, 101n1, 198
Jordan Smith, Daniel, 103
justice: corruption and, 103; developing
countries and, 56–57; environmental is-
sues and, 34, 43, 44t, 45t, 51–55; impar-
tiality and, 12–13, 16–25, 30; low trust-

corruption-inequality trap and, 153,
161; preservation of society and, 215;
quality of government and, 3, 5, 6n2,
12–13, 16–25, 30, 42, 56; reciprocity
and, 43, 102, 110, 117, 145, 166–68; rule
of law and, 42 (see also rule of law);
welfare state and, 121, 129–30
Justice as Impartiality (Barry), 16

Kaijser, Arne, 220
Karklins, Rasma, 100–101, 190
Katz, Michael B., 153
Katzenstein, Peter J., 220
Kaufmann, Daniel: corruption and, 60;
preserving society and, 207–8, 218;
quality of government and, 8, 24, 37,
41–42
Kayser, Mark, 48
Kazakhstan, 59n3
Keefer, Philip, 6, 8, 132, 214–15, 217
Kenworthy, Lane, 120
Kenya, 106
Khama, Seretse, 206
Khan, Mushtaq H., 41
kickbacks, 3, 31
King, Desmond, xii
Klomp, Jeroen, 65–66
Kluegel, James R., 157
Knack, Stephen, 6, 132, 147, 156, 215, 217
Knight, Jack, 216
Kornai, János, 6, 36, 59, 124, 158
Korpi, Walter, 120–23, 127, 131, 152, 158,
213
Koshechkina, Tatyana Y., 160
Kraay, Art, 8, 37, 42, 47–48
Krause, Matthias, 3
Krishna, Anirudh, 70
Krugman, Paul, 11
Kudamatsu, Masayuki, 43
Kuenzi, Michelle, 149
Kumlin, Staffan, x, 15n6, 43; low trust-
corruption-inequality trap and, 150,
152, 158–59; political legitimacy and,
93; social trust and, 169; welfare state
and, 128
Kurer, Oscar, 15
Kurzman, Charles, 26
Kuznets curve, 52
Kwon, Huck-ju, 204
Kyrgyzstan, 59n3

25620506R00176

Made in the USA
Lexington, KY
30 August 2013